The Programmers' Guide to osCommerce:

The Nuts and Bolts

of osCommerce Customization

The Programmers' Guide to osCommerce:

The Nuts and Bolts

of osCommerce Customization

By Myles O'Reilly

Lulu, Inc.
http://www.lulu.com

The Programmers' Guide to osCommerce: The Nuts and Bolts of osCommerce Customization

Contents

INTRODUCTION

Open source programming is nothing short of a revolution in the computing world. Along with the increasingly widespread use of the Linux operating system during the late 1990s came the realization that by allowing programmers to read, modify, and redistribute code, progress in the adaptability, functionality, and improvement of software takes place at a rate far superior to that seen in the development of code closed to public manipulation. While open source programming was, by tradition, fairly commonplace in the realm of the World Wide Web, we are now witnessing its spread to the commercial sector as technological giants like IBM, Apple, Novell, and Sharp are jumping on the open source bandwagon.

Open source has been well defined by principle proponents of the open source movement, such as the Open Source Initiative. In order to qualify as open source, software must be distributed freely and without impediment, and this distribution must be available in source code as well as in a compiled form. Any derived works must also be freely and openly distributed, and discrimination against persons, professions, specific products, and other software is not permitted.

osCommerce is a package built along these lines. Operating under an open source General Public License, osCommerce stands tall as the leading solution for online storefront creation and maintenance. With no cost to them, osCommerce provides storeowners with exceptional functionality, from download to installation to implementation. Only five years after its introduction, osCommerce boasts over 85,000 community members, from users to developers—in line with the open source philosophy, this widespread use has since created a large osCommerce community, whose contributions to the further development of the software have resulted in over 3,000 "contributions," or adaptations and additional functional modules, to the software.

These contributions have aided osCommerce in becoming more powerful, more adaptive, and more capable of meeting the demands of online storefronts. The software can run without any special requirements on just about any platform and is fully customizable in terms of localization, appearance, and functionality; in fact, it is the surprisingly simple customization capabilities of osCommerce that make this package so incredibly attractive to so many international users.

Now in version 2.2, the software is mature and ripe for the picking, so whether you are upgrading from an older version or are looking around for the right online commerce software to fit your needs, we are thrilled that you have decided to give osCommerce your consideration.

This book focuses on osCommerce's hallmark of customizability and, with detailed explanations, code samples, and informative, step-by-step graphics, will serve as an invaluable guide to your osCommerce experience, from installation to user-side customization. We hope that by reading this book, you will be convinced to join the over 7,700 live stores that currently take advantage of the endless opportunities that osCommerce has to offer.

osCommerce Installation

In keeping with its overall design, osCommerce makes installation and upgrading a breeze for the programming professional. In this chapter you will learn how to use the tools provided within the osCommerce package to quickly deploy the system on your server. Using a previously created database of merchandise, the built-in installation interface included with osCommerce simplifies database integration to a series of button clicks, although we include all the coding details for a more comprehensive treatment. If you already use an older version of osCommerce, this chapter contains a separate section devoted to explaining the upgrade process.

By way of customization, this chapter also contains detailed information on changing the look and feel of the installation interface. After reviewing a thorough code analysis, you will learn how to change the layout and style of the interface and even how to add or delete an installation step.

1.1. osCommerce Package

Suppose that you have developed a Web application on your local computer, and now, you want to upload and deploy your application on a remote server. If you are a Web developer, you must know the processes you will need to follow to accomplish this. For a PHP application the minimum steps you must take to deploy your Web application follow.

1. First, you need to import your database to the remote database server.
2. Then, you need to copy the application folder containing all files to the server.

3. Finally, you have to change the code for database connectivity.

You generally perform the whole task manually, step by step.

Not knowing how to import a database or to change the database connectivity code, it may be quite difficult to deploy a Web application. Keeping this problem in mind, the osCommerce developers have created an interface to deploy and configure the osCommerce application in your desired location. Using this interface, even a novice user can deploy the osCommerce package on their server.

The osCommerce package mainly consists of a folder named /catalog/, which contains all the application files, and a file named /oscommerce/catalog/install/oscommerce.sql, which contains the exported database in the form of SQL queries. You can also create such a package for any of your own applications.

1.2. BEGINNING THE INSTALLATION PROCESS

We are now going to install or deploy the osCommerce application on a local machine with the help of the included interface, but how do we get the interface?

1. Download the osCommerce-X (where "X" is the osCommerce version number) package.
2. Extract it to the folder /oscommerce/.
3. Copy the folder to the *root folder* of your local server.
4. Open a browser, type in the URL http://localhost/oscommerce/catalog/install/index.php/, and press **Enter**.

The first page of the installation interface will open (Figure 1.1). The address of this first page is http://hostname/osCommerce/catalog/install/index.php/ (replace "hostname" with your own host name). The user will see two image links, **Install** and **Upgrade**, which simply redirect the user to the pages /install.php and /upgrade.php, respectively.

Now, we can start with the installation process: continue by pressing the **Install** link (skip the **Upgrade** link for the moment). On the next page we see two check boxes: **Import Catalog Database** and **Automatic Configuration**. If the user selects the first option, the database will be imported. If it is not selected, the installation process will skip the database import section; thus

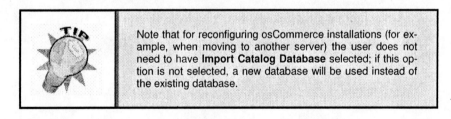

Figure 1.1. Welcome page.

no database will be created, and the new user will have to create the database and tables manually. For this reason it is recommended that for a new installation the user select the first option. Check both of the check boxes for this *first-time installation* and press the **Continue** button (Figure 1.2).

> Note that for reconfiguring osCommerce installations (for example, when moving to another server) the user does not need to have **Import Catalog Database** selected; if this option is not selected, a new database will be used instead of the existing database.

Next, a page similar to Figure 1.3 will be displayed. Here, you need to fill in all the fields with the appropriate information and press the **Continue** button. Clicking on the **Continue** button shown in Figure 1.3 posts the database configuration information. On the next page the following code, written in the /catalog/install/templates/pages/install2.php file, is executed with the posted data.

```
if (isset($HTTP_POST_VARS['DB_SERVER']) &&
!empty($HTTP_POST_VARS['DB_SERVER']) &&
isset($HTTP_POST_VARS['DB_TEST_CONNECTION'])
```

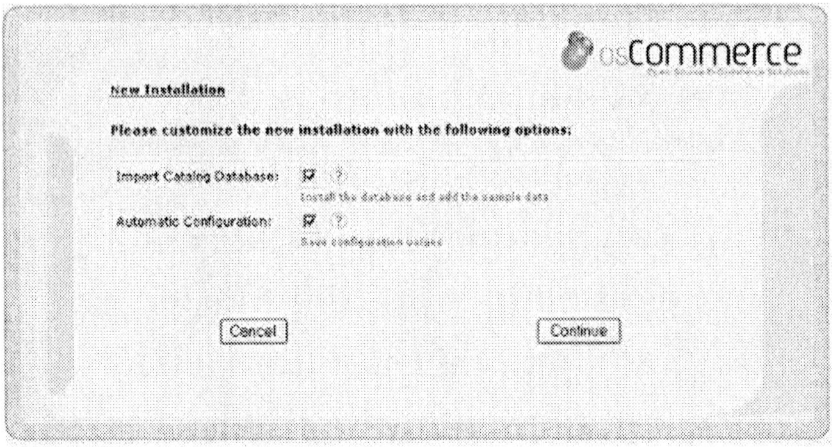

Figure 1.2. Installation Customization page.

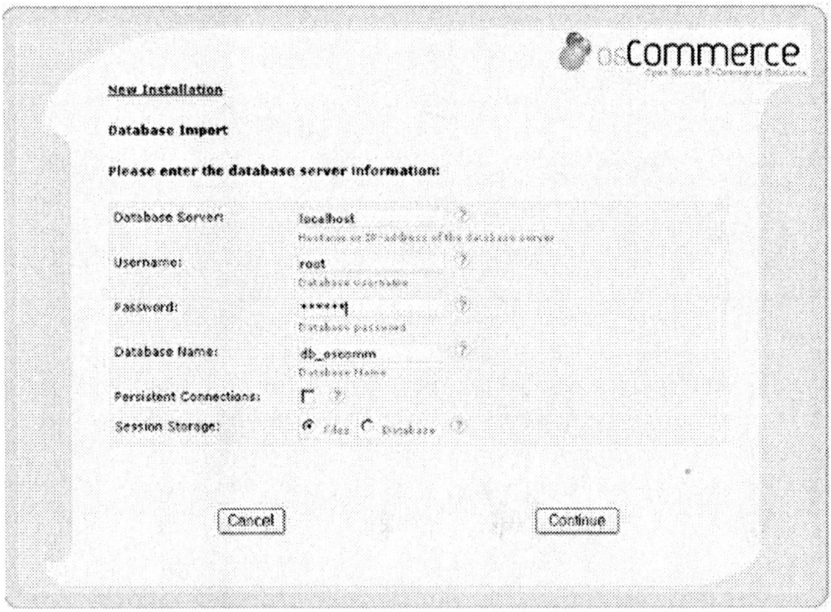

Figure 1.3. Database Import screen.

```
&& ($HTTP_POST_VARS['DB_TEST_CONNECTION'] ==
'true'))
{
    $db = array();
    $db['DB_SERVER'] =
trim(stripslashes($HTTP_POST_VARS['DB_SERVER']
));
    $db['DB_SERVER_USERNAME'] =
trim(stripslashes($HTTP_POST_VARS['DB_SERVER_U
SERNAME']));
    $db['DB_SERVER_PASSWORD'] =
trim(stripslashes($HTTP_POST_VARS['DB_SERVER_P
ASSWORD']));
    $db['DB_DATABASE'] =
trim(stripslashes($HTTP_POST_VARS['DB_DATABASE
']));

    $db_error = false;
    osc_db_connect($db['DB_SERVER'],
$db['DB_SERVER_USERNAME'],
$db['DB_SERVER_PASSWORD']);

    if ($db_error == false) {

osc_db_test_create_db_permission($db['DB_DATAB
ASE']);
    }
```

Note that **Persistent Connections** (Figure 1.3) should not be enabled for installations on shared hosting servers as it will usually degrade performance instead of improving it. It is recommended that shared hosting servers use database session storage due to security-related issues. File-based session storage improves performance but is only recommended for dedicated servers. Most Web hosting sites *do not* use dedicated servers.

1.2.1. Functions

The "osc_db_connect()" function tries to connect the database, and if it successfully connects, then the "osc_db_test_create_db_permission()" function is called to create the database, and a test table tests whether the user (provided by the form shown in Figure 1.3) has permission to create the database on the given database server. These functions are written in the /catalog/install/includes/functions/database.php file along with other database-related functions.

These two functions set the value of "$db_error" to "true" if they fail to execute successfully, and thus a message will be displayed such as that seen in Figure 1.4 (see section 1.2.2). If "$db_error" is "false," then the database information provided by the user is correct. In this case, a message will appear such as that shown in Figure 1.5, and the installation process will be ready to import or create the database on that server.

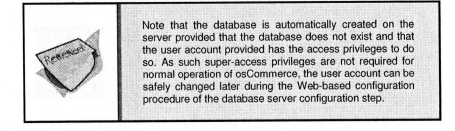

Note that the database is automatically created on the server provided that the database does not exist and that the user account provided has the access privileges to do so. As such super-access privileges are not required for normal operation of osCommerce, the user account can be safely changed later during the Web-based configuration procedure of the database server configuration step.

1.2.2. Installation Errors

If the database connection has not been made successfully, then a message "Access denied for user: 'username@hostname' (Using password: YES)" will be shown (Figure 1.4). This installation wizard verifies the information provided before proceeding to the next step to make sure that the osCommerce installation operates without any problem. Clicking on the **Back** button will redirect the user to the previous page, where they can enter the correct information in order to continue with the installation. The error messages are useful for the user and help them to fix many of the problems seen in Figure 1.4. Click on the **Cancel** button to exit the installation.

1.3. Importing a Database

Clicking on the **Continue** button, the form posts all the information provided by the user as hidden fields. On the next page the following code is executed to import the database. The code is written in the /catalog/install/templates/pages/install3.php file.

```
if (osc_in_array('database',
$HTTP_POST_VARS['install']))
{
    $db = array();
    $db['DB_SERVER'] =
trim(stripslashes($HTTP_POST_VARS['DB_SERVER']
)));
```

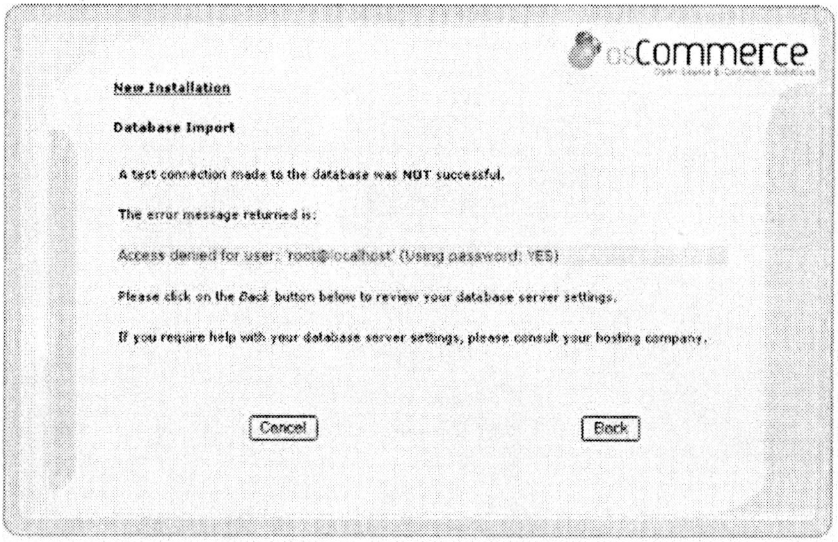

Figure 1.4. Database Import error screen.

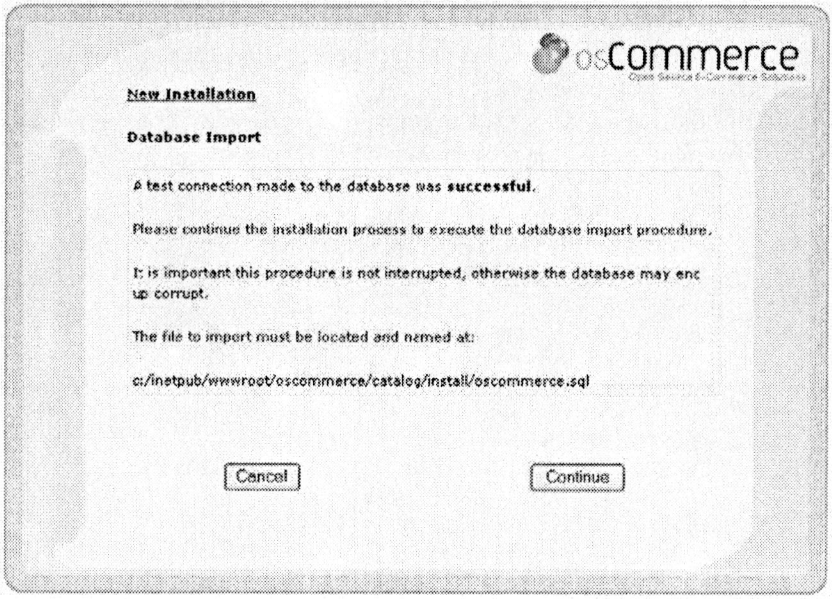

Figure 1.5. Database Configuration success screen.

```
    $db['DB_SERVER_USERNAME'] =
trim(stripslashes($HTTP_POST_VARS['DB_SERVER_U
SERNAME'])));
    $db['DB_SERVER_PASSWORD'] =
trim(stripslashes($HTTP_POST_VARS['DB_SERVER_P
ASSWORD'])));
    $db['DB_DATABASE'] =
trim(stripslashes($HTTP_POST_VARS['DB_DATABASE
'])));

    osc_db_connect($db['DB_SERVER'],
$db['DB_SERVER_USERNAME'],
$db['DB_SERVER_PASSWORD']);

    $db_error = false;
    $sql_file = $dir_fs_www_root .
'install/oscommerce.sql';

    osc_set_time_limit(0);
    osc_db_install($db['DB_DATABASE'],
$sql_file);
}
```

The function "osc_db_install ($db['DB_DATABASE'], $sql_file)" reads a file named /oscommerce.sql containing SQL queries of the database "$db['DB_DATABASE']" and then executes all the queries to create and import the database to the server (MySQL). It then creates all the tables and imports the necessary data to run the software and site. These functions are written in the /catalog/install/includes/functions/database.php file along with other database-related functions.

The file /oscommerce.sql contains the SQL scripts for the whole database. A fragment of this file is given below.

```
DROP TABLE IF EXISTS address format;
CREATE TABLE address format (
  address_format_id int NOT NULL auto
increment,
  address_format varchar(128) NOT NULL,
  address_summary varchar(48) NOT NULL,
  PRIMARY KEY (address_format_id)
);

INSERT INTO categories_description VALUES
('1', '1', 'Hardware');
INSERT INTO categories_description VALUES
('2', '1', 'Software');
INSERT INTO categories_description VALUES
('3', '1', 'DVD Movies');
```

```
INSERT INTO categories_description VALUES
('4', '1', 'Graphics Cards');
INSERT INTO categories_description VALUES
('5', '1', 'Printers');
INSERT INTO categories_description VALUES
('6', '1', 'Monitors');
```

If the database has been imported into your database server successfully, then the screen shown in Figure 1.6 will be displayed. Click on the **Continue** button for the next step.

On the next page you need to provide Web server–related information for HTTP configuration. The page is shown in Figure 1.7. Clicking on the **Continue** button, the form containing the server information provided by the user is posted along with all other data as hidden values. On the next page, two configuration files are created using the posted data: /catalog/includes/configure.php and /catalog/admin/includes/configure.php. These files contain configuration information and look like the following.

```
/*
  $Id: configure.php,v 1.14 2003/02/21
16:55:24 dgw_ Exp $

  osCommerce, Open Source E-Commerce Solutions
  http://www.oscommerce.com

  Copyright (c) 2002 osCommerce

  Released under the GNU General Public
License
*/
// define our webserver variables
// FS = Filesystem (physical)
// WS = Webserver (virtual)
  define('HTTP_SERVER', ''); // e.g.,
http://localhost or - https://localhost should
not be NULL for productive servers
  define('HTTP_CATALOG_SERVER', '');
  define('HTTPS_CATALOG_SERVER', '');
  define('ENABLE_SSL_CATALOG', 'false'); //
secure webserver for catalog module
  define('DIR_FS_DOCUMENT_ROOT',
$DOCUMENT_ROOT); // where your pages are
located on the server. if $DOCUMENT_ROOT does
not suit you, replace with your local path.
(e.g., /usr/local/apache/htdocs)
  define('DIR_WS_ADMIN', '/admin/');
  define('DIR_FS_ADMIN', DIR_FS_DOCUMENT_ROOT
. DIR_WS_ADMIN);
```

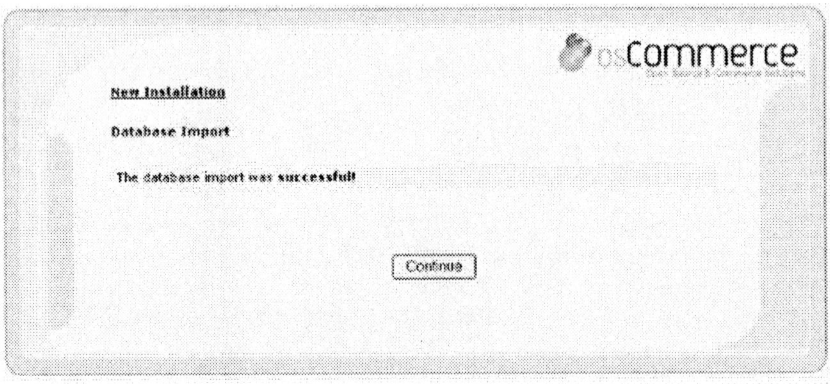

Figure 1.6. Successful Database Import screen.

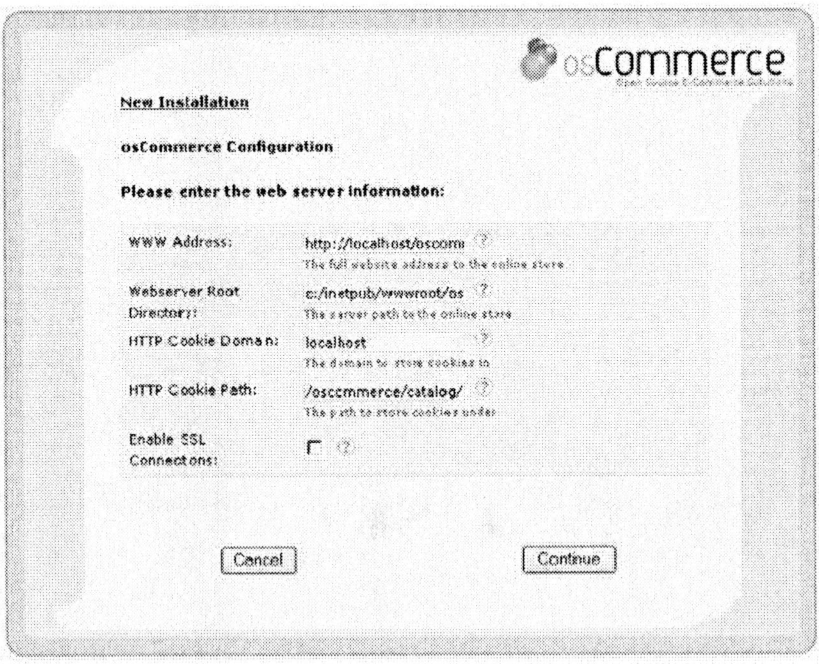

Figure 1.7. Web server Configuration screen.

```
   define('DIR_WS_CATALOG', '/catalog/');
   define('DIR_FS_CATALOG',
DIR_FS_DOCUMENT_ROOT . DIR_WS_CATALOG);
   define('DIR_WS_IMAGES', 'images/');
   define('DIR_WS_ICONS', DIR_WS_IMAGES .
'icons/');
   define('DIR_WS_CATALOG_IMAGES',
DIR_WS_CATALOG . 'images/');
   define('DIR_WS_INCLUDES', 'includes/');
   define('DIR_WS_BOXES', DIR_WS_INCLUDES .
'boxes/');
   define('DIR_WS_FUNCTIONS', DIR_WS_INCLUDES .
'functions/');
   define('DIR_WS_CLASSES', DIR_WS_INCLUDES .
'classes/');
   define('DIR_WS_MODULES', DIR_WS_INCLUDES .
'modules/');
   define('DIR_WS_LANGUAGES', DIR_WS_INCLUDES .
'languages/');
   define('DIR_WS_CATALOG_LANGUAGES',
DIR_WS_CATALOG . 'includes/languages/');
   define('DIR_FS_CATALOG_LANGUAGES',
DIR_FS_CATALOG . 'includes/languages/');
   define('DIR_FS_CATALOG_IMAGES',
DIR_FS_CATALOG . 'images/');
   define('DIR_FS_CATALOG_MODULES',
DIR_FS_CATALOG . 'includes/modules/');
   define('DIR_FS_BACKUP', DIR_FS_ADMIN .
'backups/');
// define our database connection
   define('DB_SERVER', '');
   define('DB_SERVER_USERNAME', 'mysql');
   define('DB_SERVER_PASSWORD', '');
   define('DB_DATABASE', 'osCommerce');
   define('USE_PCONNECT', 'false');
   define('STORE_SESSIONS', '');
```

Note that you should gather the following information during the preinstallation procedure: the Web server address; the location of the osCommerce installation; and the secure Web server address (optional).

Once these two files have been created, the installation process has been completed successfully. You can now get the basic server-related information and path information of different files, folders, and images by including these configuration files as and when required. Basically, in the osCommerce project, these two files are included from different files.

Please note that if the /catalog/includes/configure.php and /catalog/admin/includes/configure.php files are not created during the installation process, the project will not work; the configuration-related constants and the database connection data are defined in these two files.

When the Web server is configured successfully, the screen shown in Figure 1.8 will be displayed. The next step can be performed safely. Clicking on the **Catalog** button will display the Catalog page of the newly configured application (such as http://localhost/oscommerce/catalog/index.php/). Clicking on the **Administration Tool** button will display the Admin page of the newly configured application (such as http://localhost/oscommerce/catalog/admin/index.php/).

1.4. UPGRADING OSCOMMERCE

Now, we return to the index page of the installation wizard (see Figure 1.1). If the user wants to upgrade the application from MS1 to MS2, they will need to update the PHP files and move the data from the old database to the new database. To do this automatically, click on the **Upgrade** link. The next page will be displayed, as shown in Figure 1.9. Pressing the **Continue** button updates the database.

During the upgrade process the database attains a new version. In the new version, there are many changes to the database: some new tables are added along with the existing tables, some new fields are added in many tables, and some new data is inserted into some tables—particularly into the configuration tables. Some code fragments for the upgrade process of the database are given below. The code is written in the /catalog/install/templates/pages/upgrade_3.php file.

```
osc_db_query("alter table address_book add
customers_id int not null after
address_book_id");

osc_db_query("alter table address_book add
entry_company varchar(32) after
entry_gender");
```

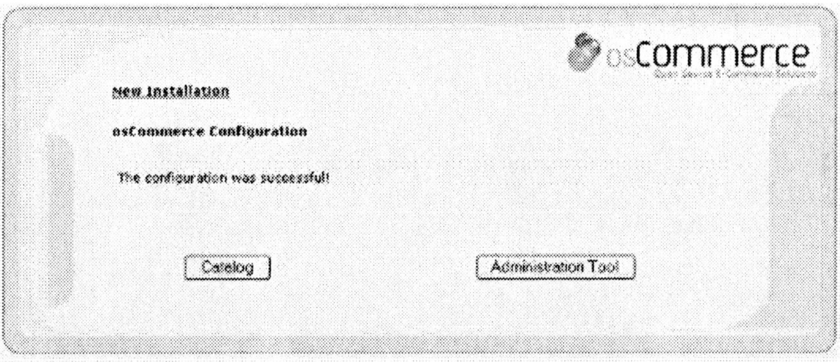

Figure 1.8. Successful Web server Configuration screen.

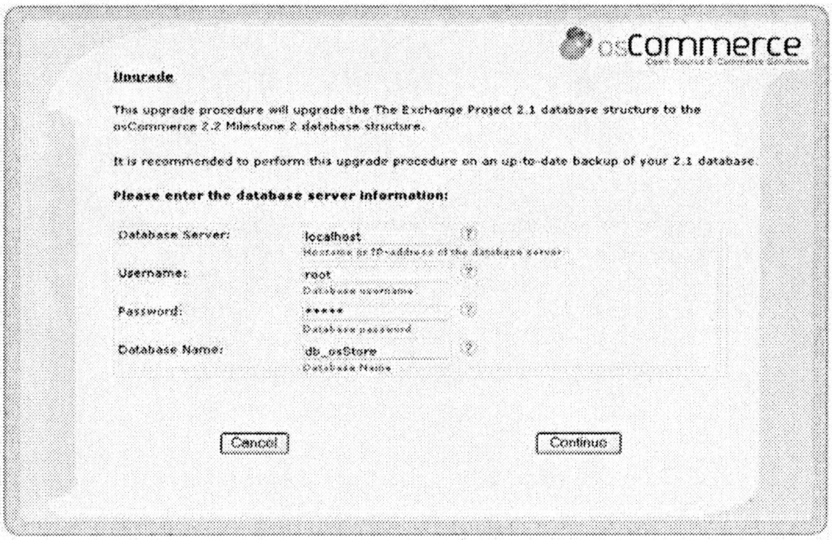

Figure 1.9. Screen for database upgrade wizard.

```
osc_db_query("alter table customers add
customers_default_address_id int(5) not null
after customers_email_address");

  $entries_query = osc_db_query("select
address_book_id, customers_id from
address_book_to_customers");

  while ($entries =
osc_db_fetch_array($entries_query)) {

    osc_db_query("update address_book set
customers_id = '" . $entries['customers_id'] .
"' where address_book_id = '" .
$entries['address_book_id'] . "'");

  }


$customer_query = osc_db_query("select
customers_id, customers_gender,
customers_firstname, customers_lastname,
customers_street_address, customers_suburb,
customers_postcode, customers_city,
customers_state, customers_country_id,
customers_zone_id from customers");

  while ($customer =
osc_db_fetch_array($customer_query)) {

    osc_db_query("insert into address_book
(customers_id, entry_gender, entry_company,
entry_firstname, entry_lastname,
entry_street_address, entry_suburb,
entry_postcode, entry_city, entry_state,
entry_country_id, entry_zone_id) values ('" .
$customer['customers_id'] . "', '" .
$customer['customers_gender'] . "', '', '" .
addslashes($customer['customers_firstname']) .
"', '" .
addslashes($customer['customers_lastname']) .
"', '" .
addslashes($customer['customers_street_address
']) . "', '" .
addslashes($customer['customers_suburb']) .
"', '" .
addslashes($customer['customers_postcode']) .
"', '" .
```

```
addslashes($customer['customers_city']) . "',
'" . addslashes($customer['customers_state'])
. "', '" . $customer['customers_country_id'] .
"', '" . $customer['customers_zone_id'] .
"')");
$address_book_id = osc_db_insert_id();
osc_db_query("update customers set
customers_default_address_id = '" .
$address_book_id . "' where customers_id = '"
. $customer['customers_id'] . "'");
  }
osc_db_query("alter table address_book add
index idx_address_book_customers_id
(customers_id)");
osc_db_query("drop table
address_book_to_customers");
```

So, we are now able to install or upgrade the osCommerce package.

1.5. INSTALLATION INTERFACE

Now, let us see how the installation interface works and which files are used in the installation and upgrade processes. Three files are included; these three files contain all the functions that will be called throughout the installation process and are located in the folder /catalog/install/includes/functions/. The first file is /catalog/install/index.php, which contains the following code.

```
require('includes/application.php'); //
application.php contains only the code for
//including another 3 files
//Setting the variables that will be used in
the templates/main_page.php page.
$page_file = 'index.php';
$page_title = 'Welcome';
$page_contents = 'index.php';
require('templates/main_page.php');
```

The above code is self-explanatory; we just need to know the contents of the /application.php file and the functional details of the /main_page.php file. The /catalog/install/includes/application.php file contains the following code.

```
// Set the level of error reporting
  error_reporting(E_ALL & ~E_NOTICE);
// Check if register_globals is enabled.
```

```
// Since this is a temporary measure this
message is hardcoded. The requirement //will
be removed before 2.2 is finalized.
 if (function_exists('ini_get')) {
ini_get('register_globals') or exit('FATAL
ERROR: register_globals is disabled in
php.ini, please enable it!');
}
 //ws comments: Customizing two general
purpose function of PHP for OSC
require('includes/functions/general.php');
//ws comments: Containing all database related
functions that will be called from //different
pages.
require('includes/functions/database.php');
//ws comments: Containing the functions that
generate HTML Form Elements //runtime.
require('includes/functions/html_output.php');
```

For better understanding, let us look at the code more closely.

```
require('includes/application.php'); //
application.php contains only the code for
//including another 3 files
//Setting the variables that will be used in
the templates/main_page.php page.
$page_file = 'index.php';
$page_title = 'Welcome';
$page_contents = 'index.php';
require('templates/main_page.php');
```

After calling the file /application.php, some variables are set that will be used in the /main_page.php file. To send some parameter to a page or file while calling it, set some variable with the parameter values before calling the file, and use these variables inside that file. Then, again, a file /main_page.php will be included. As the name suggests, this is the main page of the installation wizard. Let us see what is inside this page.

```
<!DOCTYPE HTML PUBLIC "-//W3C//DTD HTML 4.0
Transitional//EN">
<html>
<head>
<title>osCommerce :// Open Source E-Commerce
Solutions</title>
<meta name="ROBOTS" content="NOFOLLOW">
<link rel="stylesheet" type="text/css"
href="templates/main_page/stylesheet.css">
```

```
<script language="javascript"
src="templates/main_page/javascript.js"></scri
pt>
</head>

<body text="#000000" bgcolor="#ffffff"
leftmargin="0" topmargin="0" marginheight="0"
marginwidth="0">
<?php
require('templates/main_page/header.php'); ?>
<table cellspacing="0" cellpadding="0"
width="100%" border="0" align="center">
  <tr>
    <td width="5%" class="leftColumn"
valign="top"
background="images/layout/left_column_backgrou
nd.gif"><img
src="images/layout/left_column_top.gif"></td>
    <td width="85%" valign="top"><?php
require('templates/pages/' . $page_contents);
?></td>
    <td width="5%" class="rightColumn"
valign="top"><img
src="images/layout/right_column_upper_curve.gi
f" width="47"></td>
  </tr>
</table>
<?php
require('templates/main_page/footer.php'); ?>
</body>
</html>
```

At the start of the "<body>" tag a page named /header.php is included, and at the bottom, another file named /footer.php is included. These files contain the HTML code for handling layout-related issues only. These two files are located in the folder /catalog/install/templates/main_page/.

1.5.1. Changing or Deleting the Copyright

Open the page /catalog/install/templates/main_page/footer.php and edit the copyright-related portion as you wish.

1.5.2. Changing the Style and Layout

You will find all the layout-related codes in the files /main_page.php, /header.php, and /footer.php. You can change the HTML as you wish, and you can change the images related to the layout from these pages. To change the style, you have to edit the CSS file named /catalog/install/templates/ main_page/stylesheet.css. This file has been included in /main_page.php, as

seen in the above code. There is also a JS file named /catalog/install/
templates/main_page/javascript.js, which has been included in this page. This
file contains the general functions used throughout the installation process,
such as the function responsible for hiding and showing the details of the value
needed to fill up the form's elements.

Now, let us look at the content of /main_page.php again. Look at the
line "<?php require('templates/pages/' . $page_contents); ?>"; remember that
before calling the page we set the value of "$page_contents" to "index.php"?
Let us go to the page /catalog/install/templates/pages/index.php. It contains
only two links to redirect the user to the starting page of either installation or
upgrading (Figure 1.1).

So, we see how a page is displayed in the browser. For the next pages
the same technique is applied:

1. Set the variable "$page_contents" to the name of the page
    you want to display, along with other variables.
2. Then, call the page /main_page.php to display that page.

Now, on the index page, if you click the **Install** link, the /catalog/install/
install.php page will be shown on the screen. Let us look inside the
/catalog/install/install.php file.

1.5.3. Install Page

The code contained inside the /install.php file follows.

```php
require('includes/application.php');

$page_file = 'install.php';
$page_title = 'Installation';

switch ($HTTP_GET_VARS['step']) {
  case '2':
    if (osc_in_array('database',
$HTTP_POST_VARS['install'])) {
        $page_contents = 'install_2.php';
    } elseif (osc_in_array('configure',
$HTTP_POST_VARS['install'])) {
        $page_contents = 'install_4.php';
    } else {
        $page_contents = 'install.php';
    }
    break;
  case '3':
    if (osc_in_array('database',
$HTTP_POST_VARS['install'])) {
```

```
        $page_contents = 'install_3.php';
    } else {
      $page_contents = 'install.php';
    }
    break;
  case '4':
    if (osc_in_array('configure',
$HTTP_POST_VARS['install'])) {
        $page_contents = 'install_4.php';
    } else {
      $page_contents = 'install.php';
    }
    break;
case '5':
if (osc_in_array('configure',
$HTTP_POST_VARS['install'])) {
if (isset($HTTP_POST_VARS['ENABLE_SSL']) &&
($HTTP_POST_VARS['ENABLE_SSL'] == 'true')) {
$page_contents = 'install_5.php';
} else {
$page_contents = 'install_6.php';
}
} else {
$page_contents = 'install.php';
}
break;
case '6':
if (osc_in_array('configure',
$HTTP_POST_VARS['install'])) {
$page_contents = 'install_6.php';
} else {
$page_contents = 'install.php';
}
break;
case '7':
if (osc_in_array('configure',
$HTTP_POST_VARS['install'])) {
$page_contents = 'install_7.php';
} else {
$page_contents = 'install.php';
}
break;
default:
$page_contents = 'install.php';
}

require('templates/main_page.php');
```

Here, in the last line the page /main_page.php is called. Before calling it the variable "$page_contents" has been set to a value of a file name. This value is set according to the value of "$HTTP_GET_VARS['step']." You can see that inside the switch statements, different file names are set to the variable "$page_contents" as different cases. The value of the query string is set inside the /install_X.php files, and according to the query string, the next page is called in the installation process.

1.5.4. Adding or Removing an Installation Step

To add or remove an installation step, perform the following tasks:

1. First, create the file for that step, e.g., /install_M.php.
2. Save the file in the folder named /catalog/install/ templates/pages/ along with other files.
3. Add an uppercase "M" inside the switch statement.
4. Update the query string of the previous page with "?step=M."
5. Set the query string for the next page to the query string that was previously used in the preceding page.
6. To remove a step, just delete the case for that step, and set the query string of the previous page to the next page.

For the upgrade process the same steps should be followed.

Administration

As a storeowner, your most frequent interaction with osCommerce will be through the administrative area of the package, and this chapter will ensure that you are not left hanging when it comes to managing the administrative details of your online storefront. Throughout the chapter, customization of the administrative side of osCommerce is given frequent attention in order to allow the storeowner to optimize their experience with and use of the package.

Optimization takes several forms in this chapter; we discuss not only layout and the other physical changes that can be made to the administrative section, but also how to customize your store to cater to your needs as an administrator. For example, the administrative side of osCommerce supports multilingual systems, and you can customize the interface to display in your own, native language. While osCommerce comes with a host of useful tools, you can create your own tools if you find yourself with an additional administrative need, and in this chapter, we tell you how this is done.

osCommerce is adaptable to the needs of storeowners around the world, and this chapter will discuss how the package can be customized to meet the demands of localization. You will learn how to set tax rates, languages, and currencies according to your locale and the locale of your clientele. In addition, you will learn how to install and implement the payment, shipping, and other purchase-related options available to you, which you can tailor according to your requirements.

As your store grows, adding additional products to your product database, setting prices for these products, and holding specials, sales, and other promotional events can be done with ease using osCommerce. This chapter contains a section devoted to the addition of new products and the manipulation of product attributes to set prices for your products, establish sale prices, and automate the customization of your product pricing according to specified product variables. We even discuss how to manage the product review system and how to alert your customers to upcoming, new products.

Finally, the administrative side of osCommerce endows the store-owner with many practical tools. In addition to valuable reporting tools that can help the storeowner to gauge sales progress, other tools exist that help them to communicate with customers, manage files, and back up important data. You will find a thorough discussion of these tools within this chapter.

2.1. INDEX PAGE

The index page of the Admin interface is shown in Figure 2.1.

2.1.1. Changing the Index Page Content

You can find all the code and CSS for this page in the file /catalog/admin/index.php, and you can delete from this file all the code for the links that you do not want to show. There are a total of four boxes on the left side; let us consider the case of the osCommerce box. The following code is responsible for showing this box.

Figure 2.1. First page, Admin tool.

```php
$heading = array();
  $contents = array();

  $heading[] = array('params' =>
'class="menuBoxHeading"',
                     'text'  => 'osCommerce');

  $contents[] = array('params' =>
'class="infoBox"',
                      'text'  => '<a
href="http://www.oscommerce.com"
target="_blank">' . BOX_ENTRY_SUPPORT_SITE .
'</a><br>' .
                                  '<a
href="http://www.oscommerce.com/community.php/
forum" target="_blank">' .
BOX_ENTRY_SUPPORT_FORUMS . '</a><br>' .
                                  '<a
href="http://www.oscommerce.com/community.php/
mlists" target="_blank">' .
BOX_ENTRY_MAILING_LISTS . '</a><br>' .
                                  '<a
href="http://www.oscommerce.com/community.php/
bugs" target="_blank">' .
BOX_ENTRY_BUG_REPORTS . '</a><br>' .
                                  '<a
href="http://www.oscommerce.com/community.php/
faq" target="_blank">' . BOX_ENTRY_FAQ .
'</a><br>' .
                                  '<a
href="http://www.oscommerce.com/community.php/
irc" target="_blank">' .
BOX_ENTRY_LIVE_DISCUSSIONS . '</a><br>' .
                                  '<a
href="http://www.oscommerce.com/community.php/
cvs" target="_blank">' .
BOX_ENTRY_CVS_REPOSITORY . '</a><br>' .
                                  '<a
href="http://www.oscommerce.com/about.php/port
al" target="_blank">' .
BOX_ENTRY_INFORMATION_PORTAL . '</a>');

  $box = new box;
  echo $box->menuBox($heading, $contents);
```

At the beginning, two arrays are created.

```php
$heading = array();
$contents = array();
```

Then, these arrays are populated with values, and finally, an object "$box" of the class "box" is created, and the method "menuBox()" is called, passing the arrays as parameters.

```
echo $box->menuBox($heading, $contents);
```

This method returns the HTML for that box as a string, which gets printed by the "echo" statement.

Now, if you want to delete the whole box, then you have to comment out or delete at least the last line, or you can comment out or delete all of the code shown above.

```
// echo $box->menuBox($heading, $contents);
```

Now, save and refresh the index page. The whole osCommerce box will disappear!

Two types of boxes are shown on the left side: menu boxes and table boxes. The last one is a table box; the other three are menu boxes. If you want to add or remove a link or menu item from a particular box, then you have to set the value of the "$contents" array in such a way.

2.1.2. Changing the Index Page Style and Layout

The CSS code for style is written in the /catalog/admin/index.php page itself. You can edit the CSS according to your requirements and can change the style accordingly. To change the layout of the page, you have to edit the HTML of the page.

2.1.3. Removing the Administrative Tools Menu

The following code is responsible for setting the content of the Administrative Tools menu:

```
$cat = array(array('title' =>
BOX_HEADING_CONFIGURATION,
                      'image' =>
'configuration.gif',
                      'href'   =>
tep_href_link(FILENAME_CONFIGURATION,
'selected_box=configuration&gID=1'),
                      'children' =>
array(array('title' =>
BOX_CONFIGURATION_MYSTORE, 'link' =>
tep_href_link(FILENAME_CONFIGURATION,
'selected_box=configuration&gID=1')),
```

```
array('title' => BOX_CONFIGURATION_LOGGING,
'link' =>
tep_href_link(FILENAME_CONFIGURATION,
'selected_box=configuration&gID=10')),

array('title' => BOX_CONFIGURATION_CACHE,
'link' =>
tep_href_link(FILENAME_CONFIGURATION,
'selected_box=configuration&gID=11')))),
....................... .
....................... .

....................... .
....................... .

array('title' => BOX_HEADING_REPORTS,
                 'image' => 'reports.gif',
                 'href' =>
tep_href_link(FILENAME_STATS_PRODUCTS_PURCHASE
D, 'selected_box=reports'),
      'children' => array(array('title' =>
REPORTS_PRODUCTS, 'link' =>
tep_href_link(FILENAME_STATS_PRODUCTS_PURCHASE
D, 'selected_box=reports')),

array('title' => REPORTS_ORDERS, 'link' =>
tep_href_link(FILENAME_STATS_CUSTOMERS,
'selected_box=reports')))),
                array('title' =>
BOX_HEADING_TOOLS,
                 'image' => 'tools.gif',
'href' => tep_href_link(FILENAME_BACKUP,
'selected_box= tools'),
      'children' => array(array('title' =>
TOOLS_BACKUP, 'link' =>
tep_href_link(FILENAME_BACKUP,
'selected_box=tools')),
                array('title' =>
TOOLS_BANNERS, 'link' =>
tep_href_link(FILENAME_BANNER_MANAGER,
'selected_box=tools')),

array('title' => TOOLS_FILES, 'link' =>
tep_href_link(FILENAME_FILE_MANAGER,
'selected_box=tools')))));
```

A multidimensional array "$cat" is set throughout the code we see above. This array contains eight other array elements, one for every administrative tool. To add another administrative tool to the index page, add an array element in the "$cat" array. Similarly, to remove a tool from this page, delete the array element that is responsible for that tool. Figure 2.2 displays the index page again, where the left box, osCommerce, has been removed and an additional administrative tool, Administrator, has been added to the middle menu.

Once the array "$cat" is set, it needs to display in the browser. Here is the code that will display the content of the array in the browser.

```php
<?php
  $col = 2;
  $counter = 0;
  for ($i = 0, $n = sizeof($cat); $i < $n;
$i++) {
  $counter++;
  if ($counter < $col) {
  echo '                    <tr>' . "/n";
    }

    echo '                    <td><table
border="0" cellspacing="0" cellpadding="2">' .
"/n" .
            '                            <tr>' . "/n" .
            '                            <td><a
```

Figure 2.2. Modified index page.

```
href="' . $cat[$i]['href'] . '">' .
tep_image(DIR_WS_IMAGES . 'categories/' .
$cat[$i]['image'], $cat[$i]['title'], '32',
'32') . '</a></td>' . "/n" .
'<td><table border="0" cellspacing="0"
cellpadding="2">' . "/n" .
<tr>' . "/n" .
' <td class="main"><a href="' .
$cat[$i]['href'] . '" class="main">' .
$cat[$i]['title'] . '</a></td>' . "/n" .
</tr>' . "/n" .
<tr>' . "/n" .
<td class="sub">';

    $children = '';
    for ($j = 0, $k =
sizeof($cat[$i]['children']); $j < $k; $j++) {
        $children .= '<a href="' .
$cat[$i]['children'][$j]['link'] . '"
class="sub">' .
$cat[$i]['children'][$j]['title'] . '</a>, ';
    }
    echo substr($children, 0, -2);

    echo '</td> ' . "/n" .
        ' </tr>' . "/n" .
        '
</table></td>' . "/n" .
        ' </tr>' . "/n" .
        ' </table></td>' . "/n";

    if ($counter >= $col) {
      echo ' </tr>' . "/n";
      $counter = 0;
    }
  }
}
?>
```

2.2. LANGUAGE ISSUES

At the right side of the index page you see a drop-down list for Language. Once you select a language from that list, the page gets refreshed, and you can see all the headings in your selected language.

2.2.1. Multilanguage Support System

To make use of the multilanguage support facility, you will need to define all constants in different languages. For the Admin section, please see the /catalog/admin/includes/languages/ folder (Figure 2.3 shows an image of this folder). In the figure you can see that there are three folders and three files. Please observe the naming convention: it must be followed if you want to add a new language (see section 2.2.2).

Whenever the language of the interface is changed, only the headings, buttons, and link text as well as some static contents of the page will be modified accordingly. The content that is coming from the database will not be changed into the new language.

The files contain some constants that are common to the entire Admin section. In the file /english.php the constants are set with the values in English. Similarly, in the file /german.php the constants are set with the values in German.

Each folder contains some files and subfolders with the same name. Let us look at the folder named /english/ (Figure 2.4). This folder contains all the constants set in the English language. All the files inside the folder contain only constants. Here, also notice the naming convention; for example, all the constants required for the /catalog/admin/configuration.php file are defined in the /configuration.php file. Here is the code in the /configuration.php file of the /english/ folder.

```
define('TABLE_HEADING_CONFIGURATION_TITLE',
'Title');
define('TABLE_HEADING_CONFIGURATION_VALUE',
'Value');
define('TABLE_HEADING_ACTION', 'Action');

define('TEXT_INFO_EDIT_INTRO', 'Please make
any necessary changes');
define('TEXT_INFO_DATE_ADDED', 'Date Added:');
define('TEXT_INFO_LAST_MODIFIED', 'Last
Modified:');
```

The other two folders contain the same file, which just defines the same constants in the respective language. For example, here is the code in the /configuration.php file of the /espanol/ folder.

```
define('TABLE_HEADING_CONFIGURATION_TITLE',
'T&iacute;tulo');
define('TABLE_HEADING_CONFIGURATION_VALUE',
'Valor');
```

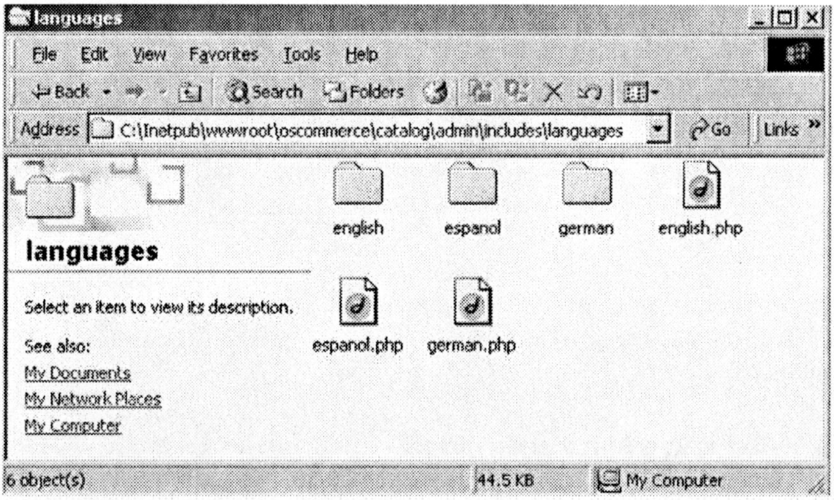

Figure 2.3. Directory structure for language.

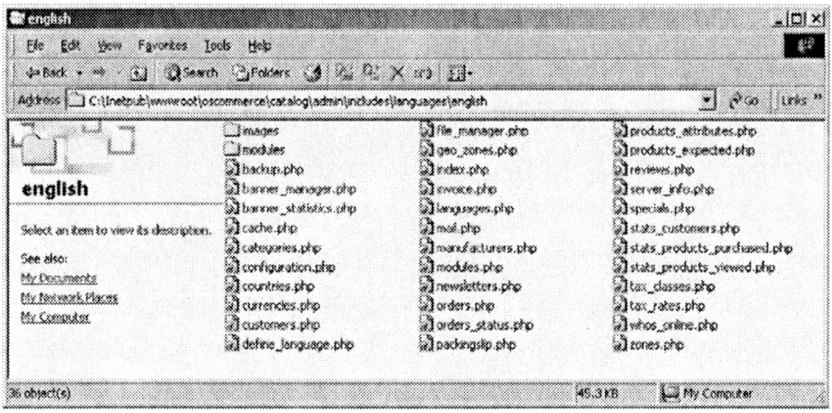

Figure 2.4. Folder /english/, containing all constants written in English.

```
define('TABLE_HEADING_ACTION', 'Acci&oacute;n');

  define('TEXT_INFO_EDIT_INTRO', 'Haga los
  cambios necesarios');
  define('TEXT_INFO_DATE_ADDED', 'Fecha de
  Alta:');
  define('TEXT_INFO_LAST_MODIFIED', 'Ultima
  Modificaci&oacute;n:');
```

These are all the files needed to make the site multilingual. Now, finally, we need to know the database structure for the language setup. There is a table named "languages" that contains all the information about the languages (Figure 2.5).

2.2.2. Adding a New Language

If you have gone through section 2.2.1, then you must be eager to add a new language to your package. Let us verify whether we understand the methodology presented in section 2.2.1 by adding a new language to our package.

Suppose that we want to add a language English1. Suppose that the rules for this language are the same as for English, except that in the English1 language, each word ends with a "1." For example, the sentence "I don't know other languages" will appear in English1 as "I1 don't1 know1 other1 languages1." Let us now follow the steps:

1. Add a new row in the "languages" table, as shown in Figure 2.6.
2. Add a file /english1.php and a folder /english1/ to the folder /catalog/admin/ includes/languages/, as in Figure 2.7.
3. Change the values of all constants that were defined inside the /english1.php file and in the other files in the /english1/ folder from English to English1.

Here is a portion of the /english1.php file that was changed from /english.php.

```
// categories box text in
includes/boxes/catalog.php
define('BOX_HEADING_CATALOG', 'Catalog1');
define('BOX_CATALOG_CATEGORIES_PRODUCTS',
'Categories1/Products1');
define('BOX_CATALOG_CATEGORIES_PRODUCTS_ATTRIB
UTES', 'Products1 Attributes1');
define('BOX_CATALOG_MANUFACTURERS',
'Manufacturers1');
define('BOX_CATALOG_REVIEWS', 'Reviews1');
define('BOX_CATALOG_SPECIALS', 'Specials1');
```

←T→	languages_id	name	code	image	directory	sort_order
□ ✐ ✗	1	English	en	icon.gif	english	1
□ ✐ ✗	2	Deutsch	de	icon.gif	german	2
□ ✐ ✗	3	Español	es	icon.gif	espanol	3

Figure 2.5. Default "languages" table.

←T→	languages_id	name	code	image	directory	sort_order
□ ✐ ✗	1	English	en	icon.gif	english	1
□ ✐ ✗	2	Deutsch	de	icon.gif	german	2
□ ✐ ✗	3	Español	es	icon.gif	espanol	3
□ ✐ ✗	4	English1	n1	icon.gif	english1	4

Figure 2.6. Modified "languages" table.

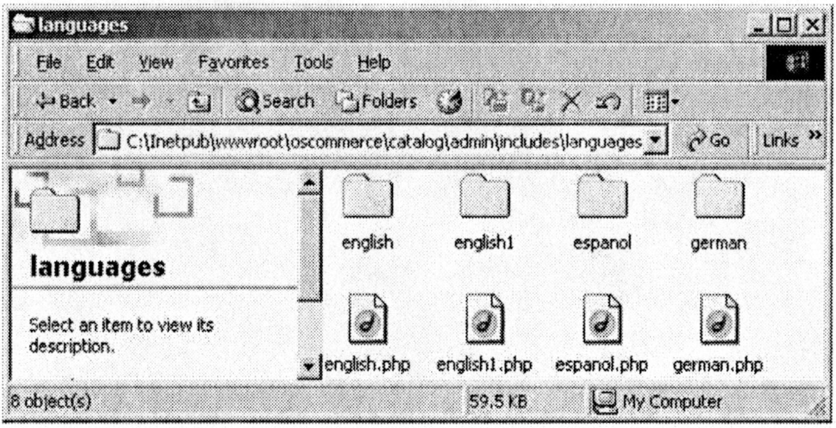

Figure 2.7. Modified /languages/ folder.

```
define('BOX_CATALOG_PRODUCTS_EXPECTED', 'Products1
        Expected1');

// customers box text in
includes/boxes/customers.php
define('BOX_HEADING_CUSTOMERS', 'Customers1');
define('BOX_CUSTOMERS_CUSTOMERS',
'Customers1');
define('BOX_CUSTOMERS_ORDERS', 'Orders1');
```

A "1" was added to the end of each English word. For a real language you
need to change the values into that language. You can now see the language-
changing effect in the Admin section. To see the effect in the Catalog section,
just follow steps 2 and 3 for the folder /catalog/includes/languages/.

Following the above few steps, you can access a version of the software in your native language. One thing that you should keep in mind is that
everything inside the /english1/ folder needs to be changed to English1; this
includes even the images of the buttons inside the /catalog/admin/includes/
languages/english1/images/buttons/ folder so that the image for the **Back**
button should be changed to **Back1**, as shown in Figure 2.8. Let us see how
the index page looks now (Figure 2.9).

But where are the links inside the Order1 box? Look at Figure 2.2:
there we can see that the Order box contains three links and shows some statistics of order status. The name of the order status, e.g., "pending," "delivered," etc., are coming from a table "orders_status." The query that fetches the
order status data from the table is written inside the following code, in the
/catalog/admin/index.php page.

```
$orders_contents = '';
  $orders_status_query = tep_db_query("select
orders_status_name, orders_status_id from " .
TABLE_ORDERS_STATUS . " where language_id = '"
. $languages_id . "'");
  while ($orders_status =
tep_db_fetch_array($orders_status_query)) {
    $orders_pending_query =
tep_db_query("select count(*) as count from "
. TABLE_ORDERS . " where orders_status = '" .
$orders_status['orders_status_id'] . "'");
    $orders_pending =
tep_db_fetch_array($orders_pending_query);
    $orders_contents .= '<a href="' .
tep_href_link(FILENAME_ORDERS,
'selected_box=customers&status='
    . $orders_status['orders_status_id']) .
'">'
```

Figure 2.8. Changing image for new language.

Figure 2.9. Index page in English1 language.

```
. $orders_status['orders_status_name'] .
'</a>: '
    . $orders_pending['count'] . '<br>';
  }
  $orders_contents = substr($orders_contents,
0, -4);

  $heading = array();
  $contents = array();

  $heading[] = array('params' =>
'class="menuBoxHeading"',
                     'text'   =>
BOX_TITLE_ORDERS);
```

```
$contents[] = array('params' =>
'class="infoBox"',
                            'text'  =>
$orders_contents);

    $box = new box;
    echo $box->menuBox($heading, $contents);
```

The query is fetching data from the "orders_status" table with respect to a language ID, but for the language ID "n1" (for the English1 language), there is no record in the "orders_status" table. So, let us insert some rows for the English1 language by running the following queries.

```
INSERT INTO `orders_status` VALUES (1, 4,
'Pending1');
INSERT INTO `orders_status` VALUES (2, 4,
'Processing1');
INSERT INTO `orders_status` VALUES (3, 4,
'Delivered1');
```

The table now looks like that shown in Figure 2.10. Refreshing the /index.php page will show the index page with all the contents modified.

This concludes our main discussion of the language issue, but as we progress, when required, we will explain relevant language-related issues further.

orders_status_id	language_id	orders_status_name
1	1	Pending
1	2	Offen
1	3	Pendiente
2	1	Processing
2	2	in Bearbeitung
2	3	Proceso
3	1	Delivered
3	2	Versendet
3	3	Entregado
1	4	Pending1
2	4	Processing1
3	4	Delivered1

Figure 2.10. Table "order_status."

2.3. ADMINISTRATIVE TOOLS

There are eight administrative tools available in the current version. These links/menus are situated in the left pane of the Admin main page:

- Configuration
- Catalog
- Modules
- Customers
- Locations and Taxes
- Localization
- Reports
- Tools

Technically, each tool is termed as a "box." Thus in the above menu we are looking at eight boxes, i.e., configuration box, catalog box, etc. In Figure 2.11 you can see the boxes on the left side. This is the main page of the Admin area. From this page we can set the values of the default settings of all the contents of the package.

One thing you should notice is that the last configuration tool that we added to the index page, Administrator, is not shown in the left menu. We should try to display it here also, so let us find out how the left menu items have been displayed.

2.3.1. General Discussion

2.3.1.1. Adding or removing an administrative tool in the left menu

To add an administrative tool, simply include the file /catalog/admin/ includes/column_left.php in the page in which you want to show this menu. Here is the code inside the file.

```
require(DIR_WS_BOXES . 'configuration.php');
require(DIR_WS_BOXES . 'catalog.php');
require(DIR_WS_BOXES . 'modules.php');
require(DIR_WS_BOXES . 'customers.php');
require(DIR_WS_BOXES . 'taxes.php');
require(DIR_WS_BOXES . 'localization.php');
require(DIR_WS_BOXES . 'reports.php');
require(DIR_WS_BOXES . 'tools.php');
```

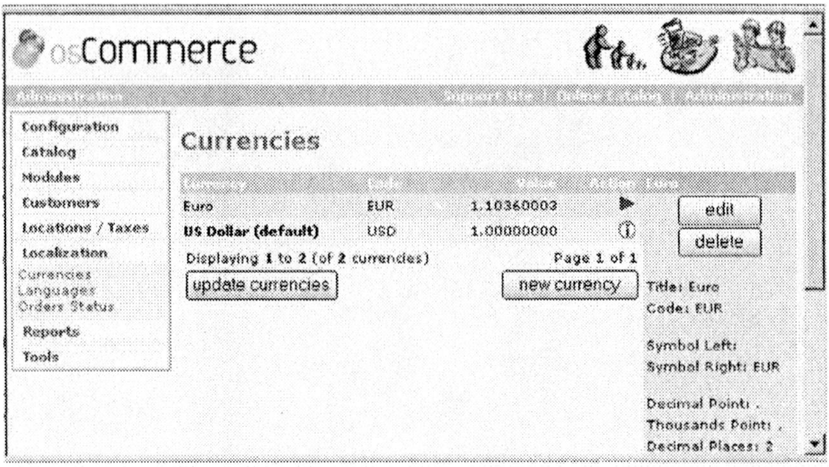

Figure 2.11. Admin main page.

The menu items are displayed in their respective files, e.g., the menu and sub-menus for Configuration are displayed in the /catalog/admin/includes/boxes/configuration.php file, etc. In contrast to above, to remove an administrative tool menu, just comment out the line that includes the file to display it.

To add an administrative tool menu, perform the following steps.

1. Add a line in the code in the appropriate position where you want to display the menu, as below.

```
require(DIR_WS_BOXES . 'configuration.php');
require(DIR_WS_BOXES . 'catalog.php');
require(DIR_WS_BOXES . 'modules.php');
require(DIR_WS_BOXES . 'customers.php');
require(DIR_WS_BOXES . 'taxes.php');
require(DIR_WS_BOXES . 'localization.php');
require(DIR_WS_BOXES . 'reports.php');
require(DIR_WS_BOXES . 'tools.php');
require(DIR_WS_BOXES . 'administrator.php');
```

The Administrator menu will be added at the bottom.

2. Create a file /administrator.php in the folder /catalog/admin/includes/boxes/ that holds the code for displaying the Administrator menu. Here is some sample code that has been written inside the /administrator.php page.

```
<!-- administrator //-->
```

```php
            <tr>
                <td>
<?php
  $heading = array();
  $contents = array();

  $heading[] = array('text'  =>
BOX_HEADING_ADMINISTRATOR,
                     'link'  =>
tep_href_link(FILENAME_ADMINISTRATOR,
'gID=16&selected_box=administrator'));

  if ($selected_box == 'administrator') {

    $contents[] = array('text'  => '<a href="'
. tep_href_link(FILENAME_ADMINISTRATOR) . '"
class="menuBoxContentLink">' .
BOX_HEADING_ADDEDIT . '</a><br>'.

        '<a href="' .
tep_href_link(FILENAME_PERMISSION) . '"
class="menuBoxContentLink">' .
BOX_HEADING_PERMISSION . '</a><br>');
  }

  $box = new box;
  echo $box->menuBox($heading, $contents);
?>
                </td>
            </tr>
<!-- administrator_eof //-->
```

To display the Administrator box at the first two arrays, "$heading" and "$contents" are set to certain values that may come from the database, or they can be written statically.

Here, two submenus were added under the Administrator menu. These are as follows.

1. BOX_HEADING_ADDEDIT
2. BOX_HEADING_PERMISSION

The values of these constants were set into all languages, /english.php, /english1.php, etc., as follows.

```php
define('BOX_HEADING_ADMINISTRATOR',
'Administrator');
define('BOX_HEADING_ADDEDIT', 'Add/Edit');
```

```
define('BOX_HEADING_PERMISSION',
'Permission');
```

Again, these two submenus are linked to the following files:

1. FILENAME_ADMINISTRATOR
2. FILENAME_PERMISSION

The values of these constants were set at the end of the /catalog/admin/ includes/filenames.php file, as follows.

```
define('FILENAME_ADMINISTRATOR',
'add_edit_admin.php');
define('FILENAME_PERMISSION',
'set_permission.php');
```

In the code above we used the function "tep_href_link()" to print the "href" attribute value of the "<a>" tag. This function, and many other such functions, are defined in the different files under the /catalog/admin/includes/ functions/ folder. All such required files have been included inside the /application_top.php file.

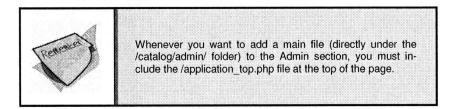

Whenever you want to add a main file (directly under the /catalog/admin/ folder) to the Admin section, you must include the /application_top.php file at the top of the page.

2.3.1.2. Adding a new page

Let us take a look at the Admin page again in order to observe the new menu. Now, the menu will appear as in Figure 2.12. It shows the Administrator box with two submenus: Add/Edit and Permission. Clicking these two submenus, the /add_edit_admin.php and /set_permission.php pages should open, respectively. However, these two files have not yet been added, so let us create the files by taking the following steps.

1. Create a new file directly under the /catalog/admin/ folder.
2. Paste the following minimum code to that file and save it.

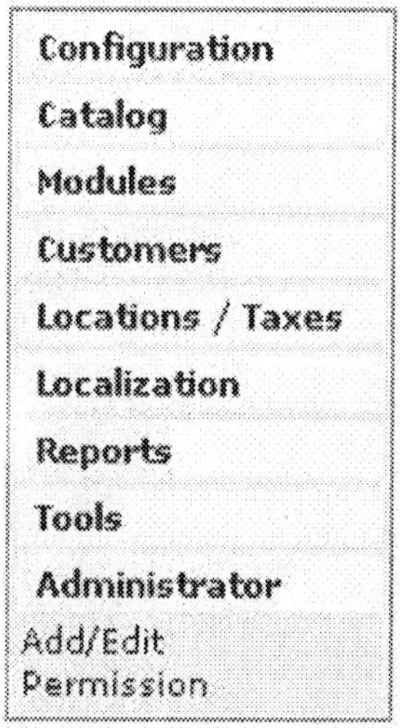

Figure 2.12. Modified left menus.

```
<?
require('includes/application_top.php');
?>
<!doctype html public "-//W3C//DTD HTML 4.01
Transitional//EN">
<html <?php echo HTML_PARAMS; ?>>
<head>
<meta http-equiv="Content-Type"
content="text/html; charset=<?php echo
CHARSET; ?>">
<title><?php echo TITLE; ?></title>
<link rel="stylesheet" type="text/css"
href="includes/stylesheet.css">
<script language="javascript"
src="includes/general.js"></script>
</head>
<body marginwidth="0" marginheight="0"
topmargin="0" bottommargin="0" leftmargin="0"
rightmargin="0" bgcolor="#FFFFFF"
onload="SetFocus();">
<!-- header //-->
<?php require(DIR_WS_INCLUDES . 'header.php');
?>
<!-- header_eof //-->

<!-- body //-->
<table border="0" width="100%" cellspacing="2"
cellpadding="2">
```

```
<tr>
    <td width="<?php echo BOX_WIDTH; ?>"
valign="top"><table border="0" width="<?php
echo BOX_WIDTH; ?>" cellspacing="1"
cellpadding="1" class="columnLeft">
<!-- left_navigation //-->
<?php require(DIR_WS_INCLUDES .
'column_left.php'); ?>
<!-- left_navigation_eof //-->
    </table></td>
<!-- body_text //-->


<!--Write the required code here-->


<!-- body_text_eof //-->
  </tr>
</table>
<!-- body_eof //-->

<!-- footer //-->
<?php require(DIR_WS_INCLUDES . 'footer.php');
?>
<!-- footer_eof //-->
<br>
</body>
</html>
<?php require(DIR_WS_INCLUDES .
'application_bottom.php'); ?>
```

This is the main code that remains the same in all the pages under the /catalog/admin/ folder.

Now, if we look at the pages /add_edit_admin.php or /set_permission.php after creating them through the above steps, they will look like Figure 2.13. This is the skeleton of a page, to which anything can be added.

Let us now discuss the above code as there are some important issues that will contribute to our understanding about how all of these things are happening. We will just discuss the highlighted lines in order to get answers to the following questions.

2.3.1.3. Including all required fields

If you want to create a new page and you want to get access to the database and all the configuration-related constants, language-related constants, database-handling functions, HTML-generating functions, and much more in

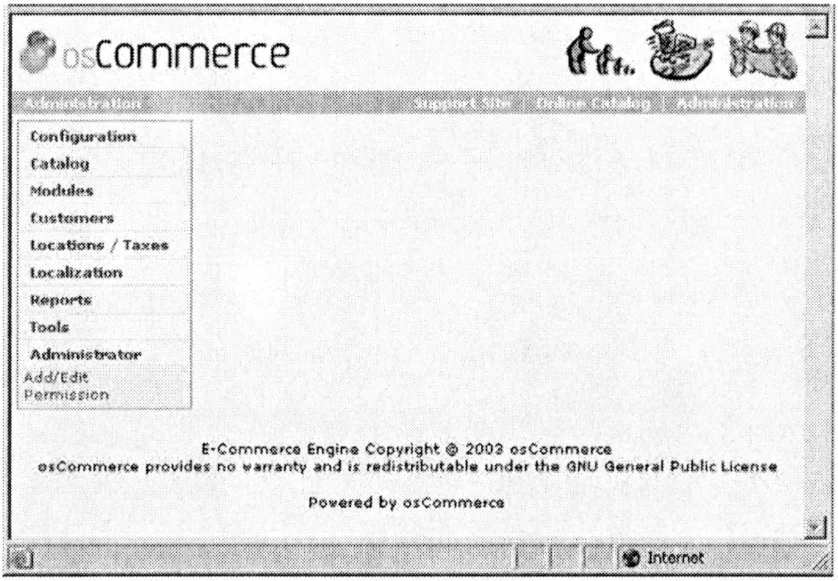

Figure 2.13. Page /add_edit_admin.php.

your page, then include the file /application_top.php. Here is a code fragment for including such files.

```
// Include application configuration
parameters
   require('includes/configure.php');
```

This file was generated during the last stage of the installation process and is used here.

There are many codes and constants defined within the /application.php file. It is recommended to go through all the content of this file. Here, only the most important code is shown.

```
// include the list of project filenames
   require(DIR_WS_INCLUDES . 'filenames.php');
// include the list of project database tables
   require(DIR_WS_INCLUDES .
'database_tables.php');
```

As the code is well commented, it is easy to understand what the files contain. Still, let us see what is written inside these files. The file /catalog/admin/ includes/filenames.php contains the following code.

```
// define the filenames used in the project
define('FILENAME_BACKUP', 'backup.php');
  define('FILENAME_BANNER_MANAGER',
'banner_manager.php');
  define('FILENAME_BANNER_STATISTICS',
'banner_statistics.php');
  define('FILENAME_CACHE', 'cache.php');

define('FILENAME_CATALOG_ACCOUNT_HISTORY_INFO'
, 'account_history_info.php');
  define('FILENAME_CATEGORIES',
'categories.php');
  define('FILENAME_CONFIGURATION',
'configuration.php');
  define('FILENAME_COUNTRIES',
'countries.php');
  define('FILENAME_CURRENCIES',
'currencies.php');
  define('FILENAME_CUSTOMERS',
'customers.php');
  define('FILENAME_DEFAULT', 'index.php');
  define('FILENAME_DEFINE_LANGUAGE',
'define_language.php');
  define('FILENAME_FILE_MANAGER',
'file_manager.php');
  define('FILENAME_GEO_ZONES',
'geo_zones.php');
  define('FILENAME_LANGUAGES',
'languages.php');
  define('FILENAME_MAIL', 'mail.php');
  define('FILENAME_MANUFACTURERS',
'manufacturers.php');
.............................
.............................
```

The file /catalog/admin/includes/database_tables.php contains the following code.

```
// define the database table names used in the
project
  define('TABLE_ADDRESS_BOOK',
'address_book');
  define('TABLE_ADDRESS_FORMAT',
'address_format');
  define('TABLE_BANNERS', 'banners');
  define('TABLE_BANNERS_HISTORY',
'banners_history');
  define('TABLE_CATEGORIES', 'categories');
```

```
 define('TABLE_CATEGORIES_DESCRIPTION',
'categories_description');
 define('TABLE_CONFIGURATION',
'configuration');
 define('TABLE_CONFIGURATION_GROUP',
'configuration_group');
 define('TABLE_COUNTRIES', 'countries');
 define('TABLE_CURRENCIES', 'currencies');
 define('TABLE_CUSTOMERS', 'customers');
```

The benefit of defining the thousands of constants used in your project is that the value of a constant can be changed without worrying about where it had been used previously. For example, suppose that the "customers" table had been used in thousands of places in your project; if you wanted to change the table name from "customers" to "customer_info," you would need to change the name in each and every place! However, if you had used the constant "TABLE_CUSTOMERS" instead of the table name "customers" in your code, you would only need to change the value of "TABLE_CUSTOMERS" from "customers" to "customer_info" in order to change the table name throughout your project.

Now, let us look at more of the code inside the /application.php file.

```
// include the database functions
  require(DIR_WS_FUNCTIONS . 'database.php');

// make a connection to the database... now
  tep_db_connect() or die('Unable to connect
to database server!');
```

All database-related functions available in PHP are customized and written in an easily accessible manner in the /catalog/admin/includes/functions/database.php file. For example, the "tep_db_connect()" function contains the following code to connect with the database.

```
function tep_db_connect($server = DB_SERVER,
$username = DB_SERVER_USERNAME, $password =
DB_SERVER_PASSWORD, $database = DB_DATABASE,
$link = 'db_link') {
    global $$link;

    if (USE_PCONNECT == 'true') {
```

```
    $$link = mysql_pconnect($server,
$username, $password);
    } else {
    $$link = mysql_connect($server,
$username, $password);
    }
    if ($$link) mysql_select_db($database);
    return $$link;
    }
```

Again, the following code includes two more important files.

```
// define our general functions used
application-wide

    require(DIR_WS_FUNCTIONS . 'general.php');
    require(DIR_WS_FUNCTIONS .
'html_output.php');
```

The /catalog/admin/includes/functions/html_output.php file contains all functions responsible for drawing the common HTML form elements, images, etc. The following function will return a form element.

More than 100 functions are contained in the /catalog/admin/includes/functions/general.php file. If you are a beginner, you might be able to learn a great deal of PHP by opening the file and examining the functions.

```
// Output a form
    function tep_draw_form($name, $action,
$parameters = '', $method = 'post', $params =
'') {
    $form = '<form name="' .
tep_output_string($name) . '" action="';
    if (tep_not_null($parameters)) {
    $form .= tep_href_link($action,
$parameters);
    } else {
    $form .= tep_href_link($action);
    }
    $form .= '" method="' .
tep_output_string($method) . '"';
    if (tep_not_null($params)) {
    $form .= ' ' . $params;
    }
```

```
$form .= '>';
return $form;
}
```

The following file contains all the session-related PHP functions, customized and written in an easily accessible manner.

```
// define how the session functions will be
used
    require(DIR_WS_FUNCTIONS . 'sessions.php');
```

The functions in the file /catalog/admin/includes/functions/session.php are customized in the following ways.

```
function tep_session_start() {
    return session_start();
}

function tep_session_register($variable) {
    return session_register($variable);
}

function
tep_session_is_registered($variable) {
    return session_is_registered($variable);
}

function tep_session_unregister($variable) {
    return session_unregister($variable);
}
```

There are also many classes that are included inside the /application_top.php file. Let us look at some code responsible for including certain class files.

```
// setup our boxes
    require(DIR_WS_CLASSES . 'table_block.php');
    require(DIR_WS_CLASSES . 'box.php');

// initialize the message stack for output
messages
    require(DIR_WS_CLASSES .
'message_stack.php');
    $messageStack = new messageStack;

// split-page-results
    require(DIR_WS_CLASSES .
'split_page_results.php');
```

```
// entry/item info classes
  require(DIR_WS_CLASSES . 'object_info.php');

// email classes
  require(DIR_WS_CLASSES . 'mime.php');

  require(DIR_WS_CLASSES . 'email.php');

// file uploading class
  require(DIR_WS_CLASSES . 'upload.php');
```

All the above class files are available in the /catalog/admin/includes/classes/ folder.

TIP

Look at the /box.php file that contains the "box" class, which is responsible for drawing the menus (or boxes) in the browser. In addition, examine all the code in all the classes—this will help you to learn how to write reusable code and much more about PHP.

Another thing you need to know is how the language-related functions are included for a particular language selected from the interface. Let us see the code inside the /application_top.php file that conditionally includes the language-related files.

```
// lets start our session
  tep_session_start();

// set the language in session variable
  if (!tep_session_is_registered('language')
|| isset($HTTP_GET_VARS['language'])) {
    if
(!tep_session_is_registered('language')) {
      tep_session_register('language');
      tep_session_register('languages_id');
    }

    include(DIR_WS_CLASSES . 'language.php');
    $lng = new language();

    if (isset($HTTP_GET_VARS['language']) &&
tep_not_null($HTTP_GET_VARS['language'])) {
      $lng-
>set_language($HTTP_GET_VARS['language']);
    } else {
      $lng->get_browser_language();
```

```
        }

        $language = $lng->language['directory'];
        $languages_id = $lng->language['id'];
    }

// include the language translations
    require(DIR_WS_LANGUAGES . $language .
'.php');
    $current_page = basename($PHP_SELF);
    if (file_exists(DIR_WS_LANGUAGES . $language
. '/' . $current_page)) {
//Includes the language file for the current
page.
        include(DIR_WS_LANGUAGES . $language . '/'
. $current_page);
    }
```

There are many more things in the /application_top.php file, but we were discussing how to include the required files to create a new page. To do so, we need not bother about the contents of the file. Simply include it in your page.

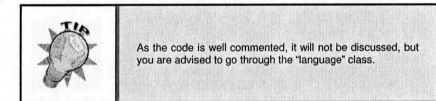

As the code is well commented, it will not be discussed, but you are advised to go through the "language" class.

2.3.1.4. Changing the look and feel of all administration pages

Each page in the Admin section includes a CSS file, as follows.

```
<link rel="stylesheet" type="text/css"
href="includes/stylesheet.css">
```

To change the color scheme, edit the /catalog/admin/includes/stylesheet.css file. Again, to change the layout, modify the HTML inside any page and inside the files /header.php and /footer.php.

2.3.1.5. Changing header and footer content

To change the content and logo of the headers and footers of the Admin section, edit the /catalog/admin/includes/header.php file. To change the copyright portion, edit the /catalog/admin/includes/footer.php file.

2.3.1.6. Adding the Administrative Tools menu

To cause the Administrative Tools menu to appear on your page, simply include the file /catalog/admin/includes/column_left.php, as follows, where you want to show the menu.

```
<?php require(DIR_WS_INCLUDES .
'column_left.php'); ?>
```

In the following sections we will discuss all the Administrative Tools in detail.

2.3.2. Configuration Menu

In this section you will learn how configuration works and where the configuration data is stored.

2.3.2.1. Configuration groups

A total of 15 configuration groups, such as My Store, Minimum Values, etc., are found in the current version. All the data for these configuration groups are stored in the "configuration_group" table of the database, the structure of which follows.

```
CREATE TABLE `configuration_group` (
  `configuration_group_id` int(11) NOT NULL
auto_increment,
  `configuration_group_title` varchar(64) NOT
NULL default '',
  `configuration_group_description`
varchar(255) NOT NULL default '',
  `sort_order` int(5) default NULL,
  `visible` int(1) default '1',
  PRIMARY KEY (`configuration_group_id`)
) TYPE=MyISAM AUTO_INCREMENT=1 ;
```

Figure 2.14 shows an image of the table contents.

2.3.2.2. Changing the contents of the Configuration menu

To change the contents of the Configuration menu, you must work directly from the database. First, open the database, then open the "configuration_group" table. Change the title of a group or change the description of a group, as you want, by editing the respective row. You can also hide a configuration group by switching the value of the "visible" field to "0" from "1."

configuration_group_id	configuration_group_title	configuration_group_description	sort_order	visible
1	My Store	General information about my store	1	1
2	Minimum Values	The minimum values for functions / data	2	1
3	Maximum Values	The maximum values for functions / data	3	1
4	Images	Image parameters	4	1
5	Customer Details	Customer account configuration	5	1
6	Module Options	Hidden from configuration	6	1

Figure 2.14. Table "configuration_group."

2.3.2.3. Adding a new Configuration menu

To add an extra menu, add an extra row for that configuration group. Figure 2.15 shows a new configuration group, Shopping Cart. This configuration group was added simply by inserting a new row into the "configuration_group" table.

2.3.2.4. Configurations

When you click a configuration group link, all the configurations under that group are listed in the middle pane of the page. Data for these configurations are stored in the "configuration" table, the structure of which follows.

Look at the query string after clicking on a configuration—it will help you to understand the data structure and the relation between configuration and configuration group.

```
CREATE TABLE `configuration` (
  `configuration_id` int(11) NOT NULL
auto_increment,
  `configuration_title` varchar(64) NOT NULL
default '',
  `configuration_key` varchar(64) NOT NULL
default '',
  `configuration_value` varchar(255) NOT NULL
default '',
  `configuration_description` varchar(255) NOT
NULL default '',
  `configuration_group_id` int(11) NOT NULL
default '0',
```

Field	Type	Function	Null	Value
configuration_group_id	int(11)			16
configuration_group_title	varchar(64)			Shopping Cart
configuration_group_description	varchar(255)			Configuring layout of the Shopping Cart
sort_order	int(5)		☐	16
visible	int(1)		☐	1

Figure 2.15. Inserting data to add new configuration group in Configuration menu.

```
`sort_order` int(5) default NULL,
`last_modified` datetime default NULL,
`date_added` datetime NOT NULL default
'0000-00-00 00:00:00',
`use_function` varchar(255) default NULL,
`set_function` varchar(255) default NULL,
PRIMARY KEY (`configuration_id`)
) TYPE=MyISAM AUTO_INCREMENT=1 ;
```

Figure 2.16 shows an image of the table contents. There are a total of 142 configurations in all 15 configuration groups in the current version.

2.3.2.5. Changing the contents in the configuration listing under a configuration group

You can change the configuration value only from the front end. To change any other configuration attribute, edit the "configuration" table for the particular configuration.

2.3.2.6. Adding a new configuration under a configuration group

To add a configuration, you will have to add a row to the "configuration" table in the database. Remember to set the appropriate "configuration_group_id" value in order to place the new configuration under a certain configuration group (see Figure 2.17).

By way of illustration, let us add a new configuration to the newly created configuration group Shopping Cart. To do so, simply add a new row to the "configuration" table (Figure 2.18). Set the value of "configuration_group_id" to 16 as it is under the Shopping Cart group. Also, set the value of "configuration value" to "false" (as we want to set the configuration value to either true or false, set the value of "set_function" to "tep_cfg_select_option(array('true', 'false')"; do not worry about the function syntax—the ending part of the function will be added at runtime according to the value selected by the user while editing this configuration).

configuration_id	configuration_title	configuration_key	
1	Store Name	STORE_NAME	SugarOnlir
2	Store Owner	STORE_OWNER	Subhamoy
3	E-Mail Address	STORE_OWNER_EMAIL_ADDRESS	subhamoy
4	E-Mail From	EMAIL_FROM	SugarOnlir
5	Country	STORE_COUNTRY	99

Figure 2.16. Table "configuration."

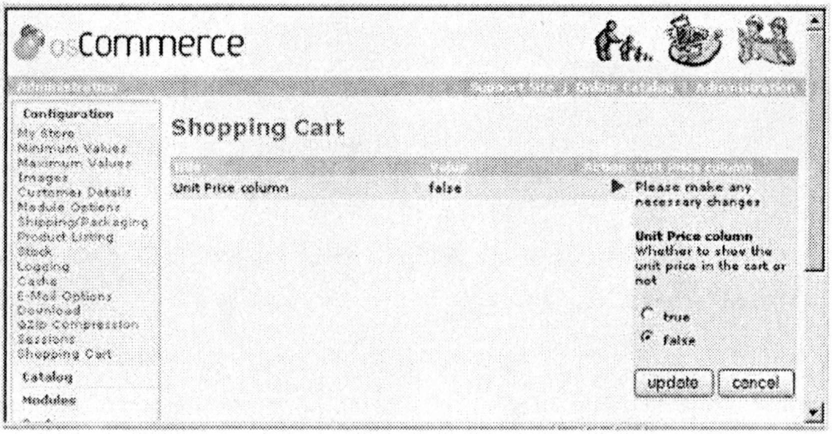

Figure 2.17. New configuration group.

Field	Type	Function	Null	Value
configuration_id	int(11)	▾		143
configuration_title	varchar(64)	▾		Unit Price column
configuration_key	varchar(64)	▾		UNIT_PRICE_COLUMN
configuration_value	varchar(255)	▾		false
configuration_description	varchar(255)	▾		Whether to show the unit price in the cart or no
configuration_group_id	int(11)	▾		16
sort_order	int(5)	▾	☐	1
last_modified	datetime	▾	☐	2005-07-06 17:18:44
date_added	datetime	▾		2005-07-06 17:15:05
use_function	varchar(255)	▾	☑	
set_function	varchar(255)	▾	☐	tep_cfg_select_option(array('true', 'false'),

Figure 2.18. Adding a new configuration.

```
tep_cfg_select_option(array('true', 'false'),
"true") or
tep_cfg_select_option(array('true', 'false'),
"false")
```

This function will draw a group of two radio buttons. Here is the code inside the function located at /catalog/admin/includes/functions/general.php.

```
function tep_cfg_select_option($select_array,
$key_value, $key = '') {
    $string = '';
    for ($i=0, $n=sizeof($select_array);
$i<$n; $i++) {
        $name = ((tep_not_null($key)) ?
'configuration[' . $key . ']' :
'configuration_value');
        $string .= '<br><input type="radio"
name="' . $name . '" value="' .
$select_array[$i] . '"';
        if ($key_value == $select_array[$i])
$string .= ' CHECKED';
        $string .= '> ' . $select_array[$i];
    }
    return $string;
}
```

When we upgrade the existing package with a newer version, these two tables also get updated.

2.3.3. Catalog Menu

Figure 2.19 shows the most common layout of the Catalog section. The Catalog section contains six subsections:

1. Categories/Products
2. Products Attributes
3. Manufacturers
4. Reviews
5. Specials
6. Products Expected

2.3.3.1. Categories/Products

Figure 2.19 shows the Categories/Products listing. Let us delete all categories and products. Now, click on the **New Category** button to add a new category. A form will open, as shown in Figure 2.20. You are required to enter the category name in four languages (the fourth language entered in Figure 2.20 is our English1 language). Figure 2.21 shows a category listing with three newly added categories.

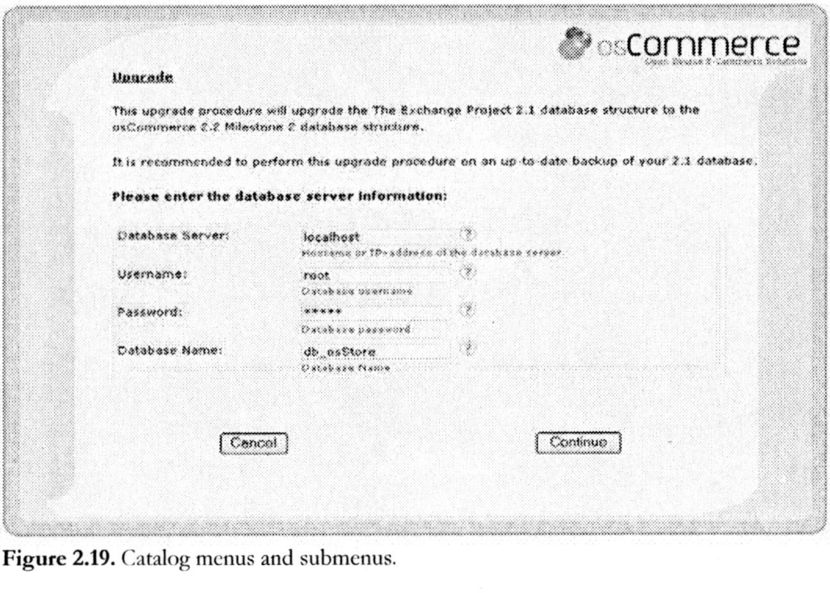

Figure 2.19. Catalog menus and submenus.

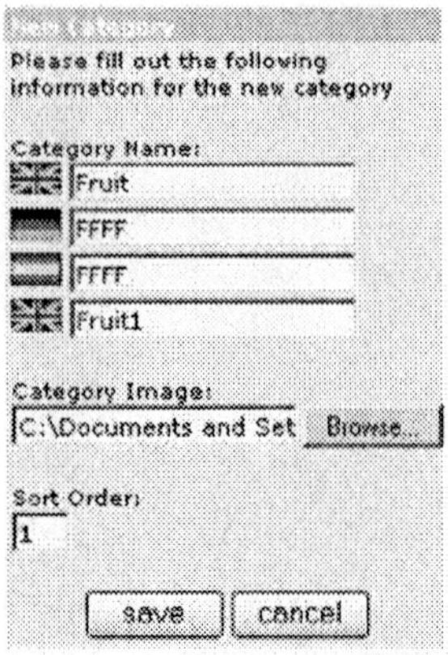

Figure 2.20. New Category form.

Figure 2.21. Category listing.

categories_id	categories_image	parent_id	sort_order	date_added	last_modified
2	homeprod2.jpg	0	2	2005-07-02 10:40:01	2005-07-02 16:02:52
21	pic085266648.JPG	0	3	2005-07-02 15:07:15	2005-07-20 15:57:41
22	img_n1.jpg	0	1	2005-07-20 15:53:02	*NULL*
23	upg.jpg	22	1	2005-07-20 16:19:19	*NULL*
24	*NULL*	22	2	2005-07-20 16:19:51	*NULL*

Figure 2.22. Table "categories."

You can click on the "Fruit" folder icon to view the categories or products under it. As there are no categories or products under the category "Fruit," the listing will be blank. Now, add another two categories, "Big Fruit" and "Small Fruit," under this category.

Information for the categories is stored in the table "categories" (Figure 2.22). (The names of the categories in all languages are stored in the "categories_description" table (Figure 2.23).) Look at the "parent_id" field: for the first three categories the "parent_id" is 0; for the next two categories the "parent_id" is 22. These are the "categories_id" of the parent category. So, whenever a new category is added, the "parent_id" field must be filled out in order to keep track of the category hierarchy. The categories having a "parent_id" of 0 are the top-level, or first-level, categories, and only those categories will be shown in the category box in the Catalog section.

In addition, products can be added under categories. Figure 2.24 shows a portion of the Add New Product form. Many different tables contain product information, but most of the product information is stored in the "products" table, the structure of which follows.

```
CREATE TABLE `products` (
  `products_id` int(11) NOT NULL
auto_increment,
  `products_quantity` int(4) NOT NULL default
'0',
  `products_model` varchar(12) default NULL,
  `products_image` varchar(64) default NULL,
  `products_price` decimal(15,4) NOT NULL
default '0.0000',
  `products_date_added` datetime NOT NULL
default '0000-00-00 00:00:00',
  `products_last_modified` datetime default
NULL,
  `products_date_available` datetime default
NULL,
  `products_weight` decimal(5,2) NOT NULL
default '0.00',
  `products_status` tinyint(1) NOT NULL
default '0',
  `products_tax_class_id` int(11) NOT NULL
default '0',
  `manufacturers_id` int(11) default NULL,
  `products_ordered` int(11) NOT NULL default
'0',
  PRIMARY KEY (`products_id`),
  KEY `idx_products_date_added`
(`products_date_added`)
)
```

categories_id	language_id	categories_name
22	1	Fruit
22	2	FFFF
22	3	FFFF
22	4	Fruit1
23	1	Big Fruit
23	2	BBBBB
23	3	BBBBBB
23	4	Big1 Fruit1
24	1	Small Fruit
24	2	sss
24	3	ssss
24	4	Small1 Fruit1

Figure 2.23. Table "categories_description."

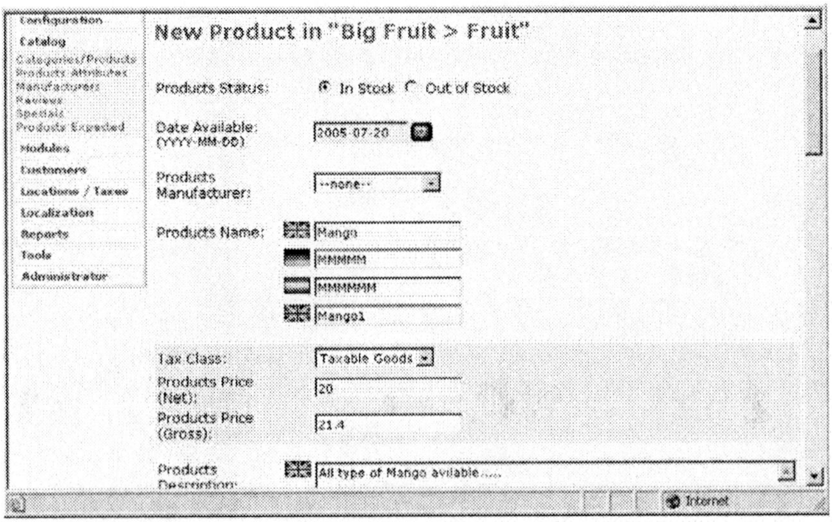

Figure 2.24. Add New Product form.

Information that was provided in multiple languages is stored in the "products_description" table (Figure 2.25), and the table shown in Figure 2.26, "products_to_categories," keeps track of the product-category mapping information.

2.3.3.2. Adding or removing a field from the Add New Product form

First, it is suggested that you open the /catalog/admin/categories.php page and take a look at the code. All the functionalities in the Catalog menu are contained inside this single page, so to keep one functionality separate from the others, each functionality has been defined inside a case under a "switch()" statement.

Now, to add or remove a form element, take the following steps:

1. Add/remove the HTML for the form element.
2. Add/remove the field in the "products" table.
3. Add/remove the required code from the appropriate case statement.

If you get an error message while going through these steps, do not worry—remember that the message will take you to the point at which you forgot to modify the code while upgrading.

To understand the logical flow of the program, you should closely observe the query string after each action from the interface. From the query string you will be able to determine which case you have to modify for a particular action.

2.3.3.3. Products Attributes

The Products Attributes page has three sections. We will discuss these sections one by one.

2.3.3.3.1. Product Options

Figure 2.27 shows a listing of the default product options. From here can be added a suitable, product-specific option; for example, suppose we want to add an option Freshness for our product Mango. We can translate the option name Freshness into different languages and press the **Insert** button to add this option. You can edit or delete an option by clicking the **Edit** or **Delete** button under the Action column, respectively. Figure 2.28 shows the Product Options edit screen. Then, after updating the field values, click the **Update** button to update, or else press **Cancel** to ignore the updates.

products_id	language_id	products_name	products_description	products_url	products_viewed
34	1	Mango	All type of Mango avilable....		0
34	2	MMMMM	AAAAAAAAAA		0
34	3	MMMMMM	AAAAAAAAAAAA		0
34	4	Mango1	All1 type1 of1 Mango1 avilable1....		0

Figure 2.25. Table "products_description."

products_id	categories_id
28	21
29	21
30	2
31	2
33	2
34	23

Figure 2.26. Table "products_to_categories."

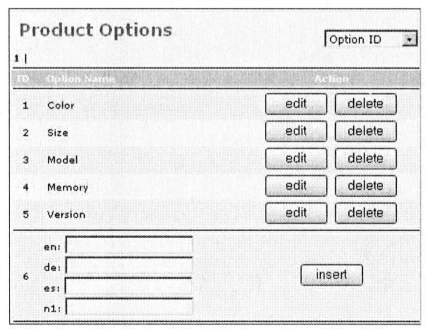

Figure 2.27. Product Options listing.

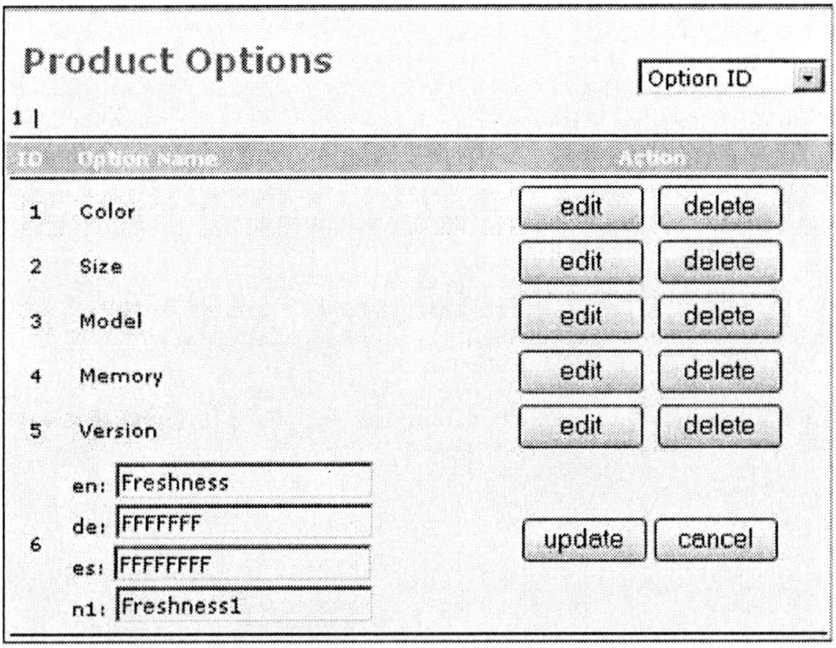

Product Options

Option ID ▾

1 |

ID	Option Name	Action	
1	Color	edit	delete
2	Size	edit	delete
3	Model	edit	delete
4	Memory	edit	delete
5	Version	edit	delete
6	en: Freshness de: FFFFFFF es: FFFFFFFF nl: Freshness1	update	cancel

Figure 2.28. Product Options edit screen.

products_options_id ▾	language_id	products_options_name
6	1	Freshness
6	2	FFFFFFF
6	3	FFFFFFFF
6	4	Freshness1
5	3	Version
5	2	Version
5	1	Version
4	1	Memory
4	2	Speicher
4	3	Memoria

Figure 2.29. Table "products_options."

Look at the functionality minutely. We can list, update, and delete elements in ASP.NET easily by Data Grid; in ASP.NET Data Grid you need not bother about how the form elements are being rendered in the same row in the editing mode nor about the table structure, but in PHP you need to do everything manually. We will see how the osCommerce programmers have done this, but before going through the code, let us see where in the database the product option values are stored: in the "products_options" table (Figure 2.29).

Now, let us go to the /catalog/admin/products_attributes.php page. In this page also, the same story has been applied to maintain the various functionalities. You just need to track the query string after each action taken from the interface, then go to the appropriate case in which the required code for that action has been written. For some actions you cannot get the information from the query string, for example, when you are submitting the form to insert an option and then the following form is being posted.

```
echo '<form name="options" action="' .
tep_href_link(FILENAME_PRODUCTS_ATTRIBUTES,
'action=add_product_options&option_page=' .
$option_page, 'NONSSL') . '"
method="post"><input type="hidden"
name="products_options_id" value="' . $next_id
. '">';

        $inputs = '';
        for ($i = 0, $n = sizeof($languages); $i
< $n; $i ++) {
$inputs .= $languages[$i]['code'] .
': <input type="text" name="option_name['
. $languages[$i]['id'] . ']"
size="20"> <br>';
        }
        ?>
    <td align="center"
class="smallText"> <?php echo $next_id;
?> </td>
                <td class="smallText"><?php
echo $inputs; ?></td>
                <td align="center"
class="smallText"> <?php echo
tep_image_submit('button_insert.gif',
IMAGE_INSERT); ?> </td>
        <?php
echo '</form>';
```

The value in the "action" attribute of the "form" tag contains the query string that was used by the "switch($action)" statement when the page was returned back, but the query string will not appear in the URL because at the last of the "case 'add_product_options':" statements the page is being redirected with some new query string.

Here is the code responsible for inserting an option into the database.

```
switch ($action) {
        case 'add_product_options':
```

```
$products_options_id =
tep_db_prepare_input($HTTP_POST_VARS['products
_options_id']);
            $option_name_array =
$HTTP_POST_VARS['option_name'];

            for ($i=0, $n=sizeof($languages);
$i<$n; $i ++) {
            $option_name =
tep_db_prepare_input($option_name_array[$langu
ages[$i]['id']]);

tep_db_query("insert into " .
TABLE_PRODUCTS_OPTIONS . "
(products_options_id, products_options_name,
language_id) values ('" .
(int)$products_options_id . "', '" .
tep_db_input($option_name) . "', '" .
(int)$languages[$i]['id'] . "')");
            }

tep_redirect(tep_href_link(FILENAME_PRODUCTS_A
TTRIBUTES, $page_info));
            break;
```

2.3.3.3.2. Option Values

The second part of the /catalog/admin/products_attributes.php page contains information on the option values (see Figure 2.30). The listing in Figure 2.30 is showing the option values inserted through the form at the bottom of the list.

To add an option value, select an option from the drop-down list on the left, then insert the value in all languages before pressing the **Insert** button. Let us add the following values to the option Freshness:

Fresh;
Packaged 5 days ago;
Packaged 1 month ago.

Figure 2.31 shows these values added. The data for the product options values are stored in the "products_options_values" table, as shown in Figure 2.32.

The code for all this functionality is written in the /catalog/admin/products_attributes.php page. Here is some sample code that is responsible for drawing the Option Values insert form.

```
echo '<form name="values" action="' .
tep_href_link(FILENAME_PRODUCTS_ATTRIBUTES,
```

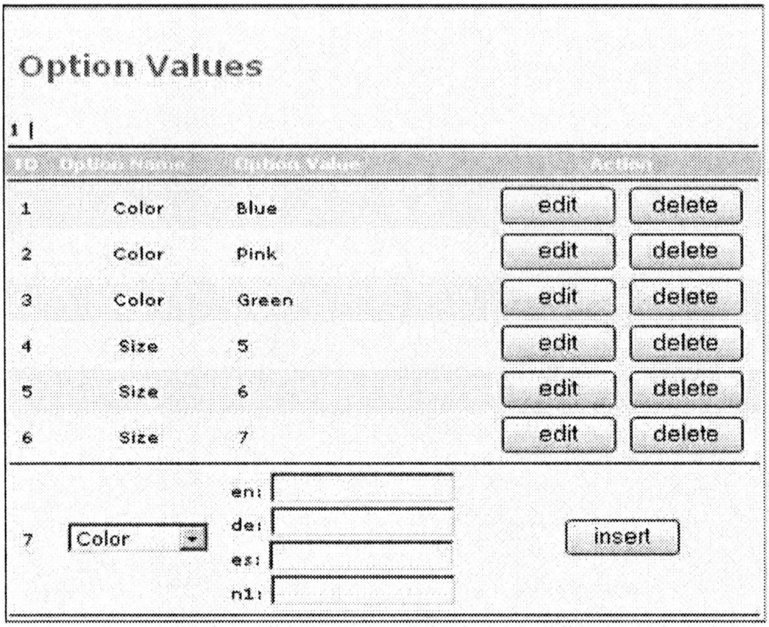

Option Values

1 |

ID	Option Name	Option Value	Action	
1	Color	Blue	edit	delete
2	Color	Pink	edit	delete
3	Color	Green	edit	delete
4	Size	5	edit	delete
5	Size	6	edit	delete
6	Size	7	edit	delete
7	Color	en: de: es: nl:	insert	

Figure 2.30. Option Values listing.

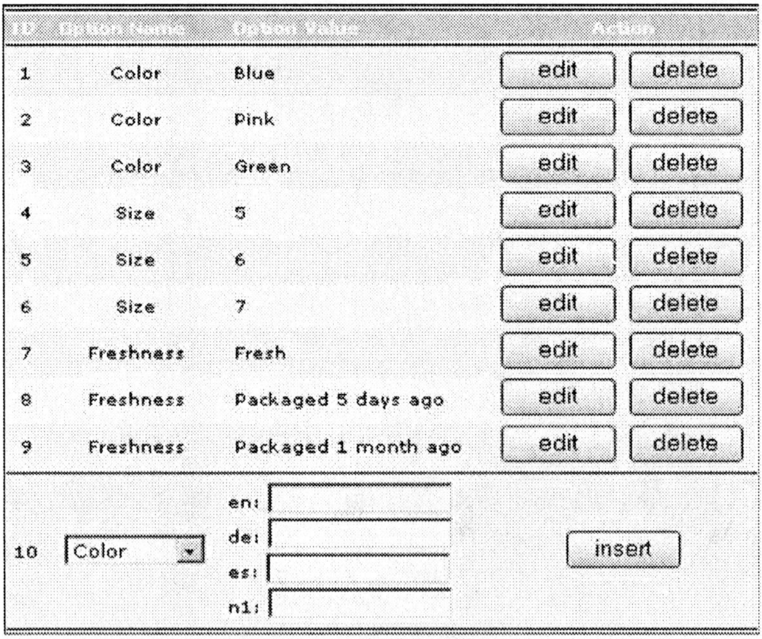

ID	Option Name	Option Value	Action	
1	Color	Blue	edit	delete
2	Color	Pink	edit	delete
3	Color	Green	edit	delete
4	Size	5	edit	delete
5	Size	6	edit	delete
6	Size	7	edit	delete
7	Freshness	Fresh	edit	delete
8	Freshness	Packaged 5 days ago	edit	delete
9	Freshness	Packaged 1 month ago	edit	delete
10	Color	en: de: es: nl:	insert	

Figure 2.31. Option Values listing: Showing values for Freshness.

products_options_values_id ▼	language_id	products_options_values_name
9	1	Packaged 1 month ago
9	2	popoppop
9	3	POPOPOPOP
9	4	Packaged1 1 month1 ago1
8	1	Packaged 5 days ago
8	2	PPPPPP
8	3	PPPPPPPP
8	4	Packaged1 5 days1 ago1
7	1	Fresh
7	2	FFFFF
7	3	FFFFFF
7	4	Fresh1

Figure 2.32. Table "products_options_values."

```php
'action=add_product_option_values&value_page=' . $value_page,
        'NONSSL') . '" method="post">';
    ?>
        <td align="center"
    class="smallText"> <?php echo $next_id;
    ?> </td>
        <td align="center"
    class="smallText"> <select
    name="option_id">
        <?php
$options = tep_db_query("select
products_options_id, products_options_name
from " . TABLE_PRODUCTS_OPTIONS . " where
language_id = '" . $languages_id . "' order by
products_options_name");
        while ($options_values =
tep_db_fetch_array($options)) {
        echo '<option name="' .
$options_values['products_options_name'] . '"
value="' .
$options_values['products_options_id'] . '">'
. $options_values['products_options_name'] .
'</option>';
        }

        $inputs = '';
```

```
        for ($i = 0, $n = sizeof($languages); $i
< $n; $i ++) {
            $inputs .= $languages[$i]['code'] .
': <input type="text" name="value_name['
. $languages[$i]['id'] . ']"
size="15"> <br>';
        }
    ?>
                </select> </td>
                <td class="smallText"><input
type="hidden" name="value_id" value="<?php
echo $next_id; ?>"><?php echo $inputs; ?></td>
    <td align="center"
class="smallText"> <?php echo
tep_image_submit('button_insert.gif',
IMAGE_INSERT); ?> </td>
        <?php
    echo '</form>';
```

The above form is posted when you click the **Insert** button. When the page is returning back, the following code is being executed to perform the insertion.

Go through the code step by step. You will learn how a drop-down list is populated and how the form elements are drawn in osCommerce.

```
    case 'add_product_option_values':
        $value_name_array =
$HTTP_POST_VARS['value_name'];
        $value_id =
tep_db_prepare_input($HTTP_POST_VARS['value_id
']);
        $option_id =
tep_db_prepare_input($HTTP_POST_VARS['option_i
d']);

        for ($i=0, $n=sizeof($languages);
$i<$n; $i ++) {
            $value_name =
`tep_db_prepare_input($value_name_array[$langu
ages[$i]['id']]);

tep_db_query("insert into " .
TABLE_PRODUCTS_OPTIONS_VALUES . "
(products_options_values_id, language_id,
products_options_values_name) values ('" .
```

products_options_values_to_products_options_id	products_options_id	products_options_values_id
1	1	1
2	1	2
3	1	3
4	2	4

Figure 2.33. Table "products_options_values_to_products_options."

```
(int)$value_id . "', '" .
(int)$languages[$i]['id'] . "', '" .
tep_db_input($value_name) . "')");
        }

tep_db_query("insert into " .
TABLE_PRODUCTS_OPTIONS_VALUES_TO_PRODUCTS_OPTI
ONS . " (products_options_id,
products_options_values_id) values ('" .
(int)$option_id . "', '" . (int)$value_id .
"')");

tep_redirect(tep_href_link(FILENAME_PRODUCTS_A
TTRIBUTES, $page_info));
break;
```

One more thing that needs to be mentioned before we move on to the next section is that there is a table named "products_options_values_to_products_options," which contains the mapping information for the "products_options_values" and "products_options" tables (Figure 2.33).

2.3.3.3.3. Products Attributes

This is the third section of the /catalog/admin/products_attributes.php page. From this section we can add, edit, and delete the product attributes of a particular product (see Figure 2.34).

To add a product attribute to a product, the form at the bottom of the listing is used. The first drop-down list contains all products, irrespective of product category. The second drop-down list contains all product options, and the third one contains all option values, irrespective of product options. From these lists, choose the appropriate combination, and then insert the price that should be added to get the product with the selected attribute. If you want to deduct some price for a particular attribute, then you have to change the plus (+) sign of the next text field to minus (−).

Suppose that for the product Mango we want to add the following attributes:

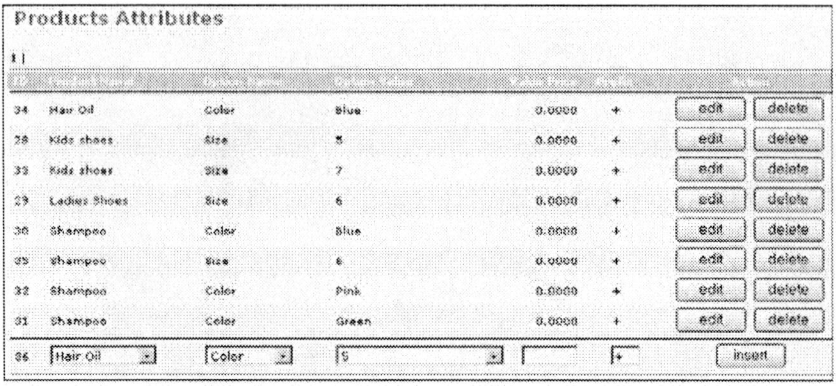

Figure 2.34. Products Attributes listing.

Mango with Freshness → Fresh will cost $1 extra;
Mango with Freshness → Packaged 5 days ago will cost
nothing extra;
Mango with Freshness → Packaged 1 month ago will cost
$1 less.

Figure 2.35 shows these attributes after adding them with the above form. Now you can see the effect of adding attributes to the Mango product in the Catalog section (see Figure 2.36). The details of the products with attributes are stored in the "products_attributes" table (Figure 2.37).

Now, let us look at some code responsible for the manipulation of the product attributes from the file /catalog/admin/products_attributes.php.

```
case 'add_product_attributes':
        $products_id =
tep_db_prepare_input($HTTP_POST_VARS['products
_id']);
        $options_id =
tep_db_prepare_input($HTTP_POST_VARS['options_
id']);
        $values_id =
tep_db_prepare_input($HTTP_POST_VARS['values_i
d']);
        $value_price =
tep_db_prepare_input($HTTP_POST_VARS['value_pr
ice']);
        $price_prefix =
tep_db_prepare_input($HTTP_POST_VARS['price_pr
efix']);
```

ID	Product Name	Option Name	Option Value	Value Price	Prefix
37	Mango	Freshness	Packaged 1 month ago	1.0000	-
39	Mango	Freshness	Packaged 5 days ago	0.0000	+
36	Mango	Freshness	Fresh	1.0000	+
31	Shampoo	Color	Green	0.0000	+
35	Shampoo	Size	6	0.0000	+
30	Shampoo	Color	Blue	0.0000	+
32	Shampoo	Color	Pink	0.0000	+
40	Hair Oil	Color	5		+

Figure 2.35. Products Attributes listing: After adding Freshness attribute to Mango.

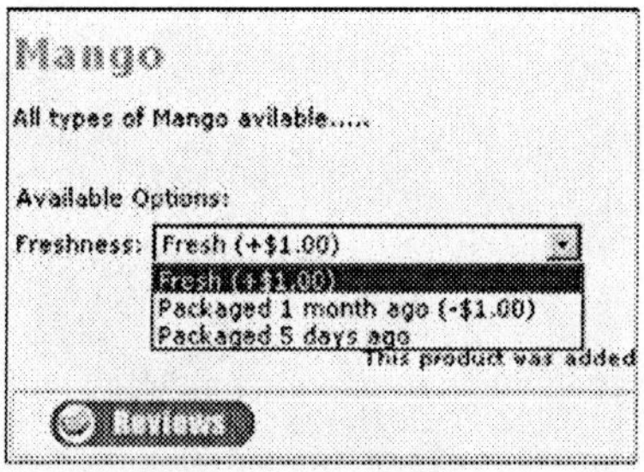

Figure 2.36. Product details view from Catalog section.

products_attributes_id	products_id	options_id	options_values_id	options_values_price	price_prefix
35	29	2	5	0.0000	+
32	29	1	2	0.0000	+
31	29	1	3	0.0000	+
30	29	1	1	0.0000	+
40	28	1	4	0.0000	+
36	34	3	7	1.0000	+
37	34	3	9	1.0000	-
39	34	3	8	0.0000	+

Figure 2.37. Table "products_attributes."

```
tep_db_query("insert into " . TABLE_PRODUCTS_ATTRIBUTES . "
values ('', '" . (int)$products_id . "', '" . (int)$options_id
. "', '" . (int)$values_id . "', '" .
tep_db_input($value_price) . "', '" .
tep_db_input($price_prefix) . "')");
                    if (DOWNLOAD_ENABLED == 'true') {
                        $products_attributes_id =
            tep_db_insert_id();
                        $products_attributes_filename =
            tep_db_prepare_input
               ($HTTP_POST_VARS['products_attributes_filen
            ame']);
                        $products_attributes_maxdays =
            tep_db_prepare_input
               ($HTTP_POST_VARS['products_attributes_maxda
            ys']);
            $products_attributes_maxcount =
            tep_db_prepare_input
            ($HTTP_POST_VARS['products_attributes_maxcount
            ']);
                        if
            (tep_not_null($products_attributes_filename))
            {
            tep_db_query("insert into " .
            TABLE_PRODUCTS_ATTRIBUTES_DOWNLOAD . " values
            (" . (int)$products_attributes_id . ", '" .
            tep_db_input($products_attributes_filename) .
            "', '" .
            tep_db_input($products_attributes_maxdays) .
            "', '" .
            tep_db_input($products_attributes_maxcount) .
            "')");
                        }
                    }

            tep_redirect(tep_href_link(FILENAME_PRODUCTS_A
            TTRIBUTES, $page_info));
            break;
```

The above code is responsible for adding a row to the "products_attributes"
table. In the code we observe that there is an "IF" block for the
"DOWNLOAD_ENABLED" option.

```
            if (DOWNLOAD_ENABLED == 'true')
```

If "DOWNLOAD_ENABLED" is set to "true" (it can be set from the Admin
> Configuration > Download section), then three more fields will be ap-

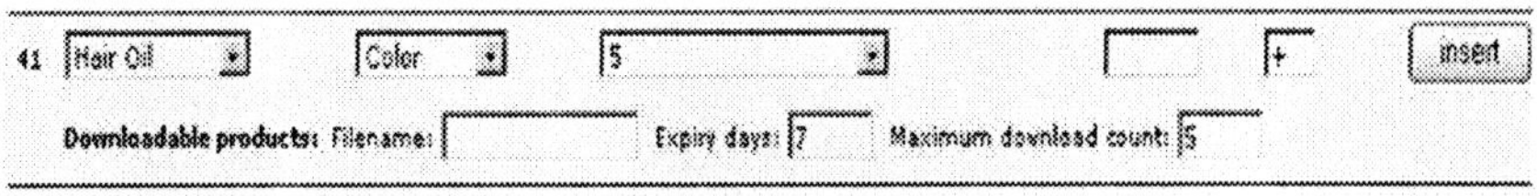

Figure 2.38. Add Product Attribute form when download option is set to "true."

products_attributes_id	products_attributes_filename	products_attributes_maxdays	products_attributes_maxcount
26	unreal.zip	7	3
40	void.zip	7	5

Figure 2.39. Table "products_attributes_download."

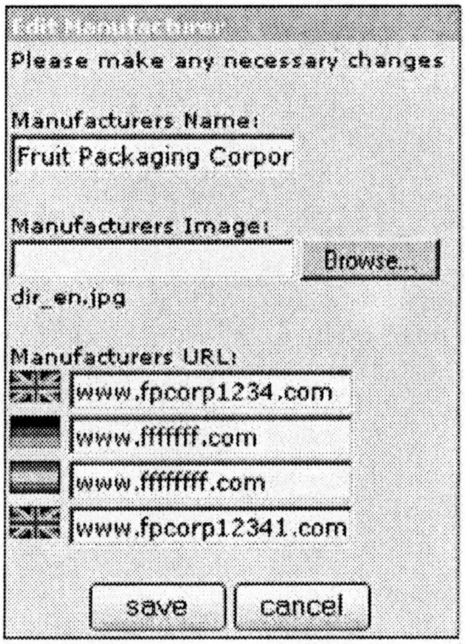

Figure 2.40. Adding new manufacturer.

pended to the Add Product Attribute form (Figure 2.38). These values are saved by the above "IF" block into the "products_attributes_ download" table (Figure 2.39).

2.3.3.4. Manufacturers

From this section you can add the product manufacturers' details using the form shown in Figure 2.40. The details of manufacturers provided in this form are stored in the "manufacturers" table, as shown in Figure 2.41. Again, some language-specific manufacturers' information is stored in the "manufacturers_info" table, as shown in Figure 2.42. The code for manipulating this manufacturers' information is written in the /catalog/admin/manufactures.php file. Here is some sample code that is responsible for inserting manufacturers' data into the above tables.

The field "url_clicked" in the "manufacturers_info" table keeps track of how many times the URL is visited by users. It is updated whenever the link is clicked by a user from the Catalog section.

```php
switch ($action) {
      case 'insert':
      case 'save':
if (isset($HTTP_GET_VARS['mID']))
$manufacturers_id = tep_db_prepare_input
($HTTP_GET_VARS['mID']);
$manufacturers_name = tep_db_prepare_input
($HTTP_POST_VARS['manufacturers_name']);
         $sql_data_array =
array('manufacturers_name' =>
$manufacturers_name);
         if ($action == 'insert')
{$insert_sql_data = array('date_added' =>
'now()');
         $sql_data_array =
array_merge($sql_data_array,
$insert_sql_data);
            tep_db_perform(TABLE_MANUFACTURERS,
$sql_data_array);
            $manufacturers_id =
tep_db_insert_id();
         } elseif ($action == 'save') {
            $update_sql_data =
array('last_modified' => 'now()');
            $sql_data_array =
array_merge($sql_data_array,
$update_sql_data);
 tep_db_perform(TABLE_MANUFACTURERS,
$sql_data_array, 'update', "manufacturers_id =
'" . (int)$manufacturers_id . "'");
         }
   if ($manufacturers_image = new
upload('manufacturers_image',
DIR_FS_CATALOG_IMAGES)) {
```

manufacturers_id ▼	manufacturers_name	manufacturers_image	date_added	last_modified
10	Fruit Packaging Corporation	dir_en.jpg	2005-07-22 13:39:48	NULL
9	Hewlett Packard	manufacturer_hewlett_packard.gif	2005-07-02 10:40:02	NULL
8	GT Interactive	manufacturer_gt_interactive.gif	2005-07-02 10:40:02	NULL
7	Sierra	manufacturer_sierra.gif	2005-07-02 10:40:02	NULL
6	Canon	manufacturer_canon.gif	2005-07-02 10:40:02	NULL
5	Logitech	manufacturer_logitech.gif	2005-07-02 10:40:02	NULL

Figure 2.41. Table "manufacturers."

manufacturers_id ▼	languages_id	manufacturers_url	url_clicked	date_last_click
10	4	www.fpcorp12341.com	0	NULL
10	3	www.fffffff.com	0	NULL
10	2	www.fffff.com	0	NULL
10	1	www.fpcorp1234.com	0	NULL
9	3	http://welcome.hp.com/country/es/spa/welcome.htm	0	NULL
9	2	http://www.hewlettpackard.de	0	NULL

Figure 2.42. Table "manufacturers_info."

```
tep_db_query("update " . TABLE_MANUFACTURERS .
" set manufacturers_image = '" .
$manufacturers_image->filename . "' where
manufacturers_id = '" . (int)$manufacturers_id
. "'");
          }
          $languages = tep_get_languages();
          for ($i=0, $n=sizeof($languages);
$i<$n; $i++) {
          $manufacturers_url_array =
$HTTP_POST_VARS['manufacturers_url'];
          $language_id = $languages[$i]['id'];

$sql_data_array = array('manufacturers_url' =>
tep_db_prepare_input($manufacturers_url_array[
$language_id]));
          if ($action == 'insert') {
             $insert_sql_data =
array('manufacturers_id' => $manufacturers_id,

'languages_id' => $language_id);
             $sql_data_array =
array_merge($sql_data_array,
$insert_sql_data);
```

```
tep_db_perform(TABLE_MANUFACTURERS_INFO,
$sql_data_array);
        } elseif ($action == 'save') {
 tep_db_perform(TABLE_MANUFACTURERS_INFO,
$sql_data_array, 'update', "manufacturers_id =
'" . (int)$manufacturers_id . "' and
languages_id = '" . (int)$language_id . "'");
        }
    }
    if (USE_CACHE == 'true') {

tep_reset_cache_block('manufacturers');
    }
    tep_redirect(tep_href_link(FILENAME_MANUFACTUR
ERS, (isset($HTTP_GET_VARS['page']) ? 'page='
. $HTTP_GET_VARS['page'] . '&' : '') . 'mID='
. $manufacturers_id));
    break;
........ . .
```

2.3.3.5. Reviews

There is a system through which customers can write product reviews. Any user can write a review of any product and can rate each product with one to five stars. The administrator can see, update, and delete such reviews from this Reviews section. Figure 2.43 shows the screen from which the administrator can update a review. The reviews are stored in two tables: the "reviews" table contains the review history (see Figure 2.44), and another table, "reviews_descriptions," contains the review note or text along with a language ID (see Figure 2.45).

The code for manipulating these reviews is written in the /catalog/admin/manufactures.php page. Here is a fraction of code that updates and deletes a review from the database.

```
if (tep_not_null($action)) {
    switch ($action) {
        case 'update':
            $reviews_id =
tep_db_prepare_input($HTTP_GET_VARS['rID']);
$reviews_rating = tep_db_prepare_input
($HTTP_POST_VARS['reviews_rating']);
$reviews_text =
tep_db_prepare_input($HTTP_POST_VARS['reviews_
text']);
tep_db_query("update " . TABLE_REVIEWS . " set
reviews_rating = '" .
tep_db_input($reviews_rating) . "',
```

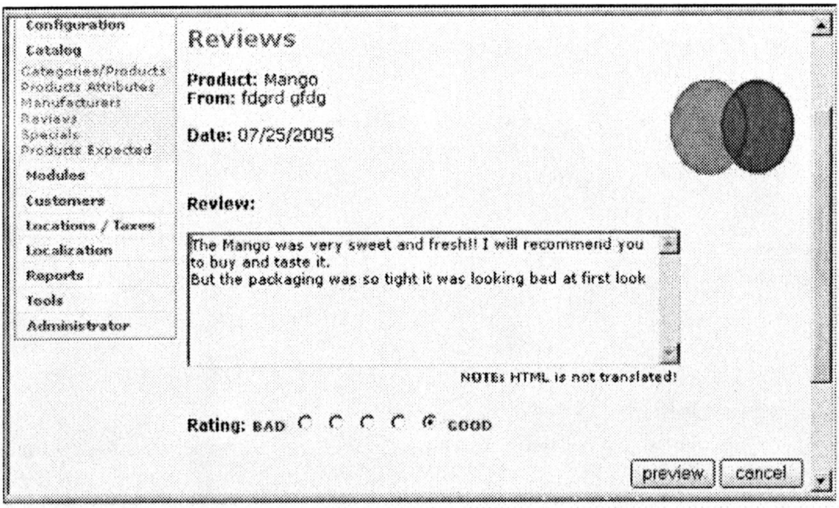

Figure 2.43. Reviews edit screen.

reviews_id	products_id	customers_id	customers_name	reviews_rating	date_added	last_modified	reviews_read
2	34	6	fdgrd gfdg	5	2005-07-25 15:08:40	2005-07-25 15:11:58	0

Figure 2.44. Table "reviews."

reviews_id	languages_id	reviews_text
2	1	The Mango was very sweet and fresh!! I will recomm...

Figure 2.45. Table "reviews_descriptions."

```
last_modified = now() where reviews_id = '" .
(int)$reviews_id . "'");
tep_db_query("update " .
TABLE_REVIEWS_DESCRIPTION . " set reviews_text
= '" . tep_db_input($reviews_text) . "' where
reviews_id = '" . (int)$reviews_id . "'");

tep_redirect(tep_href_link(FILENAME_REVIEWS,
'page=' . $HTTP_GET_VARS['page'] . '&rID=' .
$reviews_id));
     break;
     case 'deleteconfirm':
        $reviews_id =
tep_db_prepare_input($HTTP_GET_VARS['rID']);
```

```
tep_db_query("delete from " . TABLE_REVIEWS .
" where reviews_id = '" . (int)$reviews_id .
"'");
tep_db_query("delete from " .
TABLE_REVIEWS_DESCRIPTION . " where reviews_id
= '" . (int)$reviews_id . "'");

tep_redirect(tep_href_link(FILENAME_REVIEWS,
'page=' . $HTTP_GET_VARS['page']));
    break;
  }
}
```

2.3.3.6. Specials

Suppose that you want to sell a product at a special price—you'd use the Specials section to change the price. You can also set an expiry date for the special price. The product with the special price will be shown in the Catalog section up to that day. From this section you can add, edit, or delete specials for any product. Figure 2.46 shows a listing of products with a special price. The values for the specials are stored in the "specials" table (Figure 2.47). The total table contents cannot be shown here; please use your own database to get a full view of the table.

The code for manipulating these specials is written in the /catalog/admin/specials.php page. Here is a fraction of code that inserts and deletes a product's special information from the database.

```
case 'insert':
        $products_id =
tep_db_prepare_input($HTTP_POST_VARS['products
_id']);
 $products_price=tep_db_prepare_input
($HTTP_POST_VARS['products_price']);
 $specials_price =   tep_db_prepare_input
($HTTP_POST_VARS['specials_price']);
        $day =
tep_db_prepare_input($HTTP_POST_VARS['day']);
        $month =
tep_db_prepare_input($HTTP_POST_VARS['month'])
;
        $year =
tep_db_prepare_input($HTTP_POST_VARS['year']);
        if (substr($specials_price, -1) ==
'%') {
$new_special_insert_query =
tep_db_query("select products_id,
products_price from " . TABLE_PRODUCTS . "
```

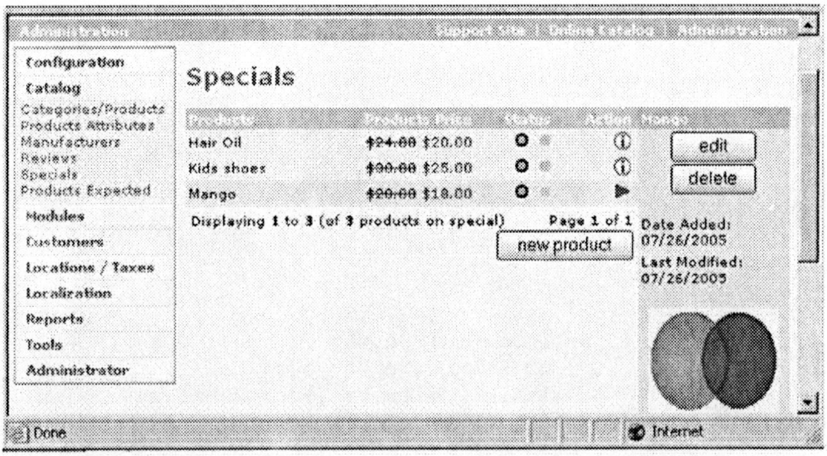

Figure 2.46. Products with special prices.

specials_id	products_id	specials_new_products_price	specials_date_added	specials_last_modified	expires_date
5	28	20.0000	2005-07-25 17:53:54	2005-07-25 17:55:38	2005-07-26 00:00:00
6	30	25.0000	2005-07-25 17:54:59	*NULL*	2005-07-27 00:00:00
7	34	18.0000	2005-07-26 13:13:49	2005-07-26 13:49:10	2005-07-26 00:00:00

Figure 2.47. Table "specials."

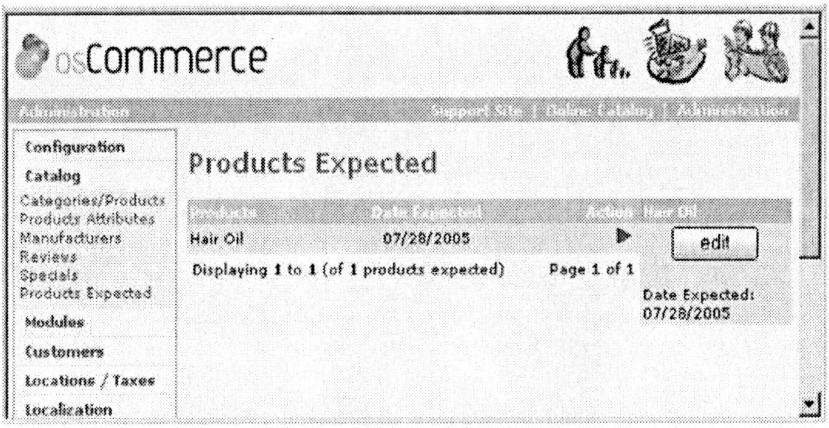

Figure 2.48. Products Expected listing.

```
where products_id = '" . (int)$products_id .
"'");
        $new_special_insert =
tep_db_fetch_array($new_special_insert_query);

        $products_price =
$new_special_insert['products_price'];
$specials_price = ($products_price -
(($specials_price / 100) *  $products_price));
        }
        $expires_date = '';
        if (tep_not_null($day) &&
tep_not_null($month) && tep_not_null($year)) {
        $expires_date = $year;
        $expires_date .= (strlen($month) ==
1) ? '0' . $month : $month;
        $expires_date .= (strlen($day) == 1)
? '0' . $day : $day;
        }
tep_db_query("insert into " . TABLE_SPECIALS .
" (products_id, specials_new_products_price,
specials_date_added, expires_date, status)
values ('" . (int)$products_id . "', '" .
tep_db_input($specials_price) . "', now(), '"
. tep_db_input($expires_date) . "', '1')");
tep_redirect(tep_href_link(FILENAME_SPECIALS,
'page=' . $HTTP_GET_VARS['page']));
break;

case 'deleteconfirm':
        $specials_id =
tep_db_prepare_input($HTTP_GET_VARS['sID']);
tep_db_query("delete from " . TABLE_SPECIALS .
" where specials_id = '" . (int)$specials_id .
"'");
tep_redirect(tep_href_link(FILENAME_SPECIALS,
'page=' . $HTTP_GET_VARS['page']));
break;
```

2.3.3.7. Products Expected

When we add a product to the Categories/Products section, we need to select a date on which the product will be available from the store. If a date later than today's date is selected, then the product will appear in the listing of the Products Expected section. Moreover, in the Catalog section a listing of upcoming products can be found at the bottom of the home page. Figure 2.48 shows a listing of the products expected in the Products Expected section.

You can edit the expected date by clicking the **Edit** button. Then, the product edit page in the Category/Product section will open.

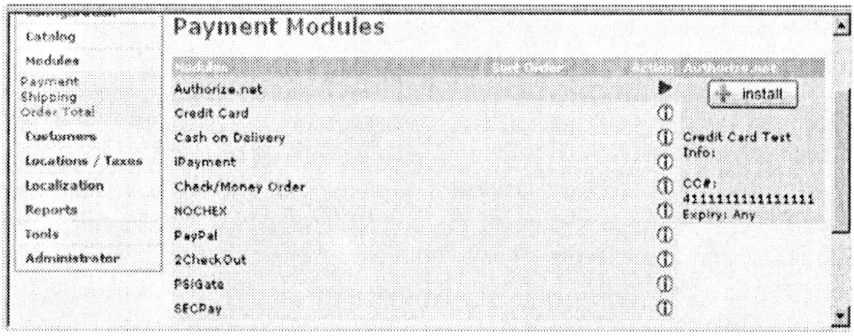

Figure 2.49. Payment Modules listing.

2.3.4. Modules Menu

This section deals with the configuration of purchase-related modules. Three modules are discussed in this section: Payment, Shipping, and Order Total.

2.3.4.1. Payment

This section discusses the several payment options available with os-Commerce. A listing of all 10 payment options is available in the current version (see Figure 2.49). You can install one or more payment modules by clicking the **Install** button corresponding to your chosen module, and you can provide users with more than one payment option. The payment module will then be installed with the default configuration settings. Once a payment module is installed, users can see the payment option during the checkout process, and users can then pay for their chosen products using that payment option.

Each and every payment module is different with respect to logic, security, implementation, etc., but they all are integrated in osCommerce through a general rule and are presented to us with a similar interface. By using the common interface, you can add or remove a payment module from your customized version, but as a general user, to activate a payment option, you just need to install one payment module and edit the default setting, if necessary. You need not know much more than that. Therefore if you are a general user, then it is enough for you to know how a payment module is activated, and thus you can skip the rest of this section. However, if you want to know the implementation details, then continue with this section.

First, let us take a look at how a payment module is installed. We will work with the credit card payment option as it is the most common. To install the credit card payment module, click on the Credit Card row, and then click on the **Install** button. By that action, the payment module for the credit card payment system will be installed with the default settings (default values are shown in Figure 2.50). You can edit the default settings by clicking the **Edit** button, as shown in Figure 2.51. If you want to disable a payment option, then you will have to remove it by clicking the **Remove** button.

Now, let us see what is actually happening and where the data is being stored for the credit card payment system. When we click the **Install** button, the following code is executed inside the file /catalog/admin/modules.php.

```
case 'install':
    case 'remove':
        $file_extension = substr($PHP_SELF,
strrpos($PHP_SELF, '.'));
        $class =
basename($HTTP_GET_VARS['module']);
        if (file_exists($module_directory .
$class . $file_extension)) {
            include($module_directory . $class .
$file_extension);
            $module = new $class;
            if ($action == 'install') {
                $module->install();
            } elseif ($action == 'remove') {
                $module->remove();
            }
        }
tep_redirect(tep_href_link(FILENAME_MODULES,
'set=' . $set . '&module=' . $class));
break;
```

Let us go through the code line by line. The code works on the following query string: "modules.php?set=payment&module=cc&action=install." The first two lines set some variable to generate a file name.

```
$file_extension = substr($PHP_SELF,
strrpos($PHP_SELF, '.'));
$class = basename($HTTP_GET_VARS['module']);
```

In our case the two variables will contain the following values.

```
$file_extension => '.php'
$class => 'cc'
```

The next two lines just include a file with the above file name.

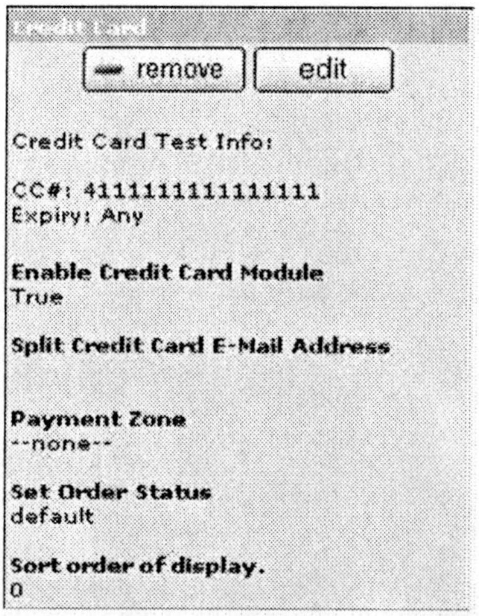

Figure 2.50. Default settings of the credit card payment module.

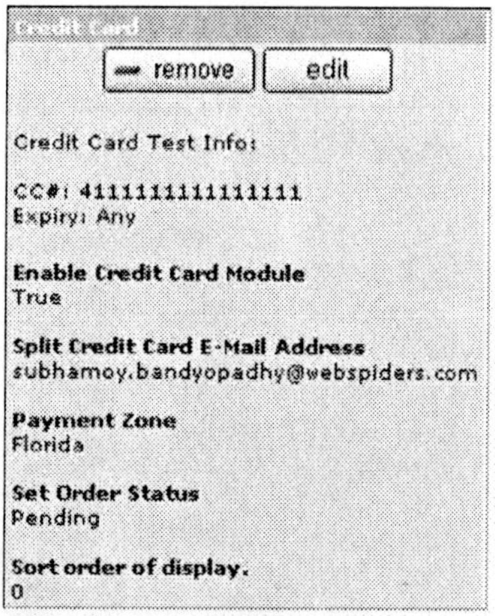

Figure 2.51. After editing the default settings of the credit card payment module.

```
if (file_exists($module_directory . $class .
$file_extension)) {
include($module_directory . $class .
$file_extension);
```

In our case the actual path for including the file will be as follows: C:/Inetpub/wwwroot/oscommerce/catalog/includes/modules/payment/cc.php. If the file /cc.php exists, then it will be included by the "include" statement.

A view of the /payment/ folder is shown in Figure 2.52; please take a look at its contents. There are 10 files for 10 payment systems. As the names suggest, each file contains a class responsible for implementing the respective payment system.

Now, let us examine the rest of the above code.

```
$module = new $class;
if ($action == 'install') {
        $module->install();
} elseif ($action == 'remove') {
        $module->remove();
}
```

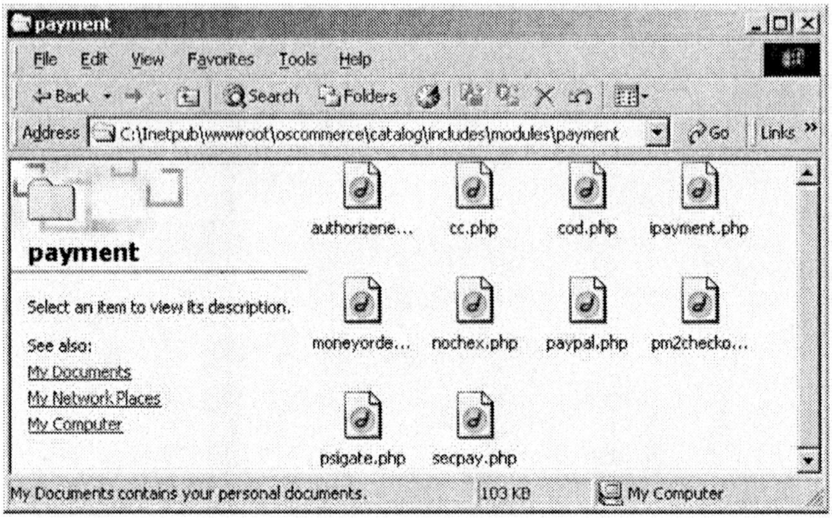

Figure 2.52. Contents of /payment/ folder.

After including the file /cc.php the class "cc" is instantiated by the statement "$module = new $class." The next lines conditionally call the member methods "install()" and "remove()" according to the action taken.

The next line redirects us to the same page with the new query string. That is why we cannot see the actual query string ("modules.php?set=payment &module=cc&action=install") on which the above code is executed. Here is the line.

```
tep_redirect(tep_href_link(FILENAME_MODULES,
'set=' . $set . '&module='.$class));
```

We have discussed the code that is responsible for installing and removing a payment component from the osCommerce site, but to gain a deeper understanding, it is necessary to go into more detail. Let us go one layer deeper and look at the content of the "cc" class. In the /cc.php file you will see the definition of the "cc" class. Here is a portion of the "cc" class (class definition and constructor "cc()").

```
class cc {
    var $code, $title, $description, $enabled;
// class constructor
    function cc() {
        global $order;
```

```
        $this->code = 'cc';
        $this->title =
MODULE_PAYMENT_CC_TEXT_TITLE;
        $this->description =
MODULE_PAYMENT_CC_TEXT_DESCRIPTION;
        $this->sort_order =
MODULE_PAYMENT_CC_SORT_ORDER;
        $this->enabled =
((MODULE_PAYMENT_CC_STATUS == 'True') ? true :
false);
        if
((int)MODULE_PAYMENT_CC_ORDER_STATUS_ID > 0) {
            $this->order_status =
MODULE_PAYMENT_CC_ORDER_STATUS_ID;
        }
        if (is_object($order)) $this-
>update_status();
    }
..................... .
```

You can go through the remainder of the code yourself. For now we will just
discuss the code for the "install()" and "remove()" methods because other
methods are responsible for performing the tasks of the Catalog section.

Here is the code for the "install()" method.

```
function install() {
    tep_db_query("insert into " .
TABLE_CONFIGURATION . " (configuration_title,
configuration_key, configuration_value,
configuration_description,
configuration_group_id, sort_order,
set_function, date_added) values ('Enable
Credit Card Module',
'MODULE_PAYMENT_CC_STATUS', 'True', 'Do you
want to accept credit card payments?', '6',
'0', 'tep_cfg_select_option(array(/'True/',
/'False/'), ', now())");
    tep_db_query("insert into " .
TABLE_CONFIGURATION . " (configuration_title,
configuration_key, configuration_value,
configuration_description,
configuration_group_id, sort_order,
date_added) values ('Split Credit Card E-Mail
Address', 'MODULE_PAYMENT_CC_EMAIL', '', 'If
an e-mail address is entered, the middle
digits of the credit card number will be sent
to the e-mail address (the outside digits are
stored in the database with the middle digits
censored)', '6', '0', now())");
```

```
    tep_db_query("insert into " .
TABLE_CONFIGURATION . " (configuration_title,
configuration_key, configuration_value,
configuration_description,
configuration_group_id, sort_order,
date_added) values ('Sort order of display.',
'MODULE_PAYMENT_CC_SORT_ORDER', '0', 'Sort
order of display. Lowest is displayed first.',
'6', '0' , now())");
    tep_db_query("insert into " .
TABLE_CONFIGURATION . " (configuration_title,
configuration_key, configuration_value,
configuration_description,
configuration_group_id, sort_order,
use_function, set_function, date_added) values
('Payment Zone', 'MODULE_PAYMENT_CC_ZONE',
'0', 'If a zone is selected, only enable this
payment method for that zone.', '6', '2',
'tep_get_zone_class_title',
'tep_cfg_pull_down_zone_classes(', now())");
    tep_db_query("insert into " .
TABLE_CONFIGURATION . " (configuration_title,
configuration_key, configuration_value,
configuration_description,
configuration_group_id, sort_order,
set_function, use_function, date_added) values
('Set Order Status',
'MODULE_PAYMENT_CC_ORDER_STATUS_ID', '0', 'Set
the status of orders made with this payment
module to this value', '6', '0',
'tep_cfg_pull_down_order_statuses(',
'tep_get_order_status_name', now())");
}
```

As per the code we see that during the installation process, five rows are added to the "configuration" table. These values are the default values for the credit card payment system.

The "remove()" method does the reverse work of the "install()" method. Here is the code.

```
function remove() {
tep_db_query("delete from " .
TABLE_CONFIGURATION . " where
configuration_key in ('" . implode("', '",
$this->keys()) . "')");
    }

function keys() {
```

```
return array('MODULE_PAYMENT_CC_STATUS',
'MODULE_PAYMENT_CC_EMAIL',
'MODULE_PAYMENT_CC_ZONE',
'MODULE_PAYMENT_CC_ORDER_STATUS_ID',
'MODULE_PAYMENT_CC_SORT_ORDER');
    }
```

The "remove()" method just deletes the configuration data for the credit card payment system with respect to the configuration keys returned by the "keys()" method.

Let us leave the "cc" class for now and look at the code from the /modules.php file that is responsible for updating the default payment configuration.

```
switch ($action) {
    case 'save':
        while (list($key, $value) =
each($HTTP_POST_VARS['configuration'])) {
tep_db_query("update " . TABLE_CONFIGURATION .
" set configuration_value = '" . $value . "'
where configuration_key = '" . $key . "'");
        }
tep_redirect(tep_href_link(FILENAME_MODULES,
'set=' . $set . '&module=' .
$HTTP_GET_VARS['module']));
break;
```

Through the above discussion we see how the credit card payment system can be installed, updated, and deleted. The story for other payment systems is the same, except for the class—each payment module uses a separate class. In each class the payment module has been implemented with a specific logic, code, and configuration.

2.3.4.2. Shipping

This section deals with the shipping cost that the customer will need to pay in order for their purchased product to be delivered. In the current version of osCommerce, there is a total of six shipping modules. You have to install the module that you want to provide to your customer. After installing you can change the default setting of that shipping module.

Figure 2.53 shows a listing of the shipping modules.

The code for handling the shipping module is written in the /catalog/admin/modules.php file. The /modules.php file actually handles the whole Modules section. The following code defines for which section (Payment/Shipping/Order Details) the page will work.

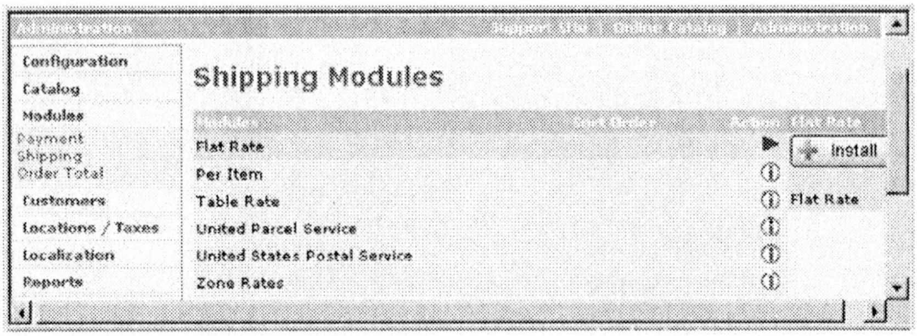

Figure 2.53. Shipping Modules listing.

```
if (tep_not_null($set)) {
    switch ($set) {
        case 'shipping':
            $module_type = 'shipping';
            $module_directory =
DIR_FS_CATALOG_MODULES . 'shipping/';
            $module_key =
'MODULE_SHIPPING_INSTALLED';
            define('HEADING_TITLE',
HEADING_TITLE_MODULES_SHIPPING);
            break;
        case 'ordertotal':
            $module_type = 'order_total';
            $module_directory =
DIR_FS_CATALOG_MODULES . 'order_total/';
            $module_key =
'MODULE_ORDER_TOTAL_INSTALLED';
            define('HEADING_TITLE',
HEADING_TITLE_MODULES_ORDER_TOTAL);
            break;
        case 'payment':
        default:
            $module_type = 'payment';
            $module_directory =
DIR_FS_CATALOG_MODULES . 'payment/';
            $module_key =
'MODULE_PAYMENT_INSTALLED';
            define('HEADING_TITLE',
HEADING_TITLE_MODULES_PAYMENT);
            break;
    }
}
```

The code is self-explanatory. The rest of the page is running with the above setting for a particular section.

Now, let us see how to install or remove a shipping component from our version. The logic is the same, and the same code is running for installing or removing a shipping module from the site.

```
case 'install':
    case 'remove':
        $file_extension = substr($PHP_SELF,
strrpos($PHP_SELF, '.'));
        $class =
basename($HTTP_GET_VARS['module']);
        if (file_exists($module_directory .
$class . $file_extension)) {
            include($module_directory . $class .
$file_extension);
            $module = new $class;
            if ($action == 'install') {
              $module->install();
            } elseif ($action == 'remove') {
              $module->remove();
            }
        }
    }tep_redirect(tep_href_link(FILENAME_MODULES,
    'set=' . $set . '&module=' . $class));
    break;
```

In this case the module directory is /catalog/includes/modules/shipping/. If we choose the Flat Rate shipping module to install, then the file /catalog/includes/modules/shipping/flat.php will be included, and the following methods will be called in order to install or remove the component.

```
function install() {
    tep_db_query("insert into " .
TABLE_CONFIGURATION . " (configuration_title,
configuration_key, configuration_value,
configuration_description,
configuration_group_id, sort_order,
set_function, date_added) values ('Enable Flat
Shipping', 'MODULE_SHIPPING_FLAT_STATUS',
'True', 'Do you want to offer flat rate
shipping?', '6', '0',
'tep_cfg_select_option(array(/'True/',
/'False/'), ', now())");
    tep_db_query("insert into " .
TABLE_CONFIGURATION . " (configuration_title,
configuration_key, configuration_value,
configuration_description,
configuration_group_id, sort_order,
date_added) values ('Shipping Cost',
'MODULE_SHIPPING_FLAT_COST', '5.00', 'The
```

```
shipping cost for all orders using this
shipping method.', '6', '0', now())");
      tep_db_query("insert into " .
TABLE_CONFIGURATION . " (configuration_title,
configuration_key, configuration_value,
configuration_description,
configuration_group_id, sort_order,
use_function, set_function, date_added) values
('Tax Class',
'MODULE_SHIPPING_FLAT_TAX_CLASS', '0', 'Use
the following tax class on the shipping fee.',
'6', '0', 'tep_get_tax_class_title',
'tep_cfg_pull_down_tax_classes(', now())");
      tep_db_query("insert into " .
TABLE_CONFIGURATION . " (configuration_title,
configuration_key, configuration_value,
configuration_description,
configuration_group_id, sort_order,
use_function, set_function, date_added) values
('Shipping Zone', 'MODULE_SHIPPING_FLAT_ZONE',
'0', 'If a zone is selected, only enable this
shipping method for that zone.', '6', '0',
'tep_get_zone_class_title',
'tep_cfg_pull_down_zone_classes(', now())");
      tep_db_query("insert into " .
TABLE_CONFIGURATION . " (configuration_title,
configuration_key, configuration_value,
configuration_description,
configuration_group_id, sort_order,
date_added) values ('Sort Order',
'MODULE_SHIPPING_FLAT_SORT_ORDER', '0', 'Sort
order of display.', '6', '0', now())");
    }


function remove() {
tep_db_query("delete from " .
TABLE_CONFIGURATION . " where
configuration_key in ('" . implode("', '",
$this->keys()) . "')");
    }

    function keys() {
 return array('MODULE_SHIPPING_FLAT_STATUS',
'MODULE_SHIPPING_FLAT_COST',
'MODULE_SHIPPING_FLAT_TAX_CLASS',
'MODULE_SHIPPING_FLAT_ZONE',
'MODULE_SHIPPING_FLAT_SORT_ORDER');
    }
```

You can get these methods inside the "flat" class in the /flat.php file. All the functionality of the code is the same as discussed in section 2.3.4.1.

The content of the /catalog/includes/modules/shipping/ folder is shown in Figure 2.54. All types of shipping modules are implemented in these separate files.

2.3.4.3. Order Total

This section deals with the order total calculation and order total configuration. There is a total of five types of order total in the Order Total module. The installing, removing, and updating of order total values is the same as discussed in sections 2.3.4.1 and 2.3.4.2. Figure 2.55 displays the listing of all available order statuses.

You can get all the classes for the Order Total section inside the /catalog/includes/modules/order_total/ folder. All types of Order Total module are implemented by the separate files inside that folder (Figure 2.56).

2.3.5. Customer Menu

This section deals with customer and order details, and hence there are two modules under this section: Customers and Orders.

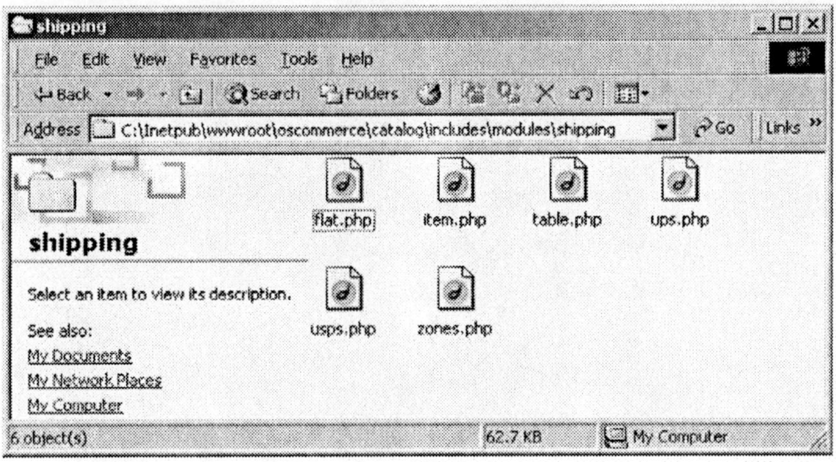

Figure 2.54. Contents of /shipping/ folder.

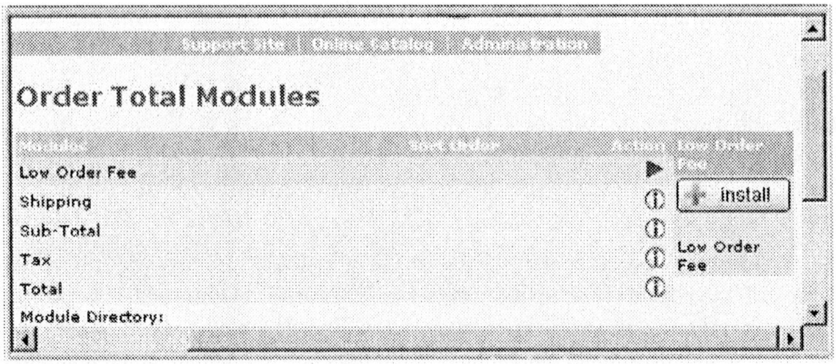

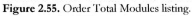

Figure 2.55. Order Total Modules listing.

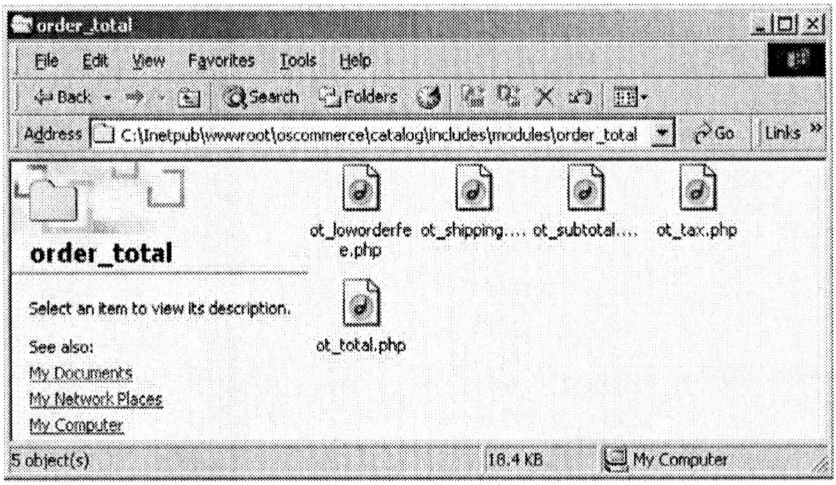

Figure 2.56. Contents of /order_total/ folder.

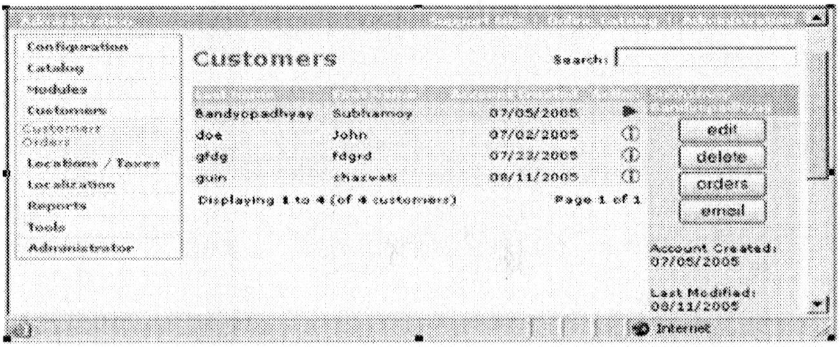

Figure 2.57. Customers list.

2.3.5.1. Customers

This section shows the list of those customers that have created accounts (Figure 2.57 shows the customers list). The administrator can edit customer details; for this action the code is written in file /catalog/admin/customers.php. The customer can be edited or deleted by clicking the **Edit** or **Delete** button on the right side of the customer list, respectively. Figure 2.58 is a partial view of the form that will open when the **Edit** button is clicked.

When the **Update** button (present at the bottom of the Edit Customer form) is clicked, the following code is executed.

```
if (tep_not_null($action)) {
    switch ($action) {
      case 'update':
        $customers_id =
tep_db_prepare_input($HTTP_GET_VARS['cID']);
        $customers_firstname =
tep_db_prepare_input($HTTP_POST_VARS['customer
s_firstname']);
        $customers_lastname =
tep_db_prepare_input($HTTP_POST_VARS['customer
s_lastname']);
        $customers_email_address =
tep_db_prepare_input($HTTP_POST_VARS['customer
s_email_address']);
        $customers_telephone =
tep_db_prepare_input($HTTP_POST_VARS['customer
s_telephone']);
        $customers_fax =
tep_db_prepare_input($HTTP_POST_VARS['customer
s_fax']);
        $customers_newsletter =
tep_db_prepare_input($HTTP_POST_VARS['customer
s_newsletter']);

        ................................................. .
        ................................................. .
```

When the customer information is updated, the effect will be seen in the following tables: "customers," "customers_info," and "address_book" (see Figures 2.59, 2.60, and 2.61, respectively).

2.3.5.2. Orders

This section lists the orders made by registered customers. Here, the administrator can see the customer name, the total amount of the order, the

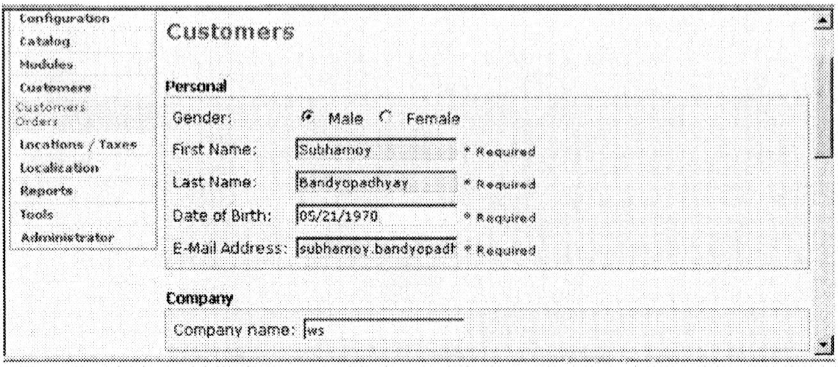

Figure 2.58. Edit Customers form.

customers_id	customers_gender	customers_firstname	customers_lastname	customers_dob
1 m		John	doe	2001-01-01 00:00:00
5 m		Subhamoy	Bandyopadhyay	1970-05-21 00:00:00
6 m		fdgrd	gfdg	1970-05-21 00:00:00
7 f		shaswati	guin	1950-01-01 00:00:00

Figure 2.59. Table "customers."

customers_info_id	customers_info_date_of_last_logon	customers_info_number_of_logons	customers_info_date_acce
1 0000-00-00 00:00:00		0	2005-07-02 10:40:02
2 NULL		0	2005-07-02 11:09:35
3 NULL		0	2005-07-05 13:31:33
5 2005-07-27 12:32:03		3	2005-07-05 17:19:19
6 NULL		0	2005-07-23 15:34:43
7 2005-08-12 10:24:18		1	2005-08-11 11:33:27

Figure 2.60. Table "customers_info."

address_book_id	customers_id	entry_gender	entry_company	entry_firstname	entry_lastname	entry_street_address
1	1 m		ACME Inc.	John	Doe	1 Way Street
2	2 m		WS	Subhamoy	banerjee	dhakuria
3	3 m		WS	Subhamoy	Bandyopadhyay	ffffwww
5	5 m		ws	Subhamoy	Bandyopadhyay	sssssssssss

Figure 2.61. Table "address_book."

date of purchase, and the order status. The administrator can update the order status (i.e., Delivered, Pending, Processing) and can also add comments. Figure 2.62 shows the Orders list.

When an order is updated, the following code is executed; the code is written in /catalog/admin/orders.php.

```
$action = (isset($HTTP_GET_VARS['action']) ?
     $HTTP_GET_VARS['action'] : '');

if (tep_not_null($action)) {
switch ($action) {
  case 'update_order':
$oID =
tep_db_prepare_input($HTTP_GET_VARS['oID']);
$status =
tep_db_prepare_input($HTTP_POST_VARS['status']
);
$comments =
tep_db_prepare_input($HTTP_POST_VARS['comments
']);

$order_updated = false;
$check_status_query = tep_db_query("select
customers_name, customers_email_address,
orders_status, date_purchased from " .
TABLE_ORDERS . " where orders_id = '" .
(int)$oID . "'");
$check_status =
tep_db_fetch_array($check_status_query);
```

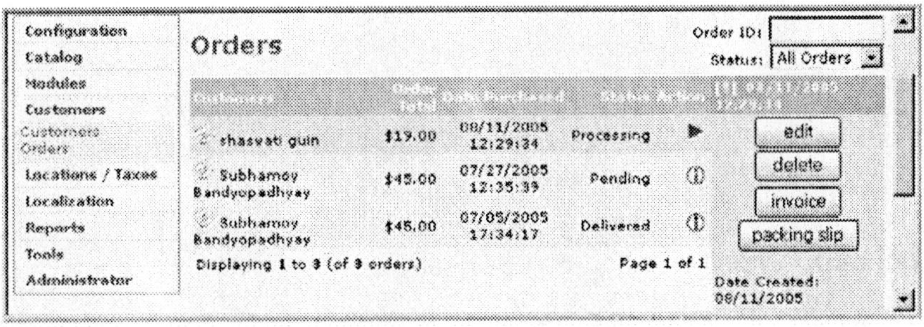

Figure 2.62. Orders list.

```
if ( ($check_status['orders_status'] !=
$status) || tep_not_null($comments)) {
tep_db_query("update " . TABLE_ORDERS . " set
orders_status = '" . tep_db_input($status) .
"', last_modified = now() where orders_id = '"
. (int)$oID . "'");

$customer_notified = '0';
if (isset($HTTP_POST_VARS['notify']) &&
($HTTP_POST_VARS['notify'] == 'on')) {
$notify_comments = '';
if (isset($HTTP_POST_VARS['notify_comments'])
&& ($HTTP_POST_VARS['notify_comments'] ==
'on')) {
$notify_comments =
sprintf(EMAIL_TEXT_COMMENTS_UPDATE, $comments)
. "/n/n";
  }
}
```

When the administrator updates an order, the "order_status" field of the "orders" table (Figure 2.63) will be updated, and a comment will be added to the "orders_status_history" table (Figure 2.64).

By clicking on the **Invoice** button, the invoice slip of the selected order can be seen, which contains a list of the purchased products and their costs; the code for this is written in /catalog/admin/invoice.php. Also, by clicking the **Packing Slip** button, the administrator can see a packing slip of the selected order, which only includes the names of the products ordered and not the payment details; the code for this is written in /catalog/admin/packingslip.php. Both files will open in a new browser window, and both are printable.

2.3.6. Locations/Taxes Menu

This section consists of the following modules: Countries, Zones, Tax Zones, Tax Classes, and Tax Rates.

2.3.6.1. Countries

This section shows the list of countries with an ISO code (Figure 2.65). The administrator can add, edit, and delete countries. To edit or insert a country, the following code is executed, which is written in /catalog/admin/countries.php.

orders_id	customers_id	customers_name	customers_company	customers_street_address	customers_suburb
1	5	Subhamoy Bandyopadhyay	ws	$$$$$$$$$$	$$$$$$$$$$$$
2	5	Subhamoy Bandyopadhyay	ws	$$$$$$$$$$	$$$$$$$$$$$$
3	7	shaswati guin	ws	$$$$$	$$$$$

Figure 2.63. Table "orders."

orders_status_history_id	orders_id	orders_status_id	date_added	customer_notified	comments
1	1	1	2005-07-05 17:34:17	1	Please Send it ASAP
2	1	3	2005-07-05 17:50:47	1	
3	2	1	2005-07-27 12:35:39	1	
4	3	1	2005-08-11 12:29:34	1	

Figure 2.64. Table "orders_status_history."

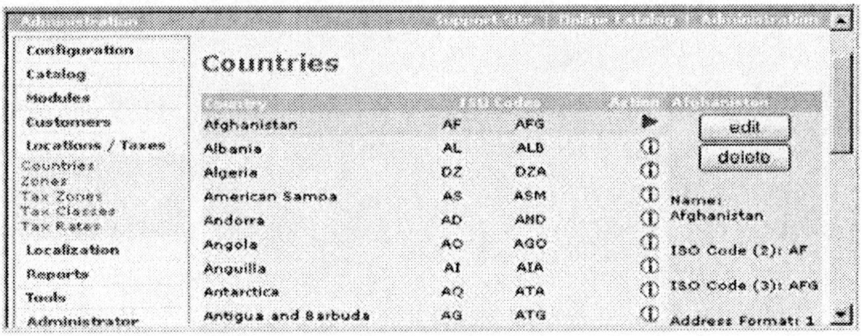

Figure 2.65. Countries list.

countries_id	countries_name	countries_iso_code_2	countries_iso_code_3	address_format_id
1	Afghanistan	AF	AFG	1
2	Albania	AL	ALB	1
3	Algeria	DZ	DZA	1

Figure 2.66. Table "countries."

```
$action = (isset($HTTP_GET_VARS['action']) ?
$HTTP_GET_VARS['action'] : '');

  if (tep_not_null($action)) {
    switch ($action) {
      case 'insert':
        $countries_name =
tep_db_prepare_input($HTTP_POST_VARS['countrie
s_name']);
        $countries_iso_code_2 =
tep_db_prepare_input($HTTP_POST_VARS['countrie
s_iso_code_2']);
        $coutries_iso_code_3 =
tep_db_prepare_input($HTTP_POST_VARS['countrie
s_iso_code_3']);
        $address_format_id =
tep_db_prepare_input($HTTP_POST_VARS['address_
format_id']);

        tep_db_query("insert into " .
TABLE_COUNTRIES . " (countries_name,
countries_iso_code_2, countries_iso_code_3,
address_format_id) values ('" .
tep_db_input($countries_name) . "', '" .
tep_db_input($countries_iso_code_2) . "', '" .
tep_db_input($countries_iso_code_3) . "', '" .
(int)$address_format_id . "')");


tep_redirect(tep_href_link(FILENAME_COUNTRIES)
);
        break;
      case 'save':
        $countries_id =
tep_db_prepare_input($HTTP_GET_VARS['cID']);
        $countries_name =
tep_db_prepare_input($HTTP_POST_VARS['countrie
s_name']);
        $countries_iso_code_2 =
tep_db_prepare_input($HTTP_POST_VARS['countrie
s_iso_code_2']);
        $countries_iso_code_3 =
tep_db_prepare_input($HTTP_POST_VARS['countrie
s_iso_code_3']);
        $address_format_id =
tep_db_prepare_input($HTTP_POST_VARS['address_
format_id']);

        tep_db_query("update " .
TABLE_COUNTRIES . " set countries_name = '" .
tep_db_input($countries_name) . "',
```

```
countries_iso_code_2 = '" .
tep_db_input($countries_iso_code_2) . "',
countries_iso_code_3 = '" .
tep_db_input($countries_iso_code_3) . "',
address_format_id = '" .
(int)$address_format_id . "' where
countries_id = '" . (int)$countries_id . "'");


tep_redirect(tep_href_link(FILENAME_COUNTRIES,
'page=' . $HTTP_GET_VARS['page'] . '&cID=' .
$countries_id));
        break;
```

The "countries" table, shown in Figure 2.66, is used when a new country is added or an existing country is updated.

2.3.6.2. Zones

This section shows the list of zones with related countries and codes (Figure 2.67). The administrator can add or edit zones using the code written in /catalog/admin/zones.php. The "zones" table, shown in Figure 2.68, is used when a new zone is added or an existing zone is updated. The "zone_country_id" field corresponds to the "country_id" of the "countries" table.

2.3.6.3. Tax Zones

This module is required to calculate the appropriate tax rate value based on where the order is placed (Figure 2.69). If no tax zones match the origin of the purchase, then no tax is applied to the order. The tax zones can be added, edited, and deleted by the administrator. The code is written in /catalog/admin/geo_zones.php.

```
$action = (isset($HTTP_GET_VARS['action']) ?
$HTTP_GET_VARS['action'] : '');

  if (tep_not_null($action)) {
    switch ($action) {
      case 'insert_zone':
        $geo_zone_name =
tep_db_prepare_input($HTTP_POST_VARS['geo_zone
_name']);
        $geo_zone_description =
tep_db_prepare_input($HTTP_POST_VARS['geo_zone
_description']);
```

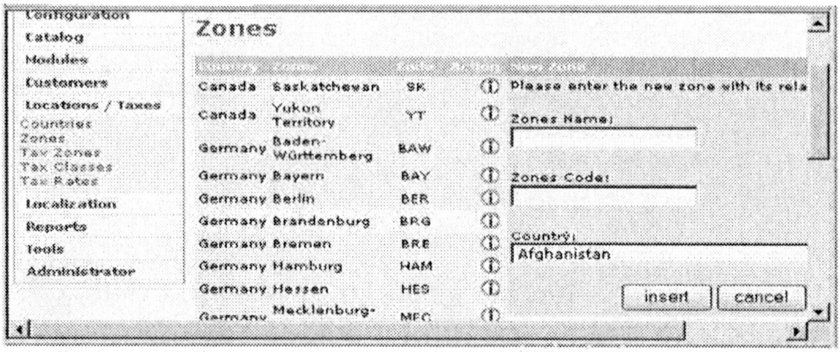

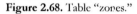

Figure 2.67. Zones list with Insert action.

zone_id	zone_country_id	zone_code	zone_name
1	223	AL	Alabama
2	223	AK	Alaska
3	223	AS	American Samoa

Figure 2.68. Table "zones."

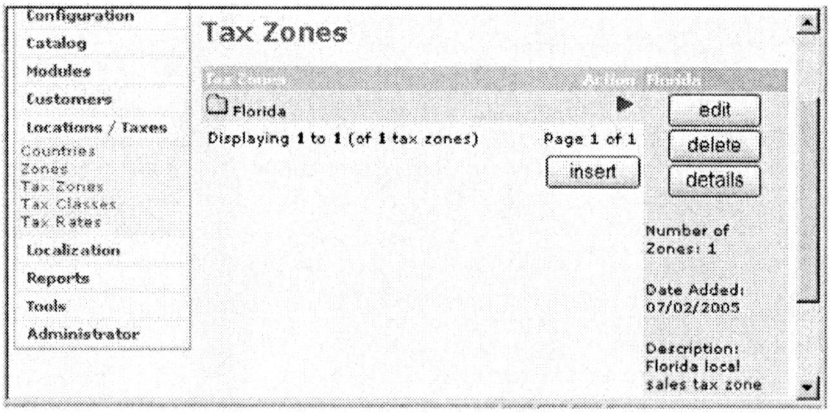

Figure 2.69. Tax Zones.

geo_zone_id	geo_zone_name	geo_zone_description	last_modified	date_added
1	Florida	Florida local sales tax zone	NULL	2005-07-02 10:40:02

Figure 2.70. Table "geo_zones."

```
        tep_db_query("insert into " .
TABLE_GEO_ZONES . " (geo_zone_name,
geo_zone_description, date_added) values ('" .
tep_db_input($geo_zone_name) . "', '" .
tep_db_input($geo_zone_description) . "',
now())");
        $new_zone_id = tep_db_insert_id();


tep_redirect(tep_href_link(FILENAME_GEO_ZONES,
'zpage=' . $HTTP_GET_VARS['zpage'] . '&zID=' .
$new_zone_id));
        break;
      case 'save_zone':
        $zID =
tep_db_prepare_input($HTTP_GET_VARS['zID']);
        $geo_zone_name =
tep_db_prepare_input($HTTP_POST_VARS['geo_zone
_name']);
        $geo_zone_description =
tep_db_prepare_input($HTTP_POST_VARS['geo_zone
_description']);

        tep_db_query("update " .
TABLE_GEO_ZONES . " set geo_zone_name = '" .
tep_db_input($geo_zone_name) . "',
geo_zone_description = '" .
tep_db_input($geo_zone_description) . "',
last_modified = now() where geo_zone_id = '" .
(int)$zID . "'");


tep_redirect(tep_href_link(FILENAME_GEO_ZONES,
'zpage=' . $HTTP_GET_VARS['zpage'] . '&zID=' .
$HTTP_GET_VARS['zID']));
        break;
.................................................. .
```

The "geo_zones" table, shown in Figure 2.70, is used to add, edit, or delete tax zones.

In addition, the administrator can add, edit, or delete countries under a particular zone (Figure 2.71). The code for this is written in /catalog/admin/geo_zones.php.

```
$saction = (isset($HTTP_GET_VARS['saction']) ?
$HTTP_GET_VARS['saction'] : '');
  if (tep_not_null($saction)) {
    switch ($saction) {
      case 'insert_sub':
```

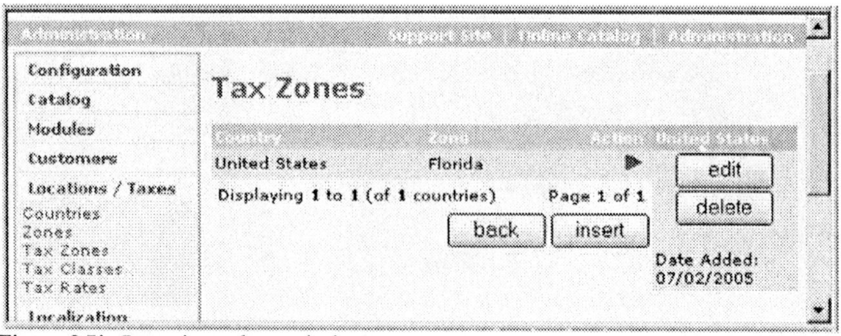

Figure 2.71. Countries under particular tax zone.

```
        $zID =
tep_db_prepare_input($HTTP_GET_VARS['zID']);
        $zone_country_id =
tep_db_prepare_input($HTTP_POST_VARS['zone_cou
ntry_id']);
        $zone_id =
tep_db_prepare_input($HTTP_POST_VARS['zone_id'
]);

        tep_db_query("insert into " .
TABLE_ZONES_TO_GEO_ZONES . " (zone_country_id,
zone_id, geo_zone_id, date_added) values ('" .
(int)$zone_country_id . "', '" . (int)$zone_id
. "', '" . (int)$zID . "', now())");
        $new_subzone_id = tep_db_insert_id();


tep_redirect(tep_href_link(FILENAME_GEO_ZONES,
'zpage=' . $HTTP_GET_VARS['zpage'] . '&zID=' .
$HTTP_GET_VARS['zID'] . '&action=list&spage='
. $HTTP_GET_VARS['spage'] . '&sID=' .
$new_subzone_id));
        break;
      case 'save_sub':
        $sID =
tep_db_prepare_input($HTTP_GET_VARS['sID']);
        $zID =
tep_db_prepare_input($HTTP_GET_VARS['zID']);
        $zone_country_id =
tep_db_prepare_input($HTTP_POST_VARS['zone_cou
ntry_id']);
        $zone_id =
tep_db_prepare_input($HTTP_POST_VARS['zone_id'
]);
```

association_id	zone_country_id	zone_id	geo_zone_id	last_modified	date_added
1	223	18	1	NULL	2005-07-02 10:40:02

Figure 2.72. Table "zones_to_geo_zones."

```
       tep_db_query("update  " .
TABLE_ZONES_TO_GEO_ZONES . " set geo_zone_id =
'" . (int)$zID . "', zone_country_id = '" .
(int)$zone_country_id . "', zone_id = " .
(tep_not_null($zone_id) ? "'" . (int)$zone_id
. "'" : 'null') . ", last_modified = now()
where association_id = '" . (int)$sID . "'");
```

The "zones_to_geo_zones" table, shown in Figure 2.72, is used when a new tax zone is added or an existing tax zone is edited.

2.3.6.4. Tax Classes

With this module, products are assigned a tax class, which inherits the tax zone and tax rate relationships. Tax classes can be created, edited, and deleted (Figure 2.73). To add, edit, and delete tax classes, the following code is used, written in /catalog/admin/tax_classes.php.

```
switch ($action) {
    case 'insert':
        $tax_class_title =
tep_db_prepare_input($HTTP_POST_VARS['tax_clas
s_title']);
        $tax_class_description =
tep_db_prepare_input($HTTP_POST_VARS['tax_clas
s_description']);

        tep_db_query("insert into " .
TABLE_TAX_CLASS . " (tax_class_title,
tax_class_description, date_added) values ('"
. tep_db_input($tax_class_title) . "', '" .
tep_db_input($tax_class_description) . "',
now())");

tep_redirect(tep_href_link(FILENAME_TAX_CLASSE
S));
        break;
    case 'save':
```

Figure 2.73. Tax Classes.

```
        $tax_class_id =
tep_db_prepare_input($HTTP_GET_VARS['tID']);
        $tax_class_title =
tep_db_prepare_input($HTTP_POST_VARS['tax_clas
s_title']);
$tax_class_description =
tep_db_prepare_input($HTTP_POST_VARS['tax_clas
s_description']);

tep_db_query("update " . TABLE_TAX_CLASS . "
set tax_class_id = '" . (int)$tax_class_id .
"', tax_class_title = '" .
tep_db_input($tax_class_title) . "',
tax_class_description = '" .
tep_db_input($tax_class_description) . "',
last_modified = now() where tax_class_id = '"
. (int)$tax_class_id . "'");

tep_redirect(tep_href_link(FILENAME_TAX_CLASSE
S, 'page=' . $HTTP_GET_VARS['page'] . '&tID='
. $tax_class_id));
        break;
    case 'deleteconfirm':
        $tax_class_id =
tep_db_prepare_input($HTTP_GET_VARS['tID']);
tep_db_query("delete from " . TABLE_TAX_CLASS
. " where tax_class_id = '" .
(int)$tax_class_id . "'");
tep_redirect(tep_href_link(FILENAME_TAX_CLASSE
S, 'page=' . $HTTP_GET_VARS['page']));
            break;
    }
```

tax_class_id	tax_class_title	tax_class_description	last_modified	date_added
1	Taxable Goods	The following types of products are included non-f..	2005-07-02 10:40:02	2005-07-02 10:40:02

Figure 2.74. Table "tax_class."

The "tax_class" table, shown in Figure 2.74, is used to store the data for the tax classes.

2.3.6.5. Tax Rates

Tax rates depend upon the tax zone and tax classes. Tax rates can be added, edited, and deleted (Figure 2.75). Tax rate calculations are based on the priority of multiple tax rates defined in a tax class, and priority can be set. Multiple tax rates defined with the same priority values are added to form a final tax rate percentage value, and multiple tax rates with different priority values are compounded together in priority order to form a final tax rate percentage value. Priorities are needed when multiple tax rates in a tax class exist wherein residents of a country need to pay a national sales tax rate, with residents of a particular state also needing to pay a local tax rate.

To enter a new tax rate tax class, zones are selected from a drop-down list, and a tax rate, a description, and a priority are entered in the text boxes, as shown in Figure 2.76. The code is written in /catalog/admin/tax_rates.php.

```
switch ($action) {
    case 'insert':
        $tax_zone_id =
tep_db_prepare_input($HTTP_POST_VARS['tax_zone
_id']);
        $tax_class_id =
tep_db_prepare_input($HTTP_POST_VARS['tax_clas
s_id']);
        $tax_rate =
tep_db_prepare_input($HTTP_POST_VARS['tax_rate
']);
        $tax_description =
tep_db_prepare_input($HTTP_POST_VARS['tax_desc
ription']);
        $tax_priority =
tep_db_prepare_input($HTTP_POST_VARS['tax_prio
rity']);

        tep_db_query("insert into " .
TABLE_TAX_RATES . " (tax_zone_id,
```

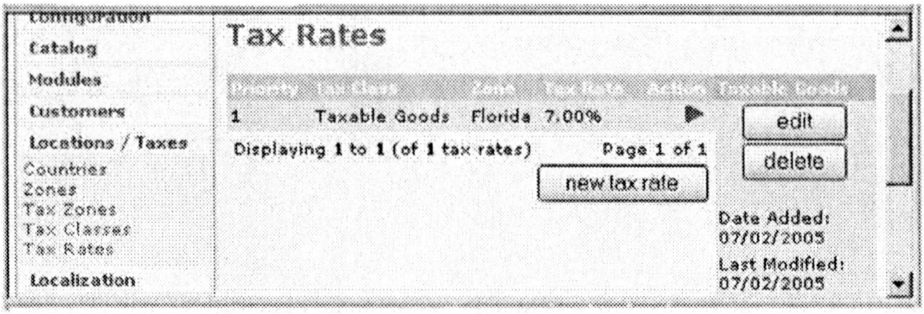

Figure 2.75. Tax Rates.

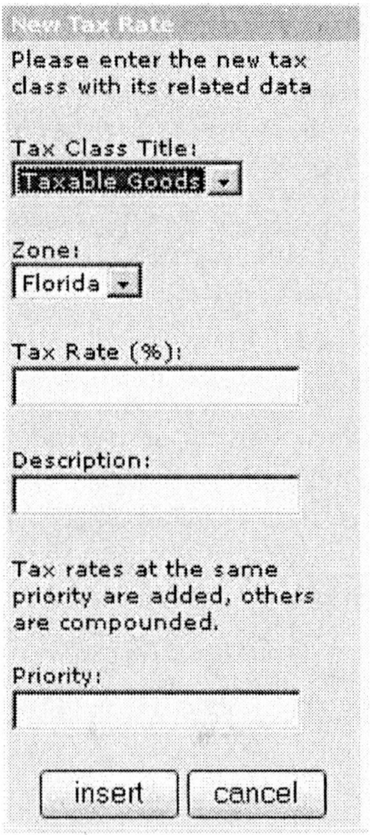

Figure 2.76. New Tax Rate form.

```
tax_class_id, tax_rate, tax_description,
tax_priority, date_added) values ('" .
(int)$tax_zone_id . "', '" .
(int)$tax_class_id . "', '" .
tep_db_input($tax_rate) . "', '" .
tep_db_input($tax_description) . "', '" .
tep_db_input($tax_priority) . "', now())");


tep_redirect(tep_href_link(FILENAME_TAX_RATES)
);
        break;
    case 'save':
    ..............................................................
..................................................
........................................
```

The "tax_rates" table, shown in Figure 2.77, is used to save the data for tax rates.

2.3.7. Localization Menu

This section consists of the following three modules: Currencies, Languages, and Orders Status.

2.3.7.1. Currencies

Different currencies are used in different countries. While in the current version of osCommerce, two currencies are installed by default (the U.S. dollar and the E.U. euro), other currencies can be installed as well. Figure 2.78 shows the currency list.

To install or insert new currency, click on the **New Currency** button, and a form will open to the right side of the currency list (Figure 2.79). The currencies that are already installed can be edited. The code is written in /catalog/admin/currencies.php.

```
switch ($action) {
    case 'insert':
    case 'save':
        if (isset($HTTP_GET_VARS['cID']))
      $currency_id =
tep_db_prepare_input($HTTP_GET_VARS['cID']);
        $title =
tep_db_prepare_input($HTTP_POST_VARS['title'])
;
        $code =
tep_db_prepare_input($HTTP_POST_VARS['code']);
```

tax_rates_id	tax_zone_id	tax_class_id	tax_priority	tax_rate	tax_description	last_modified	date_added
1	1	1	1	7.0000	FL TAX 7.0%	2005-07-02 10:40:02	2005-07-02 10:40:02

Figure 2.77. Table "tax_rates."

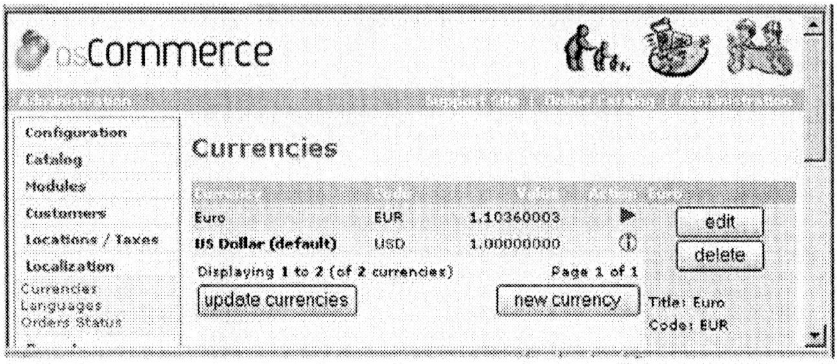

Figure 2.78. Currencies list.

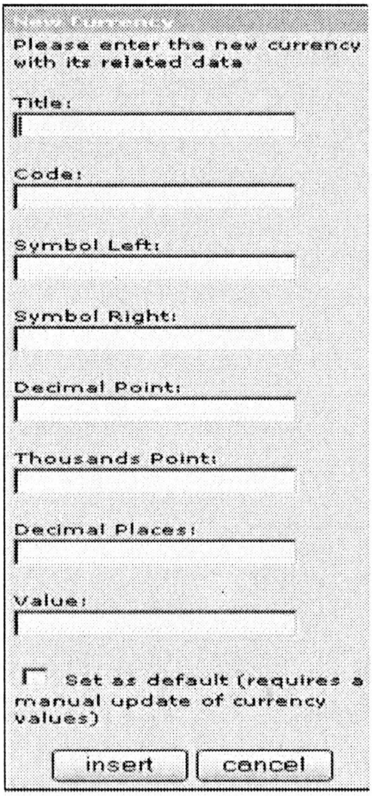

Figure 2.79. New Currency form.

```
        $symbol_left =
tep_db_prepare_input($HTTP_POST_VARS['symbol_l
eft']);
        $symbol_right =
tep_db_prepare_input($HTTP_POST_VARS['symbol_r
ight']);
        $decimal_point =
tep_db_prepare_input($HTTP_POST_VARS['decimal_
point']);
        $thousands_point =
tep_db_prepare_input($HTTP_POST_VARS['thousand
s_point']);
        $decimal_places =
tep_db_prepare_input($HTTP_POST_VARS['decimal_
places']);
        $value =
tep_db_prepare_input($HTTP_POST_VARS['value'])
;

        $sql_data_array = array('title' =>
$title,
                                'code' =>
$code,
                                'symbol_left'
=> $symbol_left,
                                'symbol_right'
=> $symbol_right,

'decimal_point' => $decimal_point,

'thousands_point' => $thousands_point,

'decimal_places' => $decimal_places,
                                'value' =>
$value);

    if ($action == 'insert') {

   tep_db_perform(TABLE_CURRENCIES,
$sql_data_array);
                    $currency_id =
tep_db_insert_id();
       }
     elseif ($action == 'save') {
  tep_db_perform(TABLE_CURRENCIES,
$sql_data_array, 'update', "currencies_id = '"
. (int)$currency_id . "'");
       }
        If (isset($HTTP_POST_VARS['default'])
&& HTTP_POST_VARS['default']      == 'on')) {
```

```
        tep_db_query("update " .
TABLE_CONFIGURATION . " set
configuration_value = '" . tep_db_input($code)
. "' where configuration_key =
'DEFAULT_CURRENCY'");
                            }


tep_redirect(tep_href_link(FILENAME_CURRENCIES
, 'page=' . $HTTP_GET_VARS['page'] . '&cID=' .
$currency_id));
        break;
```

If the currency is selected as a default currency at the time of insertion or editing, then the "configuration" table is updated (Figure 2.80). Otherwise, the data is saved in the "currencies" table only (Figure 2.81).

While the currencies are updated, the corresponding currency exchange rates need to be updated. All the values of the exchanges rates can be updated by using the **Update Currencies** button (shown in Figure 2.78). All currencies will be referenced to the default currency. The following code is executed when the **Update Currencies** button is clicked.

```
case 'update':
        $server_used =
CURRENCY_SERVER_PRIMARY;

        $currency_query = tep_db_query("select
currencies_id, code, title from " .
TABLE_CURRENCIES);
        while ($currency =
tep_db_fetch_array($currency_query)) {
            $quote_function = 'quote_' .
CURRENCY_SERVER_PRIMARY . '_currency';
            $rate =
$quote_function($currency['code']);

            if (empty($rate) &&
(tep_not_null(CURRENCY_SERVER_BACKUP))) {
                $messageStack-
>add_session(sprintf(WARNING_PRIMARY_SERVER_FA
ILED,        CURRENCY_SERVER_PRIMARY,
$currency['title'], $currency['code']),
'warning');

                $quote_function = 'quote_' .
CURRENCY_SERVER_BACKUP . '_currency';
                $rate =
$quote_function($currency['code']);
```

configuration_id	configuration_title	configuration_key	configuration_value	configuration_description
84	Default Currency	DEFAULT_CURRENCY	USD	Default Currency

Figure 2.80. Table "configuration."

currencies_id	title	code	symbol_left	symbol_right	decimal_point	thousands_point	decimal_places	value
1	US Dollar	USD	$				2	1.00000000
2	Euro	EUR		EUR	.	.	2	1.10360003

Figure 2.81. Table "currencies."

```
                    $server_used =
CURRENCY_SERVER_BACKUP;
           }

           if (tep_not_null($rate)) {
               tep_db_query("update " .
TABLE_CURRENCIES . " set value = '" . $rate .
"', last_updated = now() where currencies_id =
'" . (int)$currency['currencies_id'] . "'");

                  $messageStack-
>add_session(sprintf(TEXT_INFO_CURRENCY_UPDATE
   D, $currency['title'], $currency['code'],
           $server_used), 'success');
           } else {
               $messageStack-
>add_session(sprintf(ERROR_CURRENCY_INVALID,
$currency['title'], $currency['code'],
$server_used), 'error');
           }
       }

tep_redirect(tep_href_link(FILENAME_CURRENCIES
, 'page=' .         $HTTP_GET_VARS['page'] .
'&cID=' . $HTTP_GET_VARS['cID']));
       break;
```

The constants "CURRENCY_SERVER_PRIMARY" and "CUR-RENCY_SERVER_BACKUP" are defined in the /includes/application_top.php file as follows.

```
// Define how do we update currency exchange
rates
// Possible values are 'oanda' 'xe' or ''
```

```
define('CURRENCY_SERVER_PRIMARY', 'oanda');
define('CURRENCY_SERVER_BACKUP', 'xe');
```

Using the two constants defined above, two functions are created in the case of an update to the currencies, as given below.

```
$quote_function = 'quote_' .
CURRENCY_SERVER_PRIMARY . '_currency';
$quote_function = 'quote_' .
CURRENCY_SERVER_BACKUP . '_currency';
$rate =
$quote_function($currency['code']);
e.g. $rate=quote_oanda_currency(EUR);
```

The two functions "onada" and "xe" are given below and are defined in the /includes/functions/localization.php file.

```
function quote_oanda_currency($code, $base =
DEFAULT_CURRENCY) {
$page =
file('http://www.oanda.com/convert/fxdaily?val
ue=1&redirected=1&exch=' . $code .
'&format=CSV&dest=Get+Table&sel_list=' .
$base);

    $match = array();

    preg_match('/(.+),(/w{3}),([0-9.]+),([0-
9.]+)/i', implode('', $page), $match);

    if (sizeof($match) > 0) {
        return $match[3];
    } else {
        return false;
                                }
    }


    function quote_xe_currency($to, $from =
DEFAULT_CURRENCY) {
        $page =
file('http://www.xe.net/ucc/convert.cgi?Amount
=1&From=' . $from . '&To=' . $to);

    $match = array();

    preg_match('/[0-9.]+/s*' . $from .
'/s*=/s*([0-9.]+)/s*' . $to . '/', implode('',
$page), $match);
```

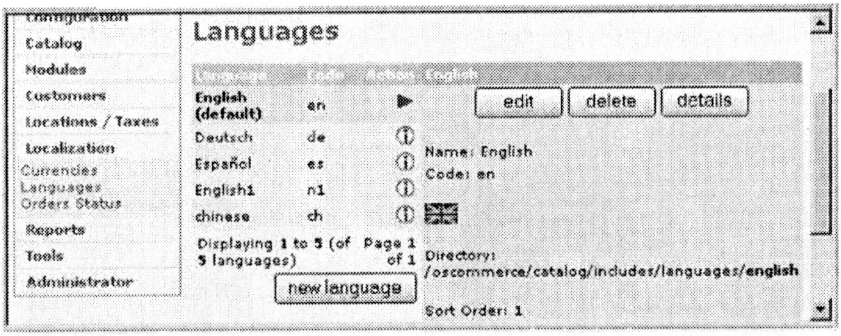

Figure 2.82. Languages list.

```
if (sizeof($match) > 0) {
    return $match[1];
} else {
    return false;
}
}
```

These two functions return an updated exchange rate with respect to the default currency (here, the default currency is USD) using the primary exchange rate server (onada) via xe.

2.3.7.2. Languages

As discussed in section 2.2, languages can be added and updated manually, but here, you will see how to add and manipulate languages through the interface. Figure 2.82 represents the list of languages. The administrator can add, edit, and delete languages using the buttons **New Language**, **Edit**, and **Delete**. When these buttons are clicked, the code written in /catalog/admin/languages.php is executed.

In the case of adding a new language the data is inserted in the following tables:
"languages," "categories_description," "products_description," "products_options," "products_options_values," "manufacturers_info," and "orders_status." At the time of editing a language the data of the "languages" and "configuration" tables are updated. If the language is set to the default language at the time of adding or editing, then the "configuration_value" of the "configuration" table is updated, where the "configuration_key" is equal to the "DEFAULT_LANGUAGE." When a language is deleted by clicking the **Delete** button, the data from the "languages" table is deleted, and also, related

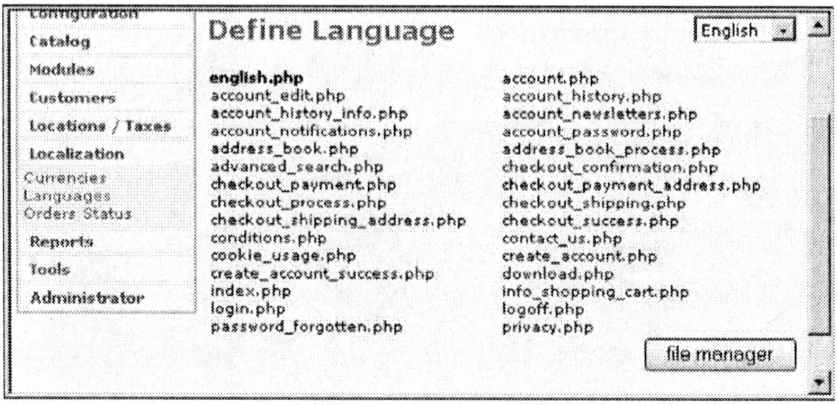

Figure 2.83. File list where constants of selected languages are present.

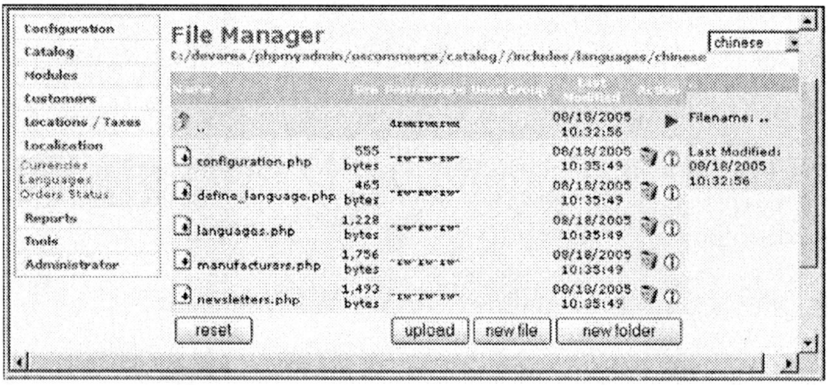

Figure 2.84. File Manager.

information regarding that language is deleted from the "catego-ries_description," "products_description," "products_options," "products_options_values," "manufacturers_info," and "orders_status" tables.

If the **Details** button is clicked, the code written in the /catalog/admin/define_language.php file is executed (Figure 2.83).

Suppose that we add a new language (Chinese), and for this a new folder /Chinese/ is needed. In addition, some files are needed in which the constants for the Chinese language are defined. For these purposes we need a File Manager (Figure 2.84). By clicking the **Upload** button, we can upload the required files, and by clicking the **New File** button, we can create a new file, writing the code in the given text area. By using the **New Folder** button, we create the required folders. Also, we can modify and delete the existing files. Figures 2.85, 2.86, and 2.87 illustrate these three actions.

2.3.7.3. Orders Status

All orders made by customers have status fields. The status of an order is defined by the administrator. The order status field is visible to both the store owner and the customer, and a customer can be notified by e-mail if the status of their order is changed. Figure 2.88 shows the Orders Status listing page under the Admin > Localization > Orders Status section.

In Figure 2.88 we can see that order status Pending is set as default and also that language-specific definitions are shown on the right side. When the **Insert, Edit,** or **Delete** buttons are clicked, then depending on the action, the code written in /catalog/admin/orders_status.php is executed. To insert or edit an order status, the following code is executed.

```
switch ($action) {
        case 'insert':
        case 'save':
          if (isset($HTTP_GET_VARS['oID']))
                  $orders_status_id =
    tep_db_prepare_input($HTTP_GET_VARS['oID']);
                $languages = tep_get_languages();
              for ($i=0, $n=sizeof($languages);
$i<$n; $i++) {
                  $orders_status_name_array =
$HTTP_POST_VARS['orders_status_name'];
                  $language_id =
$languages[$i]['id'];

              $sql_data_array =
array('orders_status_name' =>
tep_db_prepare_input($orders_status_name_array
[$language_id]));

              if ($action == 'insert') {
                if (empty($orders_status_id)) {
                  $next_id_query =
tep_db_query("select max(orders_status_id) as
orders_status_id from " . TABLE_ORDERS_STATUS
. "");
                  $next_id =
tep_db_fetch_array($next_id_query);
                  $orders_status_id =
$next_id['orders_status_id'] + 1;
                }

              $insert_sql_data =
array('orders_status_id' => $orders_status_id,
```

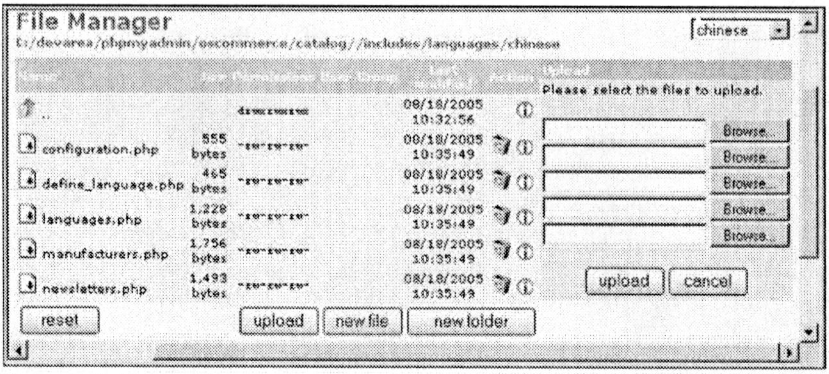

Figure 2.85. Upload files.

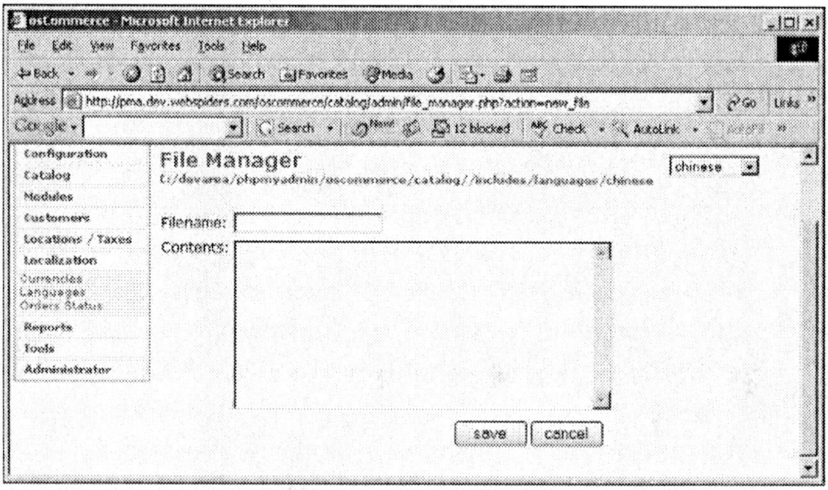

Figure 2.86. Create new file.

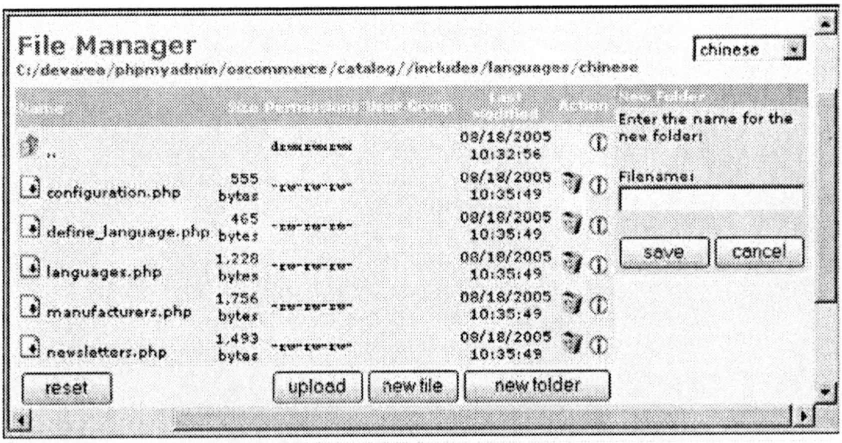

Figure 2.87. Create new folder.

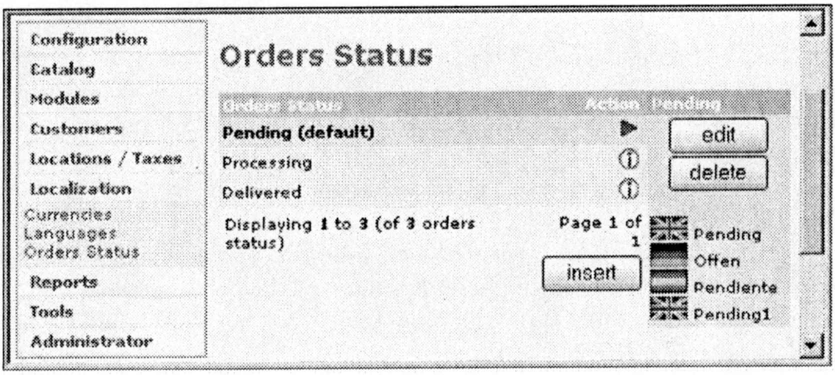

Figure 2.88. Orders Status list.

```
'language_id' => $language_id);

        $sql_data_array =
array_merge($sql_data_array,
$insert_sql_data);


tep_db_perform(TABLE_ORDERS_STATUS,
$sql_data_array);
        } elseif ($action == 'save') {

tep_db_perform(TABLE_ORDERS_STATUS,
$sql_data_array, 'update',   "orders_status_id
```

```
= '" . (int)$orders_status_id . "' and
language_id = '" . (int)$language_id . "'");
            }
        }


        if (isset($HTTP_POST_VARS['default'])
&& ($HTTP_POST_VARS['default'] == 'on')) {
            tep_db_query("update " .
TABLE_CONFIGURATION . " set
configuration_value = '" .
tep_db_input($orders_status_id) . "' where
configuration_key =
'DEFAULT_ORDERS_STATUS_ID'");
        }


    tep_redirect(tep_href_link(FILENAME_ORDERS_STA
    TUS, 'page=' . $HTTP_GET_VARS['page'] .
    '&oID=' . $orders_status_id));
        break;
```

Figure 2.89 shows the New Orders Status form. Here, order status can be inserted in the different languages installed. Also, there is a provision to set an order status as the default order status. In addition, the existing order status can be updated or deleted by clicking the **Edit** or **Delete** buttons, respectively. The data related to order status information are stored in the "orders_status" table (Figure 2.90).

If the order status is set to the default order status at the time of adding or editing, then the "configuration_value" of the "configuration" table is updated, where the "configuration_key" is equal to the "DEFAULT_ORDERS_STATUS_ID."

2.3.8. Reports Menu

Through this module the administrator can get reports about products and customers. This module has the following three subsections: Products Viewed, Products Purchased, and Customer Orders—Total.

2.3.8.1. Products Viewed

When the **Products Viewed** link is clicked, the code written in /catalog/admin/stats_products_viewed.php is executed. A list of products with the number of times each was viewed is shown in Figure 2.91. The highest-viewed product is on the top of the list. For example, from Figure 2.91 we see that the product Shampoo (English) was viewed 29 times; this means that the product was clicked 29 times. To show the highest-viewed products, the

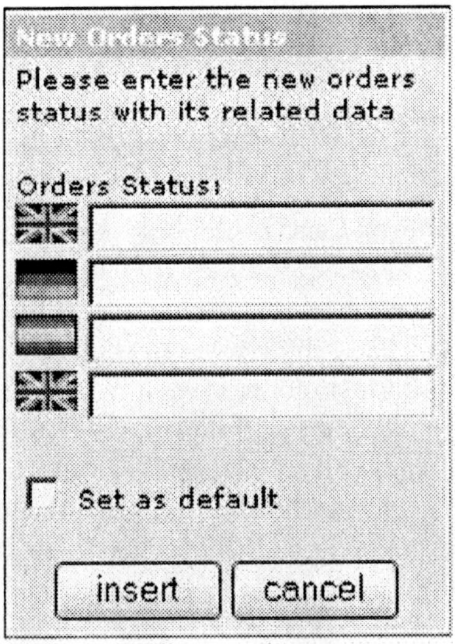

Figure 2.89. New Orders Status.

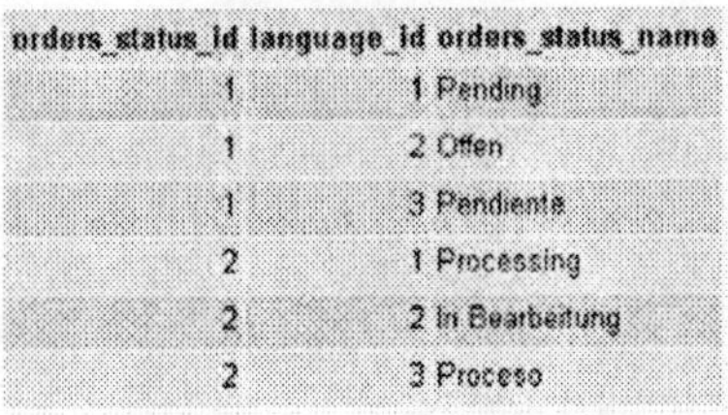

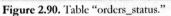

orders_status_id	language_id	orders_status_name
1	1	Pending
1	2	Offen
1	3	Pendiente
2	1	Processing
2	2	In Bearbeitung
2	3	Proceso

Figure 2.90. Table "orders_status."

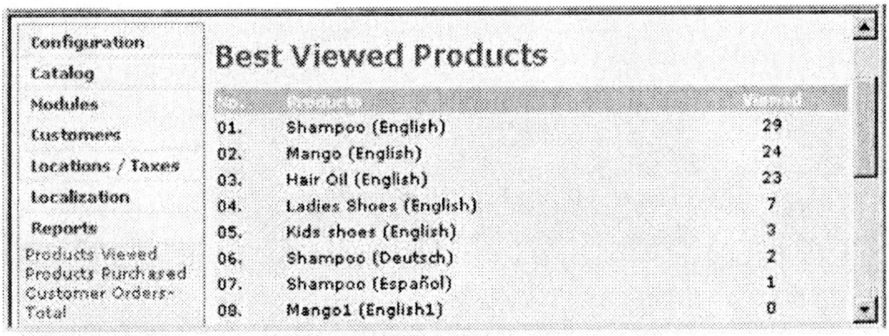

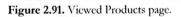

Figure 2.91. Viewed Products page.

saved data related to products are fetched from the following three tables: "products" (Figure 2.92), "products_description" (Figure 2.93), and "languages" (Figure 2.94).

2.3.8.2. Products Purchased

When the **Products Purchased** link is clicked, the code written in /catalog/admin/Stats_products_purchased.php is executed. A list of products with the number of times each was purchased is shown in Figure 2.95. The highest-purchased product (i.e., the product purchased the highest number of times) is on the top of the list. For example, in Figure 2.95, consider the product Mango. On the right side, under the purchased column, the number 40 is shown; this means that the product Mango was purchased a total of 40 times by different customers. To show the above list, the data related to products are fetched from the three tables "products," "products_description," and "languages."

products_id	products_quantity	products_model	products_image	products_price
33	4		image4s.jpg	23.0000
30	1		image5s.jpg	30.0000

Figure 2.92. Table "products."

products_id	language_id	products_name	products_description	products_url	products_viewed
30	1	Kids shoes	Best Shoes for kids		3
30	2	Kids shoes	Best Shoes for kids		0
30	3	Kids shoes	Best Shoes for kids		0
31	1	Ladies Shoes	Soft and light Shoes		7

Figure 2.93. Table "products_description."

←T→	languages_id	name	code	image	directory	sort_order
⌐ ✎ ✗	1	English	en	icon.gif	english	1
⌐ ✎ ✗	2	Deutsch	de	icon.gif	german	2
⌐ ✎ ✗	3	Español	es	icon.gif	espanol	3

Figure 2.94. Table "languages."

Configuration	**Best Products Purchased**	
Catalog		
Modules		
Customers	No. Products Purchased	
Locations / Taxes	01. Mango 40	
Localization	02. Kids shoes 8	
	03. Hair Oil 7	
Reports	04. Shampoo 6	
Products Viewed	05. Ladies Shoes 5	
Products Purchased	Displaying 1 to 5 (of 5 products) Page 1 of 1	

Figure 2.95. Products Purchased page.

Configuration	**Best Customer Orders-Total**	
Catalog		
Modules		
Customers	No. Customers Total Purchased	
Locations / Taxes	01. shaswati guin $288.00	
Localization	02. Subhamoy Bandyopadhyay $80.00	
Reports	Displaying 1 to 2 (of 2 customers) Page 1 of 1	
Products Viewed		
Products Purchased		
Customer Orders-		
Total		

Figure 2.96. Customer Orders–Total page.

2.3.8.3. Customer Orders—Total

When the **Customer Orders—Total** link is clicked, the code written in /catalog/admin/stats_customers.php is executed. Figure 2.96 shows those customers who have ordered products. The list also shows the total amount of ordered products on the right side of each customer. For example, let the customer Shaswati Guin have purchased different products on different dates, and let the total price all of those purchases be $288. The shipping cost is not included here. To show the above list, the related data is fetched from the following tables: "customers" (Figure 2.97), "orders_products" (Figure 2.98), and "orders" (Figure 2.99).

When a customer name from the customer list is clicked, the Customers section will open (Figure 2.100). This section was discussed in detail in section 2.3.5.

customers_id	customers_gender	customers_firstname	customers_lastname
1	m	John	doe
5	m	Subhamoy	Bandyopadhyay
6	m	fdgrd	gfdg
7	f	shaswati	guin

Figure 2.97. Table "customers."

orders_id	products_id	products_model	products_name	products_price	final_price	products_tax	products_quantity
1	29		Shampoo	40.0000	40.0000	0.0000	1
2	29		Shampoo	40.0000	40.0000	0.0000	1
3	34		Mango	18.0000	19.0000	0.0000	1
4	28		Hair Oil	20.0000	20.0000	0.0000	1

Figure 2.98. Table "orders_products."

orders_id	customers_id	customers_name	customers_company
1	5	Subhamoy Bandyopadhyay	ws
2	5	Subhamoy Bandyopadhyay	ws
21	7	shaswati guin	ws

Figure 2.99. Table "orders."

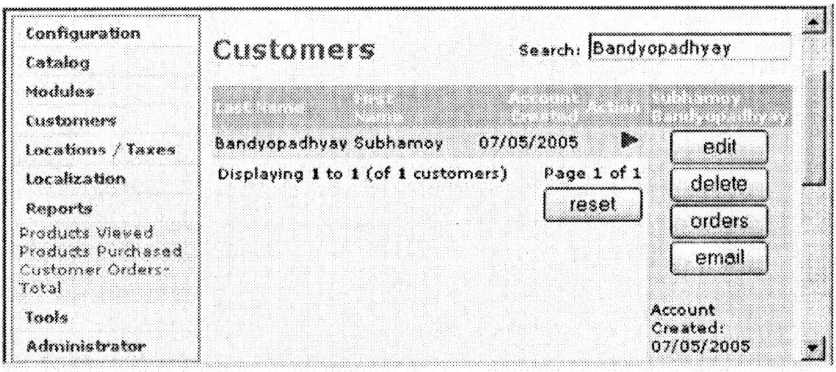

Figure 2.100. Customers section.

2.3.9. Tools

A tool provides a mechanical or mental advantage in accomplishing a task. The following tools are present in osCommerce: Database Backup, Banner Manager, Cache Control, Define Languages, File Manager, Send E-mail, Newsletter Manager, Server Information, and Who's Online.

2.3.9.1. Database Backup

The Database Backup tool allows the administrator to make backups of the database, including all customer and order information. It is best if regular backups of the database are made, but there is no tool to automatically make backups, and it should be known that in addition, most hosting sites do not make regular backups of this information unless explicitly asked.

Let us discuss how to make database backups in osCommerce. First, the backup directory needs to be created by the administrator and given permissions of 777 to give the Web server write permission for that folder. When **Database Backup** is clicked on the left side under Tools, the screen shown in Figure 2.101 appears. From Figure 2.101 it can be seen that there is no backup file of the database present on the backup manager listing page. To back up the database, click the **Backup** button. When the **Backup** button is clicked, the New Backup form shown in Figure 2.102 will open. From here we are given some choices. If we choose the "No Compression (Pure SQL)" option, a file will be created in the backups directory without any compression. If we choose the "Download only (do not store server side)" option, a backup file will not be created on the server but will be downloaded to the local computer.

If the **Backup** button is clicked, the following code, written in /catalog/admin/backup.php, is executed.

Figure 2.101. Database Backup Manager listing page (without backup file).

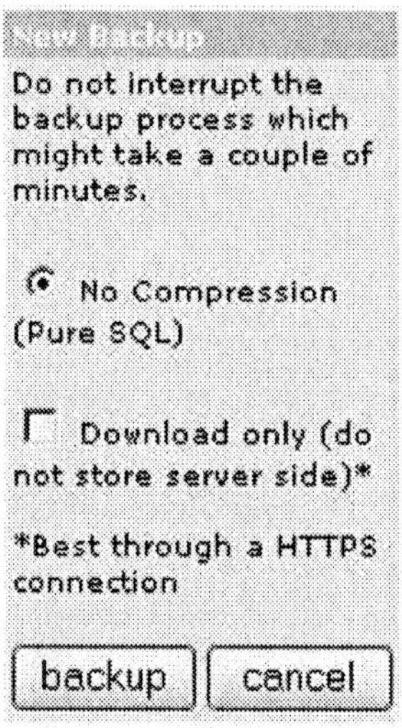

Figure 2.102. New Backup form.

```
case 'backupnow':
        tep_set_time_limit(0);
        $backup_file = 'db_' . DB_DATABASE .
'-' . date('YmdHis') . '.sql';
        $fp = fopen(DIR_FS_BACKUP .
$backup_file, 'w');

    $schema = '# osCommerce, Open Source E-
        Commerce Solutions' . "/n" .
                '#
http://www.oscommerce.com' . "/n" .
                '#' . "/n" .
                '# Database Backup For ' .
STORE_NAME . "/n" .
                '# Copyright (c) ' .
date('Y') . ' ' . STORE_OWNER . "/n" .
```

```
                '#' . "/n" .
                '# Database: ' . DB_DATABASE
. "/n" .
                '# Database Server: ' .
DB_SERVER . "/n" .
                '#' . "/n" .
                '# Backup Date: ' .
date(PHP_DATE_TIME_FORMAT) . "/n/n";
        fputs($fp, $schema);

        $tables_query = tep_db_query('show
tables');
        while ($tables =
tep_db_fetch_array($tables_query)) {
            list(,$table) = each($tables);
    schema = 'drop table if exists ' . $table .
';' . "/n" .
                    'create table ' . $table .
' (' . "/n";

        $table_list = array();
        $fields_query = tep_db_query("show
fields from " . $table);
        while ($fields =
tep_db_fetch_array($fields_query)) {
            $table_list[] = $fields['Field'];

            $schema .= ' ' . $fields['Field']
. ' ' . $fields['Type'];
```
....
....
....

If the checkbox "Download only (do not store server side)" is selected and the **Update** button is clicked, then the following code in the /backup.php file is executed.

```
case 'backupnow':
```
....
....
....
```
if (isset($HTTP_POST_VARS['download']) &&
($HTTP_POST_VARS['download'] == 'yes'))
  {
        switch ($HTTP_POST_VARS['compress'])
{
            case 'gzip':
                exec(LOCAL_EXE_GZIP . ' ' .
DIR_FS_BACKUP . $backup_file);
                $backup_file .= '.gz';
```

```
                    break;
                case 'zip':
                    exec(LOCAL_EXE_ZIP . ' -j ' .
      DIR_FS_BACKUP . $backup_file . '.zip ' .
      DIR_FS_BACKUP . $backup_file);
                    unlink(DIR_FS_BACKUP .
      $backup_file);
                    $backup_file .= '.zip';
        }
      header('Content-type: application/x-octet-
      stream');
      header('Content-disposition: attachment;
      filename=' . $backup_file);

      readfile(DIR_FS_BACKUP . $backup_file);
      unlink(DIR_FS_BACKUP . $backup_file);
          exit;
      }
```

If the radio button "No Compression (Pure SQL)" is selected, then after clicking the **Update** button the following code in /backup.php is executed.

```
case 'backupnow':
....................................................... .
....................................................... .
....................................................... .
switch ($HTTP_POST_VARS['compress']) {
case 'gzip':
exec(LOCAL_EXE_GZIP . ' ' . DIR_FS_BACKUP .
$backup_file);
break;
case 'zip':
exec(LOCAL_EXE_ZIP . ' -j ' . DIR_FS_BACKUP .
$backup_file . '.zip ' . DIR_FS_BACKUP .
$backup_file);
unlink(DIR_FS_BACKUP . $backup_file);
}

$messageStack-
>add_session(SUCCESS_DATABASE_SAVED,
'success');
```

Figure 2.103 shows the database Backup Manager listing page with the backup file. If the icon on the left side of the backup file is clicked, then the database will be downloaded to the local computer.

The administrator can restore the backup. Figure 2.104 shows the Backup Restoration form, which is opened by clicking the **Restore** button on

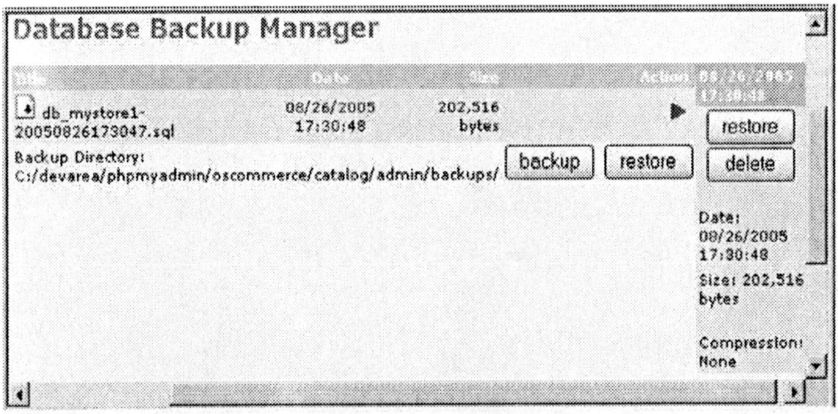

Figure 2.103. Database Backup Manager listing page (with backup file).

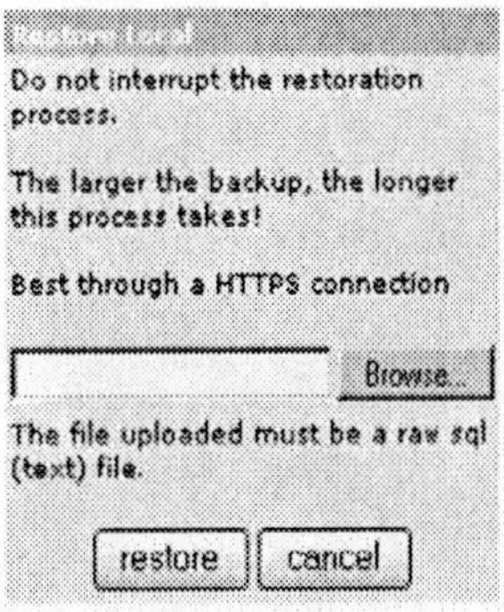

Figure 2.104. Database Backup Restore.

the right side of the backup file list. The database can be restored to a backup file that has been already saved on the server or from a local file that was previously downloaded. To restore a file that is on the server (case "restorenow" in the following code), click on the file name of the desired backup and then on **Restore**. To restore from a backup stored on the local computer (case "restorelocalnow" in the following code), press the **Restore** button listed below the file listings. This will then allow you to browse to the file where the backup is stored. When these actions are performed, the following code, written in /catalog/admin/backup.php, is executed, depending upon the case.

```
case 'restorenow':
case 'restorelocalnow':
        tep_set_time_limit(0);
```

```
if ($action == 'restorenow') {
        $read_from = $HTTP_GET_VARS['file'];

        if (file_exists(DIR_FS_BACKUP .
$HTTP_GET_VARS['file'])) {
            $restore_file = DIR_FS_BACKUP .
$HTTP_GET_VARS['file'];
            $extension =
substr($HTTP_GET_VARS['file'], -3);

            if ( ($extension == 'sql') ||
($extension == '.gz') || ($extension == 'zip')
) {
                switch ($extension) {
                  case 'sql':
                    $restore_from =
$restore_file;
                    ........................................................ . .
                    ........................................................

    }
} elseif ($action == 'restorelocalnow') {
                    $sql_file = new
upload('sql_file');

        if ($sql_file->parse() == true) {
            $restore_query =
fread(fopen($sql_file->tmp_filename, 'r'),
filesize($sql_file->tmp_filename));
                $read_from = $sql_file->filename;
            }
        }

        if (isset($restore_query)) {
            $sql_array = array();
            $sql_length =
strlen($restore_query);
            $pos = strpos($restore_query, ';');
            for ($i=$pos; $i<$sql_length; $i++)
{
                if ($restore_query[0] == '#') {
    ........................................................ .
    ........................................................

    }
        ........................................................ . .
........................................................ . .
tep_redirect(tep_href_link(FILENAME_BACKUP));
        break;
```

The database backup file can also be deleted by clicking the **Delete** button.

2.3.9.2. Banner Manager

The administrator can set image- or HTML-based banners using the Banner Manager. These banners will be displayed in the user area. Also, the Banner Manager tracks impressions and clicks on a per banner basis. Each banner is assigned a group that is used for displaying random banners in the set group. This allows certain banners to be shown throughout certain locations on the overall Web site layout. Figure 2.105 shows the Banner Manager listing page. A banner can be added, edited, or deleted by clicking the **New Banner**, **Edit**, and **Delete** buttons, respectively.

When the **New Banner** button is clicked, the form shown in Figure 2.106 will open. The following fields need to be defined: banner title (the name or title of the banner); banner URL (the destination to which a user is taken when the banner is clicked); banner group (the group to which the banner should be assigned for display purposes); scheduled date (the date on which the banner should become active—no date will cause the banner to become active when saved); and expiration date (the date on which the banner will become inactive or the number of impressions after which the banner should become inactive).

Banner images can be uploaded either by uploading the image or by writing HTML text. Image-based banners can be uploaded to the server or can be set to an image already existing on the server; also, a destination path on the server can be defined, which needs to be writeable by the Web server. HTML-based banners can be defined in the HTML text field (Figure 2.106). For example, one can write HTML and JavaScript tags to display text-, image-, or Flash-based banners.

When the **Insert** button is clicked, the following code, written in /catalog/admin/banner_manager.php, is executed.

```
case 'insert':
if (isset($HTTP_POST_VARS['banners_id']))
$banners_id =
tep_db_prepare_input($HTTP_POST_VARS['banners_
id']);
$banners_title =
tep_db_prepare_input($HTTP_POST_VARS['banners_
title']);
$banners_url =
tep_db_prepare_input($HTTP_POST_VARS['banners_
url']);
$new_banners_group =
tep_db_prepare_input($HTTP_POST_VARS['new_bann
ers_group']);
```

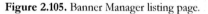

Figure 2.105. Banner Manager listing page.

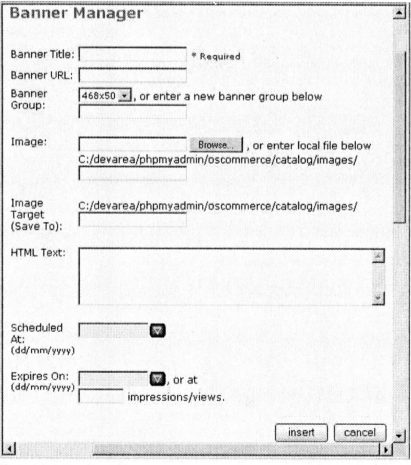

Figure 2.106. New Banner form.

```
$banners_group = (empty($new_banners_group)) ?
tep_db_prepare_input($HTTP_POST_VARS['banners_
group']) : $new_banners_group;
```
....
....
```
$banner_error = false;
        if (empty($banners_title)) {
            $messageStack-
>add(ERROR_BANNER_TITLE_REQUIRED, 'error');
            $banner_error = true;
        }
if ($banner_error == false) {
$db_image_location =
(tep_not_null($banners_image_local)) ?
$banners_image_local : $banners_image_target .
$banners_image->filename;
$sql_data_array = array('banners_title' =>
$banners_title,
'banners_url' => $banners_url,
'banners_image' => $db_image_location,
'banners_group' => $banners_group,
'banners_html_text' => $banners_html_text);

if ($action == 'insert') {
$insert_sql_data = array('date_added' =>
'now()',
'status' => '1');

$sql_data_array = array_merge($sql_data_array,
$insert_sql_data);

tep_db_perform(TABLE_BANNERS,
$sql_data_array);

$banners_id = tep_db_insert_id();

$messageStack-
>add_session(SUCCESS_BANNER_INSERTED,
'success');
}
```
....
....
```
break;
```

The related data is saved into the "banners" table (Figure 2.107).

Banners can be displayed on the front end in the footer section. To display the banners, the following code is written in /catalog/includes/footer.php.

banners_id	banners_title	banners_url	banners_image	banners_group
3	google1	http://pma.dev.webspiders.com/oscommerce/catalog/i...	eric_meyer_css.jpg	468x50
4	banner1	http://pma.dev.webspiders.com/oscommerce/catalog/i...	upldtemplate7-468.jpg	468x50

Figure 2.107. Table "banners."

```
<?php
  if ($banner = tep_banner_exists('dynamic',
'468x50')) {
?>
<br>
<table border="0" width="100%" cellspacing="0"
cellpadding="0">
  <tr>
    <td align="center"><?php echo
tep_display_banner('static', $banner); ?></td>
  </tr>
</table>
<?php
  }
?>
```

The functions "tep_banner_exists ('dynamic', '468x50')" and "tep_display_banner ('static', $banner)" are written in /catalog/includes/functions/banner.php.

```
// Check to see if a banner exists
  function tep_banner_exists($action,
$identifier) {
    if ($action == 'dynamic') {
      return tep_random_select("select
banners_id, banners_title, banners_image,
banners_html_text from " . TABLE_BANNERS . "
where status = '1' and banners_group = '" .
$identifier . "'");
    } elseif ($action == 'static') {
      $banner_query = tep_db_query("select
banners_id, banners_title, banners_image,
banners_html_text from " . TABLE_BANNERS . "
where status = '1' and banners_id = '" .
(int)$identifier . "'");
      return
tep_db_fetch_array($banner_query);
    } else {
      return false;
    }
  }
```

```
////
// Display a banner from the specified group
or banner id ($identifier)

function tep_display_banner($action,
$identifier) {
if ($action == 'dynamic') {
$banners_query = tep_db_query("select count(*)
as count from " . TABLE_BANNERS . " where
status = '1' and banners_group = '" .
$identifier . "'");
$banners = tep_db_fetch_array($banners_query);
if ($banners['count'] > 0) {
$banner = tep_random_select("select
banners_id, banners_title, banners_image,
banners_html_text from " . TABLE_BANNERS . "
where status = '1' and banners_group = '" .
$identifier . "'");
      } else {
return '<b>TEP ERROR! (tep_display_banner(' .
$action . ', ' . $identifier . ') -> No
banners with group /'' . $identifier . '/'
found!</b>';
}
} elseif ($action == 'static') {
      if (is_array($identifier)) {
        $banner = $identifier;
      } else {
$banner_query = tep_db_query("select
banners_id, banners_title, banners_image,
banners_html_text from " . TABLE_BANNERS . "
where status = '1' and banners_id = '" .
(int)$identifier . "'");
if (tep_db_num_rows($banner_query)) {
        $banner =
tep_db_fetch_array($banner_query);
} else {
return '<b>TEP ERROR! (tep_display_banner(' .
$action . ', ' . $identifier . ') -> Banner
with ID /'' . $identifier . '/' not found, or
status inactive</b>';
}
}
} else {
return '<b>TEP ERROR! (tep_display_banner(' .
$action . ', ' . $identifier . ') -> Unknown
$action parameter value - it must be either
/'dynamic/' or /'static/'</b>';
}
```

```
if
(tep_not_null($banner['banners_html_text'])) {
$banner_string = $banner['banners_html_text'];
} else {
$banner_string = '<a href="' .
tep_href_link(FILENAME_REDIRECT,
'action=banner&goto=' . $banner['banners_id'])
. '" target="_blank">' .
tep_image(DIR_WS_IMAGES .
$banner['banners_image'],
$banner['banners_title']) . '</a>';
}

tep_update_banner_display_count($banner['banne
rs_id']);

return $banner_string;
}
```

On the Banner Manager listing page, on the right side of the banner list, the administrator can see the statistics of any selected banner. Figure 2.108 is an example of the banner statistics for "banner1" over the last three days. If the icon under the action column on the banner listing page for the particular banner is clicked, then the code written in /catalog/admin/banner_ statistics.php is executed. Figure 2.109 represents the monthly statistics of banner1. The data related to banner statistics are saved into the "banners_history" table (Figure 2.110).

2.3.9.3. Cache Control

Cache Control allows the administrator to save certain areas of the Shopping Cart to a cache folder. When customers are browsing the store, the database is not queried again until the cache is expired or is reset by the administrator. The directory for holding the cache page is created during the setup procedure, and the folder is called /cache/, although it can be renamed.

If the cache folder does not exist, then create one. Now, go to Configuration > Cache (Figure 2.111). Click on **Use Cache** and set to "true." Click on **Cache Directory** and set the directory path to the cache folder.

When the **Cache Control** button on the left side of the menu is clicked, the code written in /catalog/admin/cache.php is executed. Figure 2.112 shows the cache listing page.

The following cache blocks are used in the Tools > Cache section; the code is written in /catalog/admin/includes/application_top.php.

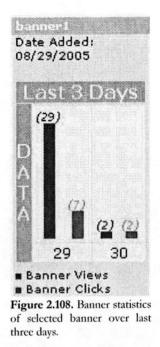

Figure 2.108. Banner statistics of selected banner over last three days.

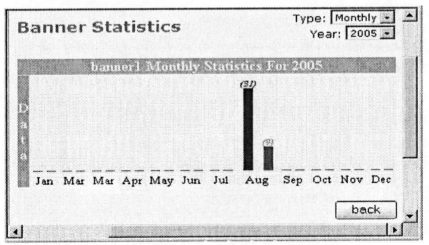

Figure 2.109. Monthly banner statistics of selected banner.

banners_history_id	banners_id	banners_shown	banners_clicked	banners_history_date
2	3	42	2	2005-08-29 10:52:00
3	4	29	7	2005-08-29 11:23:21
4	6	38	2	2005-08-29 11:25:21

Figure 2.110. Table "banners_history."

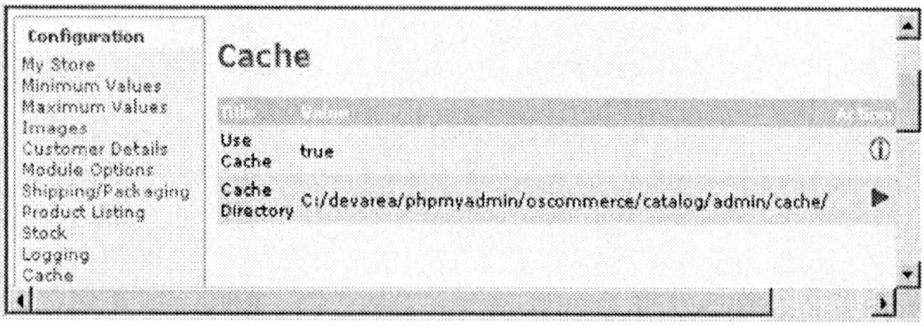

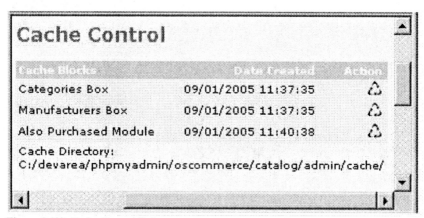

Figure 2.111. Cache Configuration page.

Figure 2.112. Cache Control listing page.

```
// ('language' in the filename is
automatically replaced by available languages)

$cache_blocks = array(
array('title' => TEXT_CACHE_CATEGORIES, 'code'
=> 'categories', 'file' => 'categories_box-
language.cache', 'multiple' => true),
array('title' => TEXT_CACHE_MANUFACTURERS,
'code' => 'manufacturers', 'file' =>
'manufacturers_box-language.cache', 'multiple'
=> true),
array('title' => TEXT_CACHE_ALSO_PURCHASED,
'code' => 'also_purchased', 'file' =>
'also_purchased-language.cache', 'multiple' =>
true)
);
```

If the language is English, then the definitions for "TEXT_CACHE_CATEGORIES," "TEXT_CACHE_MANUFACTURERS," and "TEXT_CACHE_ALSO_PURCHASED" are available in /catalog/admin/includes/languages/english.php.

```
define('TEXT_CACHE_CATEGORIES', 'Categories
Box');
define('TEXT_CACHE_MANUFACTURERS',
'Manufacturers Box');
define('TEXT_CACHE_ALSO_PURCHASED', 'Also
Purchased Module');
```

Similarly, these can be defined for other languages.

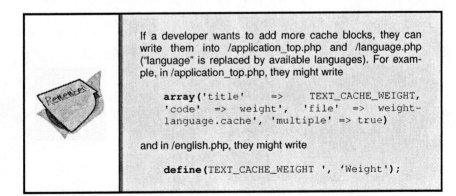

If a developer wants to add more cache blocks, they can write them into /application_top.php and /language.php ("language" is replaced by available languages). For example, in /application_top.php, they might write

```
array('title'    =>    TEXT_CACHE_WEIGHT,
'code'  =>  weight',  'file'  =>  weight-
language.cache', 'multiple' => true)
```

and in /english.php, they might write

```
define(TEXT_CACHE_WEIGHT ', 'Weight');
```

2.3.9.4. Define Languages

This module was discussed previously in section 2.2.

2.3.9.5. File Manager

This module was discussed previously in section 2.2.

2.3.9.6. Send E-mail to Customers

Figure 2.113 shows the Send E-mail to Customers form. The administrator can send e-mail to a particular customer or to all customers by selecting options from the customer drop-down box. If the **Send Mail** button is clicked, the code written in /catalog/admin/mail.php is executed.

```
if ( ($action == 'send_email_to_user') &&
isset($HTTP_POST_VARS['customers_email_address
']) && !isset($HTTP_POST_VARS['back_x']) ) {
switch
($HTTP_POST_VARS['customers_email_address']) {
case '***':
$mail_query = tep_db_query("select
customers_firstname, customers_lastname,
customers_email_address from " .
TABLE_CUSTOMERS);
$mail_sent_to = TEXT_ALL_CUSTOMERS;
break;
case '**D':
$mail_query = tep_db_query("select
customers_firstname, customers_lastname,
customers_email_address from " .
TABLE_CUSTOMERS . " where customers_newsletter
= '1'");
$mail_sent_to = TEXT_NEWSLETTER_CUSTOMERS;
break;
default:
$customers_email_address =
tep_db_prepare_input($HTTP_POST_VARS['customer
s_email_address']);

$mail_query = tep_db_query("select
customers_firstname, customers_lastname,
customers_email_address from " .
TABLE_CUSTOMERS . " where
customers_email_address = '" .
tep_db_input($customers_email_address) . "'");
$mail_sent_to =
$HTTP_POST_VARS['customers_email_address'];
break;
}
```

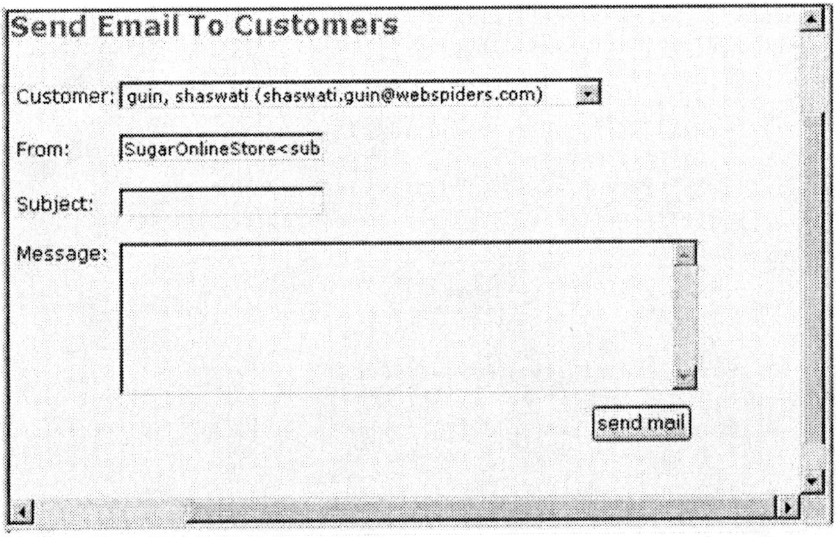

Figure 2.113. Send E-mail to Customers.

```
$from =
tep_db_prepare_input($HTTP_POST_VARS['from']);
$subject =
tep_db_prepare_input($HTTP_POST_VARS['subject'
]);
$message =
tep_db_prepare_input($HTTP_POST_VARS['message'
]);

//Let's build a message object using the email
class
$mimemessage = new email(array('X-Mailer:
osCommerce'));
// add the message to the object
$mimemessage->add_text($message);
$mimemessage->build_message();
while ($mail =
tep_db_fetch_array($mail_query)) {
$mimemessage-
>send($mail['customers_firstname'] . ' ' .
$mail['customers_lastname'],
$mail['customers_email_address'], '', $from,
$subject);
}

tep_redirect(tep_href_link(FILENAME_MAIL,
'mail_sent_to=' . urlencode($mail_sent_to)));
}
```

The functions "add_text($message)," "build_message()," "send($mail['cus-tomers_firstname'] . ' ' . $mail['customers_lastname'])," and "$mail['customers_email_address'], '', $from, $subject)" in the above code are defined in the class "email," which is written in /catalog/admin/includes/classes/email.php.

```
class email {
    var $html;
    var $text;
    var $output;
    var $html_text;
..................................................... .

.....................................................
function add_text($text = '') {
    $this->text =
tep_convert_linefeeds(array("/r/n", "/n",
"/r"), $this->lf, $text);
    }

..................................... . .
function build_message($params = '') {
    if ($params == '') $params = array();

    if (count($params) > 0) {
       reset($params);
       while(list($key, $value) =
each($params)) {
            $this->build_params[$key] = $value;
       }

..................................... .

}
function send($to_name, $to_addr, $from_name,
$from_addr, $subject = '', $headers = '') {
    $to = (($to_name != '') ? '"' . $to_name
. '" <' . $to_addr . '>' : $to_addr);
$from = (($from_name != '') ? '"' . $from_name
. '" <' . $from_addr . '>' : $from_addr);

.................................................................... .

.................................................................... .
if (EMAIL_TRANSPORT == 'smtp') {
        return mail($to_addr, $subject, $this-
>output, 'From: ' . $from . $this->lf . 'To: '
. $to . $this->lf . implode($this->lf, $this-
>headers) . $this->lf . implode($this->lf,
$xtra_headers));
        } else {
        return mail($to, $subject, $this-
>output, 'From: '.$from.$this-
```

```
>lf.implode($this->lf, $this->headers).$this-
>lf.implode($this->lf, $xtra_headers));
    }
}
```

....

....

}

2.3.9.7. Newsletter Manager

The Newsletter Manager is a system that sends e-mails to customers who have previously provided their e-mail addresses during account creation. Two newsletter modules are installed by default: one is used for sending e-mails to customers who have selected to receive newsletters, and other is for sending e-mails to customers who have selected to be notified of product updates. Figure 2.114 shows the list of newsletters.

Before a newsletter can be sent, the newsletter status needs to be locked. This will prevent unsaved changes from being missed during the mailing. Once a newsletter status has been locked, it can be sent to the targeted audience via the chosen newsletter module (Newsletter or Product Notification). When locked, a newsletter can be edited, deleted, previewed, sent, or unlocked.

Depending on the newsletter module chosen, the target audience may need to be defined before the newsletter can be sent. This is not required for the Newsletter module as the target audience is already known (customers who have chosen to receive newsletters); however, the target audience needs to be

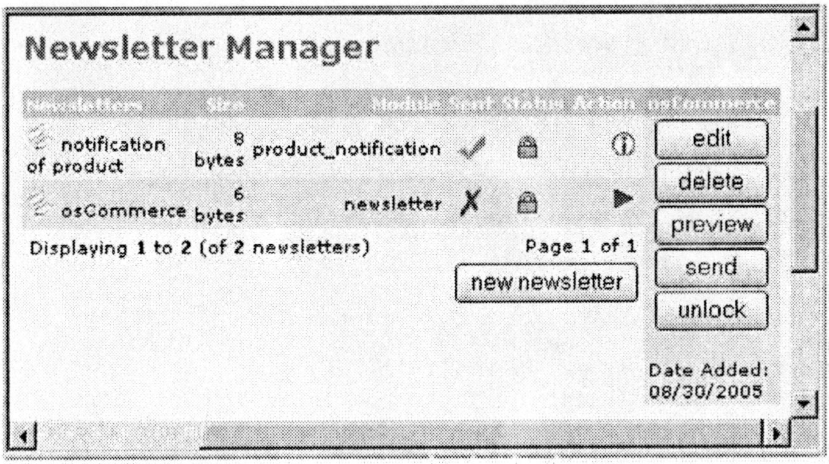

Figure 2.114. Newsletter Manager list.

defined for the Product Notification module, where the administrator must select about which products the newsletter is concerned so that customers who have selected to be notified about similar product updates can receive the newsletter. Once the target audience has been defined, a preview of the newsletter (for last minute changes) as well as the number of customers who will receive the newsletter is displayed. The newsletter can then be sent after its contents have been confirmed via the online preview.

If the **Edit, Delete, Preview, Send,** or **Unlock** buttons shown in Figure 2.114 are clicked, the code written in /catalog/admin/newsletters.php is executed, depending on the indicated action (add, edit, send, etc.). If the module of the newsletter is Product Notification, then after clicking the **Send** button (see Figures 2.115 and 2.116), the code written in /catalog/admin/ newsletters.php and /catalog/admin/includes/modules/newsletters/product_ notification.php is executed. A class named "product_notification" is defined in /product_notification.php, which is called from /admin/newsletters.php.

```
class product_notification {
var $show_choose_audience, $title, $content;
........................................................................ .

........................................................ .
function confirm() {
global $HTTP_GET_VARS, $HTTP_POST_VARS;

$audience = array();

if (isset($HTTP_GET_VARS['global']) &&
($HTTP_GET_VARS['global'] == 'true')) {
$products_query = tep_db_query("select
distinct customers_id from " .
TABLE_PRODUCTS_NOTIFICATIONS);
while ($products =
tep_db_fetch_array($products_query)) {
$audience[$products['customers_id']] = '1';
}
.............................................................. . .
.............................................................. .
$confirm_string = '<table border="0"
cellspacing="0" cellpadding="2">' . "/n" .
'   <tr>' . "/n" .
'      <td class="main"><font
color="#ff0000"><b>' .
sprintf(TEXT_COUNT_CUSTOMERS,
sizeof($audience)) . '</b></font></td>' . "/n"
.
'   </tr>' . "/n" .
.............................................................. .
.............................................................. . .
```

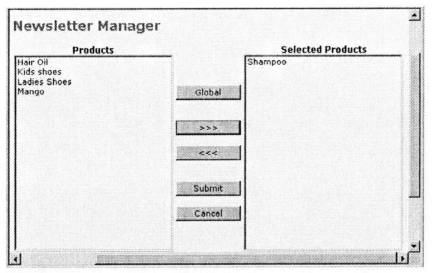

Figure 2.115. Send newsletter with the Product Notification module.

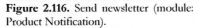

Figure 2.116. Send newsletter (module: Product Notification).

```
return $confirm_string;
}

function send($newsletter_id) {
global $HTTP_POST_VARS;
............................................................. . .
............................................................. .
$mimemessage = new email(array('X-Mailer:
osCommerce bulk mailer'));
$mimemessage->add_text($this->content);
$mimemessage->build_message();

reset($audience);
while (list($key, $value) = each ($audience))
{
$mimemessage->send($value['firstname'] . ' ' .
$value['lastname'], $value['email_address'],
'', EMAIL_FROM, $this->title);
}

$newsletter_id =
tep_db_prepare_input($newsletter_id);
tep_db_query("update " . TABLE_NEWSLETTERS . "
set date_sent = now(), status = '1' where
newsletters_id = '" .
tep_db_input($newsletter_id) . "'");
}
}
```

If the module of the newsletter is Newsletter, then after clicking the **Send** button (Figure 2.117) the code written in /catalog/admin/ newsletters.php and /catalog/admin/includes/modules/newsletters/news- letter.php is executed. A class named "newsletter" is defined in /admin/ includes/modules/newsletters/newsletter.php, which is called from /admin/ newsletters.php.

```
class newsletter {
    var $show_choose_audience, $title,
$content;

    function newsletter($title, $content) {
        $this->show_choose_audience = false;
        $this->title = $title;
        $this->content = $content;
    }

    ...........................................................
    ...........................................................
function confirm() {
        global $HTTP_GET_VARS;
```

```
        $mail_query = tep_db_query("select
count(*) as count from " . TABLE_CUSTOMERS . "
where customers_newsletter = '1'");
        $mail = tep_db_fetch_array($mail_query);

        $confirm_string = '<table border="0"
cellspacing="0" cellpadding="2">' . "/n" .
                          '  <tr>' . "/n" .
.......................................................
.......................................................
  '</table>';

        return $confirm_string;
    }

function send($newsletter_id) {
        $mail_query = tep_db_query("select
customers_firstname, customers_lastname,
customers_email_address from " .
TABLE_CUSTOMERS . " where customers_newsletter
= '1'");

        $mimemessage = new email(array('X-
Mailer: osCommerce bulk mailer'));
        $mimemessage->add_text($this->content);
        $mimemessage->build_message();
        while ($mail =
tep_db_fetch_array($mail_query)) {
            $mimemessage-
>send($mail['customers_firstname'] . ' ' .
$mail['customers_lastname'],
$mail['customers_email_address'], '',
EMAIL_FROM, $this->title);
        }

        $newsletter_id =
tep_db_prepare_input($newsletter_id);
        tep_db_query("update " .
TABLE_NEWSLETTERS . " set date_sent = now(),
status = '1' where newsletters_id = '" .
tep_db_input($newsletter_id) . "'");
    }
}
```

The data related to newsletters is saved in the "newsletters" table (Figure 2.118).

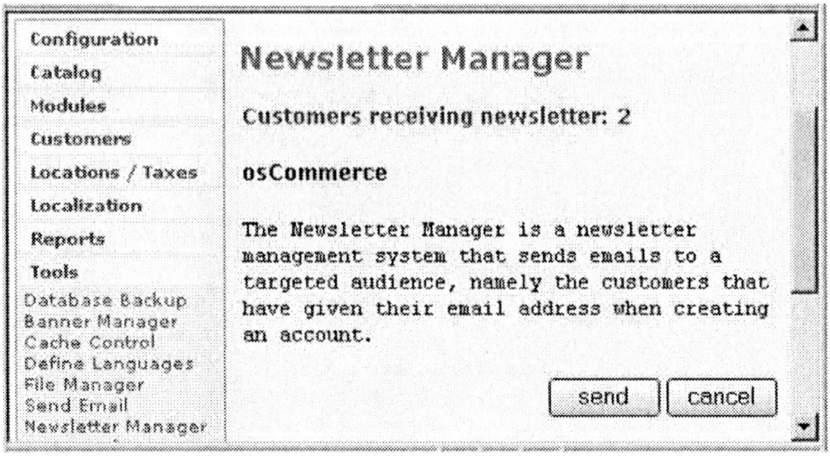

Figure 2.117. Send newsletter (module: Newsletter).

newsletters_id	title	content	module	date_added	date_sent	status	locked
1	osCommerce	The Newsletter Manager is a newsletter management ...	newsletter	2005-08-30 18:23:25	2005-08-31 11:40:26	1	1
2	notification of product	attractive offer will be given with this product	product_notification	2005-08-30 18:25:08	2005-08-31 12:34:12	1	1

Figure 2.118. Table "newsletters."

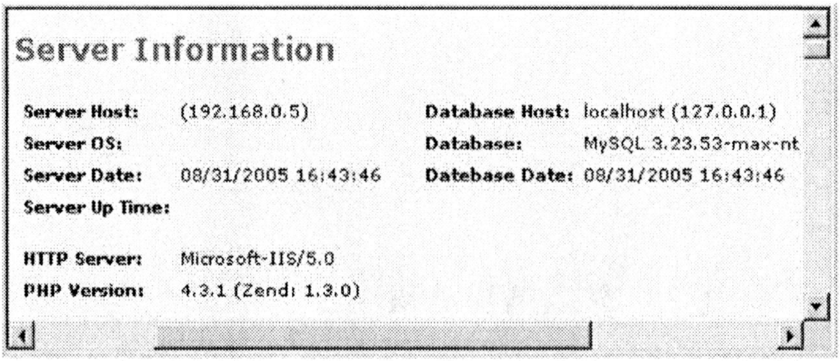

Figure 2.119. Server Information listing page.

2.3.9.8. Server Information

The Server Information page gives the administrator the details on the configuration of the Web server. When the **Server Information** link is clicked, the code written in /catalog/admin/server_info.php is executed.

```php
$system = tep_get_system_information();
..........................................................  . .
..........................................................
<tr>
<td class="smallText"><b><?php echo
TITLE_SERVER_HOST; ?></b></td>
<td class="smallText"><?php echo
$system['host'] . ' (' . $system['ip'] . ')';
?></td>
<td
class="smallText">    &nbs
p;<b><?php echo TITLE_DATABASE_HOST;
?></b></td>
<td class="smallText"><?php echo
$system['db_server'] . ' (' . $system['db_ip']
. ')'; ?></td>
</tr>
<tr>
<td class="smallText"><b><?php echo
TITLE_SERVER_OS; ?></b></td>
<td class="smallText"><?php echo
$system['system'] . ' ' . $system['kernel'];
?></td>
<td
class="smallText">    &nbs
p;<b><?php echo TITLE_DATABASE; ?></b></td>
<td class="smallText"><?php echo
$system['db_version']; ?></td>
</tr>
..........................................................
..........................................................  . .
<?php
ob_start();
phpinfo();
$phpinfo = ob_get_contents();
ob_end_clean();

$phpinfo = str_replace('border: 1px', '',
$phpinfo);
ereg('<body>(.*)</body>', $phpinfo, $regs);
echo '<table border="1" cellpadding="3"
width="600" style="border: 0px; border-color:
#000000;">' .
'  <tr><td><a
href="http://www.oscommerce.com"><img
```

```
border="0" src="images/oscommerce.gif" alt="
osCommerce " /></a><h1 class="p"> ' .
PROJECT_VERSION . '</h1></td>' .
'  </tr>' .
'</table>';
echo $regs[1];
} else {
phpinfo();
}
?>
```

....
....

The function "phpinfo()" outputs a large amount of information about the current state of the PHP. This includes information about PHP compilation options and extensions, the PHP version, server information and environment (if compiled as a module), the PHP environment, OS version information, paths, master and local values of configuration options, HTTP headers, and the PHP license (Figure 2.119). The function "tep_get_system_information()" retrieves the server information and is defined in /catalog/admin/includes/functions/general.php.

```
function tep_get_system_information() {
global $HTTP_SERVER_VARS;

$db_query = tep_db_query("select now() as
datetime");
$db = tep_db_fetch_array($db_query);

list($system, $host, $kernel) =
preg_split('/[/s,]+/', @exec('uname -a'), 5);

return array('date' =>
tep_datetime_short(date('Y-m-d H:i:s')),
'system' => $system,
'kernel' => $kernel,
'host' => $host,
'ip' => gethostbyname($host),
'uptime' => @exec('uptime'),
'http_server' =>
$HTTP_SERVER_VARS['SERVER_SOFTWARE'],
'php' => PHP_VERSION,
'zend' => (function_exists('zend_version') ?
zend_version() : ''),
'db_server' => DB_SERVER,
'db_ip' => gethostbyname(DB_SERVER),
'db_version' => 'MySQL ' .
(function_exists('mysql_get_server_info') ?
mysql_get_server_info() : ''),
```

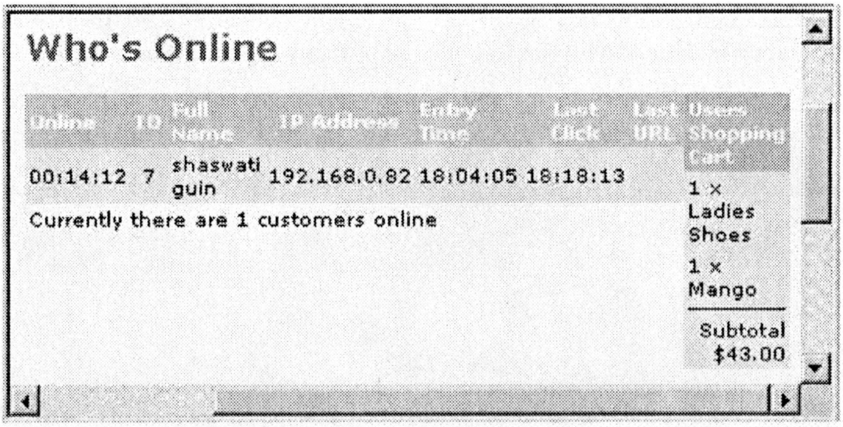

Figure 2.120. Who's Online listing page.

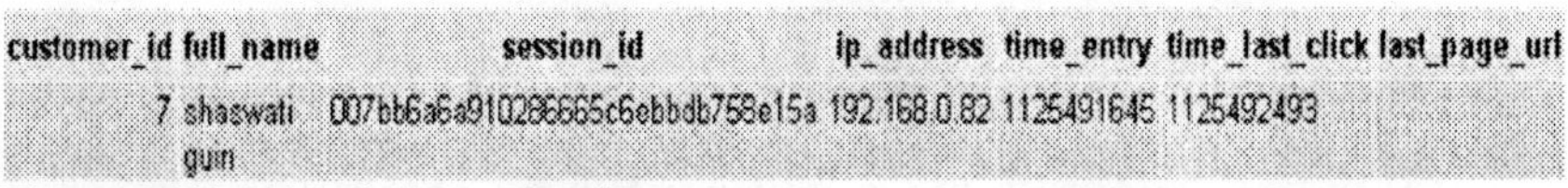

customer_id	full_name	session_id	ip_address	time_entry	time_last_click	last_page_url
7	shaswati guin	007bb6a6a910286665c6ebbdb758e15a	192.168.0.82	1125491645	1125492493	

Figure 2.121. Table "whos_online."

```
'db_date' =>
tep_datetime_short($db['datetime']));
}
```

2.3.9.9. Who's Online

The Who's Online tool is a reporting tool that shows the administrator how many visitors are currently browsing the store. If the **Who's Online** link on the left side menu is clicked, the code written in /catalog/admin/whos_online.php is executed. Figure 2.120 represents the Who's Online listing page. When a customer logs in to the site, the information is stored in the "whos_online" table (Figure 2.121). The entries are removed when time expires; expiry time is set in /whos_online.php.

```
$xx_mins_ago = (time() - 900);

tep_db_query("delete from " .
TABLE_WHOS_ONLINE . " where time_last_click <
'" . $xx_mins_ago . "'");
```

There are some functions in /whos_online.php that are called from /catalog/admin/includes/functions/sessions.php and /catalog/admin/includes/classes/sessions.php.

Catalog Area

With so many online stores operating in cyberspace today, the look, feel, and layout of your online storefront will define your customers' experiences with your company, and there is no second chance for a first impression. With that fact in mind, this chapter will give you all the information you need to customize the front end, or customer side, of your storefront.

The home page of your store will necessarily contain a wealth of text, links, graphics, and options, which the customer needs to sort through and manage. Your optimization of this home page is thus a very important factor in making a good impression as well as a sale. This chapter devotes a large amount of discussion to the customization of the layout, colors, text, header, and footer of your pages. Learn how to incorporate your company's logo, rearrange category and product boxes, alter colors, and add new elements where needed. To maximize the effectiveness of customer communications, this chapter will also show you how to create and alter the text of automated e-mail messages, both from you to your customer and from customer to customer via your store. A discussion of the use of SSL with osCommerce is included.

osCommerce provides your clientele with the ability to manage their accounts, but as the storeowner, you have some control over the functionality of this module. The shopping cart, through which customers purchase products, and all checkout and payment information are likewise customizable, and this chapter goes into detail on how to streamline these processes for your customers.

While browsing your store, customers will be confronted with a wealth of product information and options, and this chapter also covers how to arrange and customize the presentation of product listings, product information, and new products. Customers are able to comment on products they have purchased using the reviewing module supplied through osCommerce, and your control over this module is detailed in this chapter.

In designing the look and feel of your store, you will most likely want all pages to maintain a consistent layout scheme. As a final discussion, this chapter provides information and instructions on using the BTS and STS template systems available as separate contributions to the osCommerce package. These systems will help you to achieve design consistency with minimal programming effort.

3.1. CUSTOMIZING THE FRONT END

To modify the way your shop looks in a browser window, you need to understand the various sections into which the code in the /index.php file is divided. You can view this code easily in a text editor application. For example, consider the following.

```
<body marginwidth="0" marginheight="0">
<!-- header //-->
<?php require(DIR_WS_INCLUDES . 'header.php');
?>
<!-- header_eof //-->
<!-- body //-->
<table border="0" width="100%" cellspacing="3"
cellpadding="3">
<tr>
<td width=" <?php echo BOX_WIDTH; ?>"
valign="top">
<table border="0" width=" <?php echo
BOX_WIDTH; ?>" cellspacing="0"
cellpadding="2">
<!-- left_navigation //-->
<?php require(DIR_WS_INCLUDES .
'column_left.php'); ?>
<!-- left_navigation_eof //-->
<!-- body_text //-->
............................
<!-- body_text_eof //-->
    <td width="<?php echo BOX_WIDTH; ?>"
valign="top"><table border="0" width="<?php
echo BOX_WIDTH; ?>" cellspacing="0"
cellpadding="2">
<!-- right_navigation //-->
<?php require(DIR_WS_INCLUDES .
'column_right.php'); ?>
<!-- right_navigation_eof //-->
    </table></td>
  </tr>
</table>
```

```
<!-- body_eof //-->
<!-- footer //-->
<?php require(DIR_WS_INCLUDES . 'footer.php');
?>
<!-- footer_eof //-->
<br>
</body>
```

In the above code the PHP code is separated from the HTML code by the tags "<?php" and "?>." By understanding this convention, the HTML code, used in every file in osCommerce, can be edited to change the look of the application.

In order to customize the look of your store, the files shown in Figure 3.1 are needed—these are the files that comprise /index.php. The way os-Commerce dynamically generates pages allows for a consistent editing process: the same code in similar locations in all the necessary files is modified.

3.1.1. Customization of Text

For the English language the text definitions defining the catalog boxes and error messages for the osCommerce store are in the /catalog/includes/english.php file. Individual page files throughout the store, including the /index.php page, have their own text definitions in the /catalog/includes/languages/english/ folder, or in whichever language folder you are using.

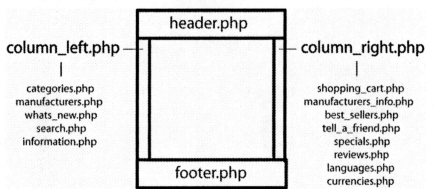

Figure 3.1. Layout of /index.php.

3.1.1.1. Index text

If you wish to change the text displayed on the home page, then modification of the file /catalog/includes/languages/english/index.php (if the language is English) is necessary. If other languages in addition to or instead of English are used, then the /index.php file will need to be changed in the other language folders.

Let the code be as follows.

```
define('TEXT_MAIN', ' This is a default setup
of the osCommerce project.........');
```

To change the text, write the above as follows.

```
define('TEXT_MAIN', ' To choose your items,
you can browse by Category or search by
Keyword');
```

We can see the effect of changes to /index.php in a browser.

If there are no products in a category at the time of browsing, then the message "There are no products to list in this category" comes up. To change this text, open the /catalog/includes/languages/english/index.php file and make the necessary modifications to the following code.

```
define('TEXT_NO_PRODUCTS', 'There are no
products to list in this category.');
```

To modify the welcome message on the index page, modify the following code in /catalog/includes/languages/english.php.

```
define('TEXT_GREETING_GUEST', 'Welcome <span
class="greetUser">Guest!</span> Would you like
to <a href="%s"><u>log yourself in</u></a>? Or
would you prefer to <a href="%s"><u>create an
account</u></a>?');
```

3.1.1.2. Heading text

Any desired changes to the text in the navigation bar of the store can be implemented in /catalog/includes/languages/english.php. In this page, all of the heading listings are present. Also, footer text, page title, and date format definitions are present here. The following code is for the header text.

```
// header text in includes/header.php
```

```
define('HEADER_TITLE_CREATE_ACCOUNT', 'Create
an Account');
define('HEADER_TITLE_MY_ACCOUNT', 'My
Account');
define('HEADER_TITLE_CART_CONTENTS', 'Cart
Contents');
define('HEADER_TITLE_CHECKOUT', 'Checkout');
define('HEADER_TITLE_TOP', 'Top');
define('HEADER_TITLE_CATALOG', 'Catalog');
define('HEADER_TITLE_LOGOFF', 'Log Off');
define('HEADER_TITLE_LOGIN', 'Log In');
```

So, if you want to change a text phrase displayed on any page, then you need to find the correct PHP file; for that you need to perform the following steps:

1. Highlight the /catalog/ folder, and, right-clicking your mouse button, select **Search**.
2. In the input box named "Search for files or folders named:" enter "*.php," or in the input box named "Containing text:" paste in your text phrase.
3. Then, open and edit the PHP file as described above.

3.1.2. Customizing the Header

The osCommerce logo is present at the top left corner of the store. You can exchange this logo for your own logo. The main logo is located in /catalog/images/oscommerce.gif. The easiest method to replace this logo is to overwrite the original with your own logo. First, use FTP to upload your logo. If you want to change the image name and alt text of your image, then find the following code in /catalog/includes/header.php.

```
<td valign="middle"><?php echo '<a href="' .
tep_href_link(FILENAME_DEFAULT) . '">' .
tep_image(DIR_WS_IMAGES . 'oscommerce.gif',
'osCommerce') . '</a>'; ?></td>
```

In the above code the current image name is /oscommerce.gif, and the current alt text of the image is "osCommerce."

As an example, let us say that your logo is called /img_logo.jpg and that your alt text is "Browse My Store"—you would rewrite the code as follows.

```
<td valign="middle"><?php echo '<a href="' .
tep_href_link(FILENAME_DEFAULT) . '">' .
tep_image(DIR_WS_IMAGES .     'img_logo.jpg',
'Browse My Store') . '</a>'; ?></td>
```

Similarly, you can change the other icon images on the right side of the header, or you can add more images to the header. In fact, you can customize the header as per your requirements.

As a further example, to change the color of the header, change the following section in the /stylesheet.css file.

```
TR.header {
   background: #ffffff;
}
```

You will get a white header background using the above code. If you want a lemon header background, then change the code to the following.

```
TR.header {
   background: #FFFFCC;
}
```

To show a banner as a header, use the following code in the /catalog/includes/header.php file (shown modified).

```
<table border="0" width="100%" cellspacing="0"
cellpadding="0">
    <tr class="header">
        <td valign="middle"><?php echo '<a
href="' . tep_href_link(FILENAME_DEFAULT) .
'">' . tep_image(DIR_WS_IMAGES .
'oscommerce.gif', 'osCommerce') . '</a>';
?></td>
        <td valign="middle" align="center">
        <?php
        if ($banner =
tep_banner_exists('dynamic', '468x50')) {
    ?>
    <br>
    <table border="0" width="100%"
cellspacing="0" cellpadding="0">
    <tr>
        <td align="center"><?php echo
tep_display_banner('static', $banner); ?></td>
    </tr>
    </table>
    <?php
            }
        ?>
    </td>
```

```
        <td align="right" valign="bottom"><?php
echo '<a href="' .
tep_href_link(FILENAME_ACCOUNT, '', 'SSL') .
'">' . tep_image(DIR_WS_IMAGES .
'header_account.gif', HEADER_TITLE_MY_ACCOUNT)
. '</a>  <a href="' .
tep_href_link(FILENAME_SHOPPING_CART) . '">' .
tep_image(DIR_WS_IMAGES . 'header_cart.gif',
HEADER_TITLE_CART_CONTENTS) .
'</a>  <a href="' .
tep_href_link(FILENAME_CHECKOUT_SHIPPING, '',
'SSL') . '">' . tep_image(DIR_WS_IMAGES .
'header_checkout.gif', HEADER_TITLE_CHECKOUT)
. '</a>'; ?>  </td>
      </tr>
    </table>
```

Using the above code, you can show a banner for a header, or you can replace this entire table set with your own. Design the table in your HTML code editor and simply copy and paste the table, replacing this one.

3.1.3. Customizing the Footer

To customize the footer section, modify the following files: /catalog/includes/footer.php, /catalog/includes/counter.php, /catalog/includes/languages/english.php, and /catalog/stylesheet.css. To show the date in long format (e.g., Monday 12 September, 2005), the following code in /footer.php is used.

```
<td class="footer">  <?php echo
strftime(DATE_FORMAT_LONG);
?>  </td>
```

To show the date in sort format (e.g., 09/12/05) instead of in long format, use the following code instead of the above code.

```
<td class="footer">  <?php echo
strftime(DATE_FORMAT_SHORT);
?>  </td>
```

"DATE_FORMAT_LONG" and "DATE_TIME_FORMAT" are defined in the /english.php file. The code is as follows.

```
@setlocale(LC_TIME, 'en_US.ISO_8859-1');
define('DATE_FORMAT_SHORT', '%m/%d/%Y'); //
this is used for strftime()
```

```
define('DATE_FORMAT_LONG', '%A %d %B, %Y'); //
this is used for strftime()
```

The function "strftime()" is a PHP function that returns a string formatted according to the given format string using the given time stamp, or the current local time if no time stamp is given. Month and weekday names and other language-dependent strings respect the current locale set with "setlocale()."

On the right side of the footer is some text that tells the customer how many times the site has been visited since the start date. For this the following code is written in /footer.php.

```
<td align="right"
class="footer">  <?php echo
$counter_now . ' ' .
FOOTER_TEXT_REQUESTS_SINCE . ' ' .
$counter_startdate_formatted;
?>  </td>
```

Functions "$counter_now" and "$counter_startdate_formatted" are defined in the /counter.php file.

```
$counter_query = tep_db_query("select
startdate, counter from " . TABLE_COUNTER);

  if (!tep_db_num_rows($counter_query)) {
    $date_now = date('Ymd');
    tep_db_query("insert into " .
TABLE_COUNTER . " (startdate, counter) values
('" . $date_now . "', '1')");
    $counter_startdate = $date_now;
    $counter_now = 1;
  } else {
    $counter =
tep_db_fetch_array($counter_query);
    $counter_startdate =
$counter['startdate'];
    $counter_now = ($counter['counter'] + 1);
    tep_db_query("update " . TABLE_COUNTER . "
set counter = '" . $counter_now . "'");
  }

  $counter_startdate_formatted =
strftime(DATE_FORMAT_LONG, mktime(0, 0, 0,
substr($counter_startdate, 4, 2),
substr($counter_startdate, -2),
substr($counter_startdate, 0, 4)));
```

Figure 3.2. Table "counter."

Here, you can change the date format. To count the total number of requests, the "counter" table, shown in Figure 3.2, is used.

To show a banner as a footer, delete or comment out the following code in the /footer.php file.

```php
<?php
  if ($banner = tep_banner_exists('dynamic',
'468x50')) {
?>
<br>
<table border="0" width="100%" cellspacing="0"
cellpadding="0" >
  <tr>
    <td align="center" ><?php echo
tep_display_banner('static', $banner); ?></td>
  </tr>
</table>
<?php
  }
?>
```

To change the text of the footer, modify the /english.php file, depending upon the constants in the /footer.php file. To change the background color, font size, etc. of the footer, modify the following code in the /stylesheet.css file.

```css
TR.footer {
  background: #bbc3d3;
}

TD.footer {
  font-family: Verdana, Arial, sans-serif;
  font-size: 10px;
  background: #bbc3d3;
  color: #ffffff;
  font-weight: bold;
}
```

3.1.4. Modifying Colors

A single CSS file controls the style and colors of your store: /catalog/ stylesheet.css. For example, consider the current code in the /stylesheet.css file.

```
.boxText { font-family: Verdana, Arial, sans-
serif; font-size: 10px; }
```

```
BODY {
   background: #ffffff;
   color: #000000;
   margin: 0px;
}
```

```
A {
   color: #000000;
   text-decoration: none;
}
A:hover {
   color: #AABBDD;
   text-decoration: underline;
}
```

```
TD.footer {
   font-family: Verdana, Arial, sans-serif;
   font-size: 10px;
   background: #bbc3d3;
   color: #ffffff;
   font-weight: bold;
}
```

You can change the colors, font sizes, font colors, margins, etc. for the entire store using this file. A detailed discussion about the customization of CSS is given in section 3.5.

3.1.5. Modifying E-mails

3.1.5.1. Tell-a-friend

When customer wants to tell someone about one of your products, then a "tell-a-friend" e-mail can be sent. To change the content of this e-mail, change the following file: /catalog/includes/languages/<your language>/tell_ a_friend.php. For example, if your language is English, then you would need to alter the section of code containing the content of the tell-a-friend e-mail in the file /catalog/includes/languages/english/tell_a_friend.php.

```
define('TEXT_EMAIL_SUBJECT', 'Your friend %s
has recommended this great product from %s');
define('TEXT_EMAIL_INTRO', 'Hi %s!' . "\n\n" .
'Your friend, %s, thought that you would be
interested in %s from %s.');
define('TEXT_EMAIL_LINK', 'To view the product
click on the link below or copy and paste the
link into your web browser:' . "\n\n" . '%s');
define('TEXT_EMAIL_SIGNATURE', 'Regards,' .
"\n\n" . '%s');
```

The above constants "TEXT_EMAIL_SUBJECT," "TEXT_EMAIL_INTRO," etc. are called in /catalog/tell_a_friend.php.

```
if ($error == false) {
        $email_subject =
sprintf(TEXT_EMAIL_SUBJECT, $from_name,
STORE_NAME);
        $email_body = sprintf(TEXT_EMAIL_INTRO,
$to_name, $from_name,
$product_info['products_name'], STORE_NAME) .
"\n\n";

  if (tep_not_null($message)) {
        $email_body .= $message . "\n\n";
        }
$email_body .= sprintf(TEXT_EMAIL_LINK,
tep_href_link(FILENAME_PRODUCT_INFO,
'products_id=' .
$HTTP_GET_VARS['products_id'])) . "\n\n" .
sprintf(TEXT_EMAIL_SIGNATURE, STORE_NAME .
"\n" . HTTP_SERVER . DIR_WS_CATALOG . "\n");

  tep_mail($to_name, $to_email_address,
$email_subject, $email_body, $from_name,
$from_email_address);
  $messageStack->add_session('header',
sprintf(TEXT_EMAIL_SUCCESSFUL_SENT,
$product_info['products_name'],
tep_output_string_protected($to_name)),
'success');

  tep_redirect(tep_href_link(FILENAME_PRODUCT_IN
FO, 'products_id=' .
$HTTP_GET_VARS['products_id']));
        }
```

3.1.5.2. Welcome e-mails

A welcome e-mail is sent when a customer creates an account. To edit the content of this e-mail, the following file is needed: /catalog/includes/ languages/english/create_account.php. Here is the code.

```
define('EMAIL_SUBJECT', 'Welcome to ' .
STORE_NAME);
define('EMAIL_GREET_MR', 'Dear Mr. %s,' .
"\n\n");
define('EMAIL_GREET_MS', 'Dear Ms. %s,' .
"\n\n");
define('EMAIL_GREET_NONE', 'Dear %s' .
"\n\n");
define('EMAIL_WELCOME', 'We welcome you to
<b>' . STORE_NAME . '</b>.' . "\n\n");
define('EMAIL_TEXT', 'You can now take part in
the <b>various services</b> we have to offer
you. Some of these services include:' . "\n\n"
. '<li><b>Permanent Cart</b> - Any products
added to your online cart remain there until
you remove them, or check them out.' . "\n" .
'<li><b>Address Book</b> - We can now deliver
your products to another address other than
yours! This is perfect to send birthday gifts
direct to the birthday-person themselves.' .
"\n" . '<li><b>Order History</b> - View your
history of purchases that you have made with
us.' . "\n" . '<li><b>Products Reviews</b> -
Share your opinions on products with our other
customers.' . "\n\n");
define('EMAIL_CONTACT', 'For help with any of
our online services, please email the store-
owner: ' . STORE_OWNER_EMAIL_ADDRESS . '.' .
"\n\n");
define('EMAIL_WARNING', '<b>Note:</b> This
email address was given to us by one of our
customers. If you did not signup to be a
member, please send an email to ' .
STORE_OWNER_EMAIL_ADDRESS . '.' . "\n");
```

The above constants "EMAIL_SUBJECT," "EMAIL_WELCOME," etc. are called in the /catalog/create_account.php file.

```
if (ACCOUNT_GENDER == 'true') {
        if ($gender == 'm') {
            $email_text =
    sprintf(EMAIL_GREET_MR, $lastname);
        } else {
```

```
            $email_text =
sprintf(EMAIL_GREET_MS, $lastname);
            }
        } else {
          $email_text =
sprintf(EMAIL_GREET_NONE, $firstname);
        }

        $email_text .= EMAIL_WELCOME .
EMAIL_TEXT . EMAIL_CONTACT . EMAIL_WARNING;
      tep_mail($name, $email_address,
EMAIL_SUBJECT, $email_text, STORE_OWNER,
STORE_OWNER_EMAIL_ADDRESS);


tep_redirect(tep_href_link(FILENAME_CREATE_ACC
OUNT_SUCCESS, '', 'SSL'));
    }
  }
```

In both the "tell-a-friend" and "welcome e-mail" cases the function "tep_mail(......,......,............)" described above is defined in /catalog/includes/functions/general.php.

```
function tep_mail($to_name, $to_email_address,
$email_subject, $email_text, $from_email_name,
$from_email_address)
 {
    if (SEND_EMAILS != 'true') return false;

    // Instantiate a new mail object
    $message = new email(array('X-Mailer:
osCommerce Mailer'));

    // Build the text version
    $text = strip_tags($email_text);
    if (EMAIL_USE_HTML == 'true') {
      $message->add_html($email_text, $text);
    } else {
      $message->add_text($text);
    }

    // Send message
    $message->build_message();
    $message->send($to_name,
$to_email_address, $from_email_name,
$from_email_address, $email_subject);
  }
```

3.1.6. Customizing the Left and Right Columns

3.1.6.1. Adding new boxes links and pages

New boxes can be added to the left or right side column by editing the /catalog/includes/column_left.php or /catalog/includes/column_right.php files, respectively. All box files are in the following directory: /catalog/includes/boxes/.

Consider the left column of the store, which contains the boxes shown in Figure 3.3. To add more boxes to this column, open /catalog/includes/boxes/information.php and save it as /catalog/includes/boxes/test.php. Then, to the /column_left.php file, add the line "require(DIR_WS_BOXES . 'test.php')"; directly below, add "require(DIR_WS_BOXES . 'information.php')." Save /column_left.php to your server, and reload the main Catalog page in your browser. You will then see two information boxes on the left (Figure 3.4). The second one was added by writing one line of code.

3.1.6.2. Changing links and text

The next step is to customize that box, and to do so, we need to modify a few more files. For this example we will be creating four links to pages called /testpage1.php, /testpage2.php, /testpage3.php, and /testpage4.php in the second information block, which was created in the previous step. Here, we will use the /shipping.php file as a base template.

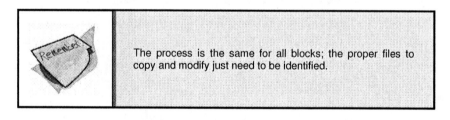

The process is the same for all blocks; the proper files to copy and modify just need to be identified.

The following files are needed: /catalog/includes/filename.php, /catalog/includes/languages/english.php, /catalog/includes/languages/english/shipping.php, /catalog/shipping.php, and /catalog/includes/boxes/test.php. In the file /catalog/includes/filenames.php, create four new define statements, as follows.

```
define('FILENAME_TESTPAGE1', 'testpage1.php');
define('FILENAME_TESTPAGE2', 'testpage2.php');
define('FILENAME_TESTPAGE3', 'testpage3.php');
define('FILENAME_TESTPAGE4', 'testpage4.php');
```

Figure 3.3. Left column boxes.

Figure 3.4. Modified view of column boxes.

Now, save the file. This is the step that creates the file name definitions so that osCommerce can build links. Next, in the file /catalog/includes/languages/english.php, write the following code.

```
// test box text in includes/boxes/test.php

define('BOX_HEADING_TEST', 'TEST BOX');
define('BOX_TEST_LINK1', 'Test Link 1');
define('BOX_TEST_LINK2', 'Test Link 2');
define('BOX_TEST_LINK3', 'Test Link 3');
define('BOX_TEST_LINK4', 'Test Link 4');
```

This step creates the link text that will go into each new link you create.

In the file /catalog/includes/languages/english/shipping.php, edit the following.

```
define('NAVBAR_TITLE', 'Shipping & Returns');
define('HEADING_TITLE', 'Shipping & Returns');
define('TEXT_INFORMATION', 'Put here your
Shipping & Returns information.');
```

It should look like this.

```
define('NAVBAR_TITLE', 'Test Page 1');
define('HEADING_TITLE', 'Test Page 1');
define('TEXT_INFORMATION', 'This is an added
simple page.');
```

Save as /catalog/includes/languages/english/testpage1.php.

Repeat the above three more times, creating /testpage2.php, /testpage3.php, and /testpage4.php. This is the step that actually creates the text that will be on each of your new pages, and in the process, it creates four new files.

In the file /catalog/shipping.php, replace "FILENAME_SHIPPING" with "FILENAME_TESTPAGE1," and save as /catalog/testpage1.php. Repeat this three more times, changing "FILENAME_TESTPAGE1" to "FILENAME_TESTPAGE2," "FILENAME_TESTPAGE3," and "FILE-NAME_TESTPAGE4" and saving as /testpage2.php, /testpage3.php, and /testpage4.php. This step creates the actual pages that will be loaded by the links. Finally, edit the file /catalog/includes/boxes/test.php to the following.

```
$info_box_contents = array();
  $info_box_contents[] = array('text' =>
BOX_HEADING_TEST);
```

```
    new infoBoxHeading($info_box_contents,
false, false);

    $info_box_contents = array();
    $info_box_contents[] = array('text' => '<a
href="' . tep_href_link(FILENAME_TESTPAGE1) .
'">' . BOX_TEST_LINK1 . '</a><br>' .

    '<a href="' .
tep_href_link(FILENAME_TESTPAGE2) . '">' .
BOX_TEST_LINK2 . '</a><br>' .

    '<a href="' .
tep_href_link(FILENAME_TESTPAGE3) . '">' .
BOX_TEST_LINK3 . '</a><br>' .

    '<a href="' .
tep_href_link(FILENAME_TESTPAGE4) . '">' .
BOX_TEST_LINK4 . '</a>');

    new infoBox($info_box_contents);
```

This changes the text that is output in the browser.

Editing of the files, at this point, is complete. Now, view the Catalog in the browser, and the new links should show up in the new block (see Figure 3.5).

3.1.6.3. Customizing look

Now, we are going to discuss modifying the font, graphics, colors, and styles of the boxes. To do this, modify the following files: /catalog/ includes/classes/boxes.php and /catalog/stylesheet.css. To give borders to the top and bottom of the box heading, modify the following code in the /stylesheet.css file.

```
TD.infoBoxHeading {
    font-family: Verdana, Arial, sans-serif;
    font-size: 10px;
    font-weight: bold;
    background: #bbc3d3;
    color: #ffffff;
}
```

The changed code follows.

```
TD.infoBoxHeading {
    font-family: Verdana, Arial, sans-serif;
    font-size: 10px;
```

Figure 3.5. Modified view of column boxes.

Figure 3.6. After giving border to heading box.

```
font-weight: bold;
background: #bbc3d3;
color: #ffffff;
border-top: 2px;
border-top-style: solid;
border-top-color: #000000;
border-bottom: 2px;
border-bottom-style: solid;
border-bottom-color: #000000;
}
```

The effect is shown in Figure 3.6. As a further example, to increase the height of the box heading, find the following code in /boxes.php.

```
$info_box_contents = array();
    $info_box_contents[] =
array(array('params' => 'height="14"
class="infoBoxHeading"',

'text' => $left_corner),
```

```
array('params' => 'width="100%" height="14"
class="infoBoxHeading"',

'text' => $contents[0]['text']),

array('params' => 'height="14"
class="infoBoxHeading" nowrap',

'text' => $right_corner));

        $this->tableBox($info_box_contents,
true);
```

Change the value of the height tag to your desired value.

You may add links or HTML without enclosing them in a box, such as button advertising, logos, or whatever else you want. To do this, add a little code to either /column_left.php or /column_right.php. Below is some sample code to add after the closing PHP tag "?>."

```
<tr>
        <td><a href="http://www.thumbshots.org"
target="_blank"><img
src="http://open.thumbshots.org/attribution.pn
g" alt="Free previews by        Thumbshots.org"
width="88" height="31" border="0" /></a>
</td>
</tr>
```

If we add the above code to /column_right.php, the right column will appear as in Figure 3.7.

3.1.6.4. Removing boxes

The boxes can be removed from the left- or right-hand columns by editing appropriate /catalog/includes/column_left.php or /catalog/includes/ column_right.php files, respectively. For example, consider the /includes/ column_left.php file.

```
require(DIR_WS_BOXES . 'whats_new.php');
require(DIR_WS_BOXES . 'search.php');
require(DIR_WS_BOXES . 'information.php');
```

To remove the search box, either its inclusion needs to be commented out or it needs to be removed entirely.

```
require(DIR_WS_BOXES . 'whats_new.php');
```

Figure 3.7. After adding link image at the bottom of right column.

```
// require(DIR_WS_BOXES . 'search.php');

require(DIR_WS_BOXES . 'information.php');
```

3.1.7. Customizing the Categories Box and All Other Boxes

To remove the left corner image from the header of the category box, change the following code in /catalog/includes/boxes/categories.php.

```
new infoBoxHeading($info_box_contents, true,
false);
```

The changed code is as follows.

```
new infoBoxHeading($info_box_contents, false,
false);
```

See Figures 3.8 and 3.9 for the old and new configurations, respectively. The "InfoBoxHeading" function is defined in the following class, which is defined in /catalog/includes/classes/boxes.php.

```
class infoBoxHeading extends tableBox {
    function infoBoxHeading($contents,
$left_corner = true, $right_corner = true,
$right_arrow = false) {
        $this->table_cellpadding = '0';

        if ($left_corner == true) {
            $left_corner = tep_image(DIR_WS_IMAGES
. 'infobox/corner_left.gif');
        } else {
            $left_corner = tep_image(DIR_WS_IMAGES
. 'infobox/corner_right_left.gif');
        }
        if ($right_arrow == true) {
            $right_arrow = '<a href="' .
$right_arrow . '">' . tep_image(DIR_WS_IMAGES
. 'infobox/arrow_right.gif', ICON_ARROW_RIGHT)
. '</a>';
        } else {
            $right_arrow = '';
        }
        if ($right_corner == true) {
            $right_corner = $right_arrow .
tep_image(DIR_WS_IMAGES .
'infobox/corner_right.gif');
        } else {
            $right_corner = $right_arrow .
tep_draw_separator('pixel_trans.gif', '11',
'14');
```

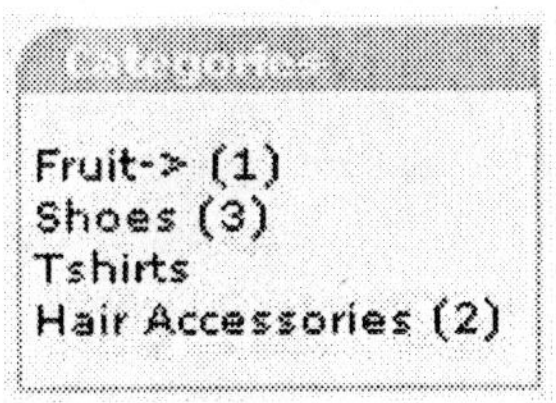

Figure 3.8. Previous view of Categories box.

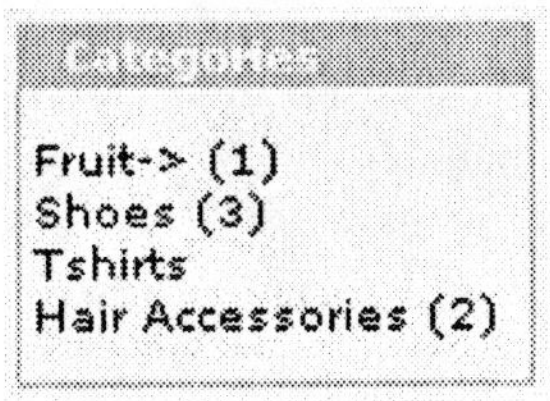

Figure 3.9. Changed view of Categories box.

```
          }

          $info_box_contents = array();
          $info_box_contents[] =
array(array('params' => 'height="14"
class="infoBoxHeading"',

          'text' => $left_corner),

          array('params' => 'width="100%" height="14"
class="infoBoxHeading"',

          'text' => $contents[0]['text']),

          array('params' => 'height="14"
class="infoBoxHeading" nowrap',

          'text' => $right_corner));

              $this->tableBox($info_box_contents,
true);
          }
      }
```

To replace the heading text of the category box with an image, edit the following code, found within the /catalog/includes/languages/english.php file.

```
// categories box text in
includes/boxes/categories.php
define('BOX_HEADING_CATEGORIES',
'Categories');
```

Replace it with the following.

```
// categories box text in
includes/boxes/categories.php
define('BOX_HEADING_CATEGORIES', '<img
src="images/categories.gif"> Categories');
```

To give a background image to the box header, use files /catalog/includes/classes/boxes.php, /catalog/includes/boxes/categories.php, and /catalog/stylesheet.css. The following code should be added to /catalog/includes/classes/boxes.php before the ending "?>" tag. This code creates a new class, which will be used in the catagories box.

```
class infoBoxHeadingCategories extends
tableBox {
```

```
    function
infoBoxHeadingCategories($contents) {
      $this->table_cellpadding = '0';

      $info_box_contents = array();
      $info_box_contents[] =
array(array('params' =>'height="20"
width="100%"
class="infoBoxHeadingCategories"',

'text' => $contents[0]['text']));

      $this->tableBox($info_box_contents,
true);
    }
   }
```

The following code in /catalog/includes/boxes/categories.php,

```
new infoBoxHeading($info_box_contents, false,
false);
```

will need to be replaced with the following:

```
new
infoBoxHeadingCategories($info_box_contents,
false, false);
```

In the above we have passed three parameters: one is "$info_box_contents," and the other two are "false" and "false." Here, we use "false" to remove the left and right corner images from the header of the categories box. We will need a new style sheet definition for the categories box in /catalog/stylesheet.css.

```
TD.infoBoxHeadingCategories {
  background: #33c3d3;
  background-image: url('images/
cat_ico.gif');
  background-repeat: no-repeat;
}
```

Also, we can add font, size, spacing, etc. according to our style sheet requirements. In Figure 3.10 we can see both effects.

If you want to display the manufacturers' box as a list rather than as a drop-down list (see Figure 3.11), follow one of the two methodologies below.

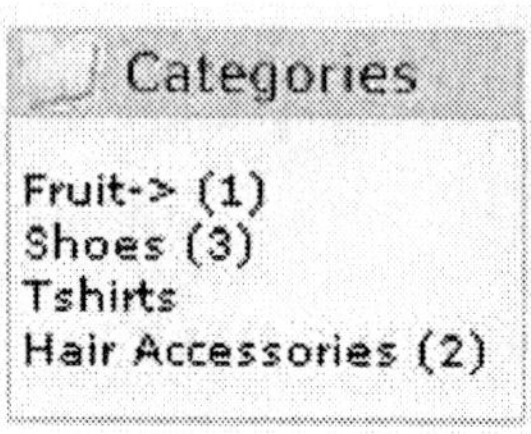

Figure 3.10. Changed view of Categories box.

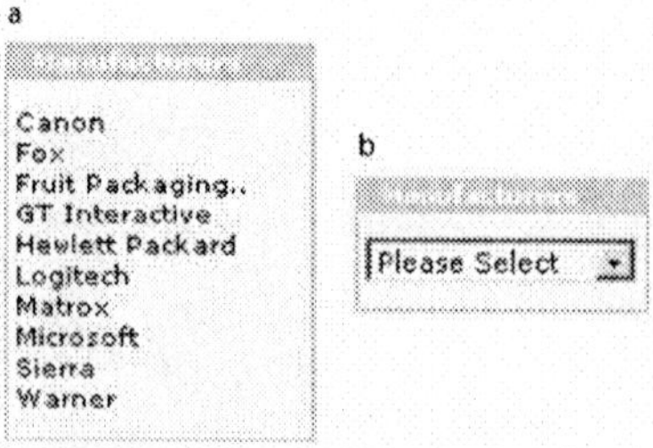

Figure 3.11. Manufacturers (a) menu and (b) drop-down box.

1. Go to Admin > Configuration > Maximum Values > Manufacturers List, and set a number as your requirement. If the number of manufacturers exceeds this number, a drop-down list will be displayed instead of the default list.

2. To show either the default or drop-down list, use either of the following codes: one for the default list and the other for the drop-down list. Then, delete or comment out either of the following two code sections in the /catalog/includes/boxes/manufacturers.php file.

```
// Display a list
        $manufacturers_list = '';
        while ($manufacturers =
tep_db_fetch_array($manufacturers_query)) {
        $manufacturers_name =
((strlen($manufacturers['manufacturers_name'])
> MAX_DISPLAY_MANUFACTURER_NAME_LEN) ?
substr($manufacturers['manufacturers_name'],
0, MAX_DISPLAY_MANUFACTURER_NAME_LEN) . '..' :
$manufacturers['manufacturers_name']);
        if
(isset($HTTP_GET_VARS['manufacturers_id']) &&
($HTTP_GET_VARS['manufacturers_id'] ==
$manufacturers['manufacturers_id']))
$manufacturers_name = '<b>' .
$manufacturers_name .'</b>';
        $manufacturers_list .= '<a href="' .
tep_href_link(FILENAME_DEFAULT,
'manufacturers_id=' .
$manufacturers['manufacturers_id']) . '">' .
$manufacturers_name . '</a><br>';
        }
```

```
        $manufacturers_list =
substr($manufacturers_list, 0, -4);

        $info_box_contents = array();
        $info_box_contents[] = array('text' =>
$manufacturers_list);

new infoBox($info_box_contents);
```

// Display a drop-down

```
        $manufacturers_array = array();
        if (MAX_MANUFACTURERS_LIST < 2) {
            $manufacturers_array[] = array('id' =>
'', 'text' => PULL_DOWN_DEFAULT);
        }

        while ($manufacturers =
tep_db_fetch_array($manufacturers_query)) {
            $manufacturers_name =
((strlen($manufacturers['manufacturers_name'])
> MAX_DISPLAY_MANUFACTURER_NAME_LEN) ?
substr($manufacturers['manufacturers_name'],
0, MAX_DISPLAY_MANUFACTURER_NAME_LEN) . '..' :
$manufacturers['manufacturers_name']);
            $manufacturers_array[] = array('id' =>
$manufacturers['manufacturers_id'],
                                           'text'
=> $manufacturers_name);
        }

        $info_box_contents = array();
        $info_box_contents[] = array('form' =>
tep_draw_form('manufacturers',
tep_href_link(FILENAME_DEFAULT, '', 'NONSSL',
false), 'get'),
                                     'text' =>
tep_draw_pull_down_menu('manufacturers_id',
$manufacturers_array,
(isset($HTTP_GET_VARS['manufacturers_id']) ?
$HTTP_GET_VARS['manufacturers_id'] : ''),
'onChange="this.form.submit();" size="' .
MAX_MANUFACTURERS_LIST . '" style="width:
100%"') . tep_hide_session_id());
        }

    new infoBox($info_box_contents);
```

To remove or change corner graphics, change the color, and add a top and bottom border as a box separator, edit the /catalog/stylesheet.css and /catalog/includes/classes/boxes.php files. To remove corner graphics, find the following code in /boxes.php.

```php
class infoBoxHeading extends tableBox {
    function infoBoxHeading($contents,
$left_corner = true, $right_corner = true,
$right_arrow = false) {
        $this->table_cellpadding = '0';

        if ($left_corner == true) {
            $left_corner = tep_image(DIR_WS_IMAGES
. 'infobox/corner_left.gif');
        } else {
            $left_corner = tep_image(DIR_WS_IMAGES
. 'infobox/corner_right_left.gif');
        }
        if ($right_arrow == true) {
            $right_arrow = '<a href="' .
$right_arrow . '">' . tep_image(DIR_WS_IMAGES
. 'infobox/arrow_right.gif', ICON_ARROW_RIGHT)
. '</a>';
        } else {
            $right_arrow = '';
        }
        if ($right_corner == true) {
            $right_corner = $right_arrow .
tep_image(DIR_WS_IMAGES .
'infobox/corner_right.gif');
        } else {
            $right_corner = $right_arrow .
tep_draw_separator('pixel_trans.gif', '11',
'14');
        }

        $info_box_contents = array();
        $info_box_contents[] =
array(array('params' => 'height="14"
class="infoBoxHeading"',

'text' => $left_corner),

array('params' => 'width="100%" height="14"
class="infoBoxHeading"',

'text' => $contents[0]['text']),

array('params' => 'height="14"
class="infoBoxHeading" nowrap',
```

```
'text' => $right_corner));

      $this->tableBox($info_box_contents,
true);
    }
  }

class contentBoxHeading extends tableBox {
    function contentBoxHeading($contents) {
        $this->table_width = '100%';
        $this->table_cellpadding = '0';

        $info_box_contents = array();
        $info_box_contents[] =
array(array('params' => 'height="14"
class="infoBoxHeading"',

    'text' => tep_image(DIR_WS_IMAGES .
'infobox/corner_left.gif')),

array('params' => 'height="14"
class="infoBoxHeading" width="100%"',

    'text' => $contents[0]['text']),

array('params' => 'height="14"
class="infoBoxHeading"',

    'text' => tep_image(DIR_WS_IMAGES .
'infobox/corner_right_left.gif')));

      $this->tableBox($info_box_contents,
true);
    }
  }
```

Now, replace the bold face paths with the file name /pixel_trans.gif. The code should look like the following.

```
class contentBoxHeading extends tableBox {
    function contentBoxHeading($contents) {
        $this->table_width = '100%';
        $this->table_cellpadding = '0';

        $info_box_contents = array();
        $info_box_contents[] = ar-
ray(array('params' => 'height="14"
class="infoBoxHeading"',
```

```
'text' => tep_image(DIR_WS_IMAGES .
'pixel_trans.gif')),
                                        ar-
ray('params' => 'height="14"
class="infoBoxHeading" width="100%"',

'text' => $contents[0]['text']),
                                        ar-
ray('params' => 'height="14"
class="infoBoxHeading"',

'text' => tep_image(DIR_WS_IMAGES .
'pixel_trans.gif')));

      $this->tableBox($info_box_contents,
true);
      }
   }


class infoBoxHeading extends tableBox {
    function infoBoxHeading($contents,
$left_corner = false, $right_corner = false,
$right_arrow = false) {
      $this->table_cellpadding = '0';

      if ($left_corner == true) {
        $left_corner = tep_image(DIR_WS_IMAGES
. 'pixel_trans.gif');
      } else {
        $left_corner = tep_image(DIR_WS_IMAGES
. 'pixel_trans.gif');
      }
      if ($right_arrow == true) {
        $right_arrow = '<a href="' .
$right_arrow . '">' . tep_image(DIR_WS_IMAGES
. 'infobox/arrow_right.gif', ICON_ARROW_RIGHT)
. '</a>';
      } else {
        $right_arrow = '';
      }
      if ($right_corner == true) {
        $right_corner = $right_arrow .
tep_image(DIR_WS_IMAGES . 'pixel_trans.gif');
      } else {
        $right_corner = $right_arrow .
tep_draw_separator('pixel_trans.gif', '11',
'14');
      }
```

```
        $info_box_contents = array();
        $info_box_contents[] = ar-
ray(array('params' => 'height="14"
class="infoBoxHeading"',

'text' => $left_corner),
                                        ar-
ray('params' => 'width="100%" height="14"
class="infoBoxHeading"',

'text' => $contents[0]['text']),
                                        ar-
ray('params' => 'height="14"
class="infoBoxHeading" nowrap',

'text' => $right_corner));

        $this->tableBox($info_box_contents,
true);
    }
  }
```

To change the color, font size, or style of boxes, modify the code written in /stylesheet.css to be like the following.

```
.infoBoxNotice {
  background: #FF8E90;
}

.infoBoxNoticeContents {
  background: #FFE6E6;
  font-family: Verdana, Arial, sans-serif;
  font-size: 10px;
}

TD.infoBoxHeading {
  font-family: Verdana, Arial, sans-serif;
  font-size: 10px;
  font-weight: bold;
  background: #FF9999;
  color: #ffffff;
  }
```

The changed code given above will result in changes in the browser view (see Figures 3.12 and 3.13).

There are individual box files in /catalog/includes/boxes/. To edit only one or two boxes, follow the steps as discussed above for the editing of the header of the category box in the left column as per your requirements.

3.1.8. Using SSL with osCommerce

In order to make SSL work with osCommerce, once your SSL is installed, set the configuration paths for https:// in /catalog/includes/configure.php and /admin/includes/configure.php, enable SSL, and the code takes care of the rest. As an example on how to set the correct configuration paths in /catalog/includes/configure.php, examine the following.

```
// Define the webserver and path parameters
// * DIR_FS_* = Filesystem directories
(local/physical)
// * DIR_WS_* = Webserver directories
(virtual/URL)

define('HTTP_SERVER',
'http://www.yourdomain.com');
define('HTTPS_SERVER',
'https://yourdomain.com');
define('ENABLE_SSL', true); // secure
webserver for catalog module
define('HTTP_COOKIE_DOMAIN',
'www.yourdomain.com');
define('HTTPS_COOKIE_DOMAIN',
'yourdomain.com');
define('HTTP_COOKIE_PATH', '/catalog/');
define('HTTPS_COOKIE_PATH', '/catalog/');
define('DIR_WS_HTTP_CATALOG', '/catalog/');
define('DIR_WS_HTTPS_CATALOG', '/catalog/');
```

Similar corrections are needed for /admin/includes/configure.php.

3.2. MY ACCOUNT

This is one of the major areas in the Catalog module. When a customer clicks on the **My Account** link, Figure 3.14 will be displayed. New customers click the **Continue** button to be taken to the Create Account page,

Figure 3.12. Changed view of (a) left and (b) right column boxes.

Figure 3.13. Changed view of New Products box.

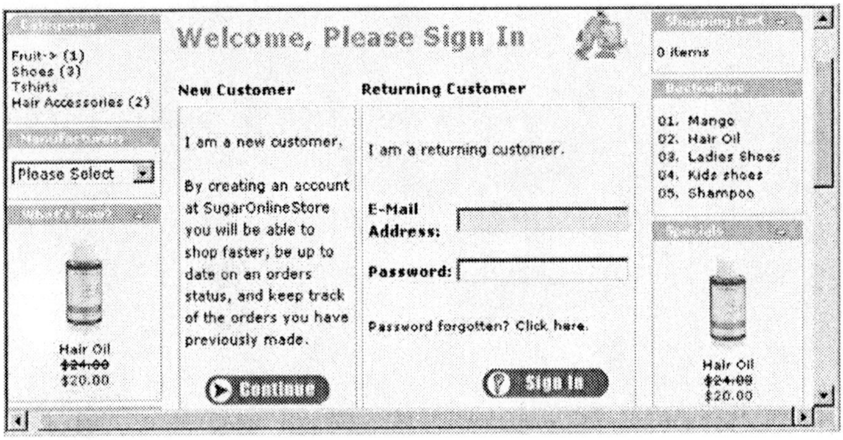

Figure 3.14. My Account page.

where they fill out the registration form to become a registered customer. The customer details are stored in the "customers" (Figure 3.15), "address_book" (Figure 3.16), and "customers_info" (Figure 3.17) tables.

When a registered customer logs in to the store, he or she will be able to see the following: My Account Information, My Orders, and E-mail Notifications.

3.2.1. My Account Information

Figure 3.18 shows the My Account Information page. This page consists of the following sections: **View or change my account information, View or change entries in my address book,** and **Change my account password.**

3.2.1.1. View or change my account information

By clicking this link, a customer can edit and view his account information. When the customer clicks the link, the code written in /catalog/account_edit.php is executed.

customers_id	customers_gender	customers_firstname	customers_lastname	customers_dob
1 m		John	doe	2001-01-01 00:00:00
5 m		Subhamoy	Bandyopadhyay	1970-05-21 00:00:00

Figure 3.15. Table "customers."

address_book_id	customers_id	entry_gender	entry_company	entry_firstname	entry_lastname	entry_street_address
5	5 m	ws		Subhamoy	Bandyopadhyay	sssssssssss
6	5 m	ws		Amit	Paul	kjdjsdjfj
8	7 f	ws		shaswati	guin	sssss

Figure 3.16. Table "address_book."

customers_info_id	customers_info_date_of_last_logon	customers_info_number_of_logons
5	2005-07-27 12:32:03	3
6	NULL	0
7	2005-09-05 16:26:26	26

Figure 3.17. Table "customers_info."

3.2.1.2. View or change entries in my address book

In the address book section the customer can add, edit, and delete personal addresses. When this link is clicked, the code written in /catalog/address_book.php is executed. Figure 3.19 shows a customer's personal address book.

When the **Add Address** button is clicked, the code written in /catalog/address_book_process.php is executed. Unlimited addresses cannot be added to the address book: the administrator sets how many addresses can be stored. Figure 3.20 shows the New Address Book Entry form. The data related to the address book is saved in the "customers" and "address_book" tables.

3.2.1.3. Change my account password

When this link is clicked, the code written in /catalog/account_password.php is executed. The following code changes the password.

```
if (isset($HTTP_POST_VARS['action']) &&
($HTTP_POST_VARS['action'] == 'process'))
  {
    $password_current =
tep_db_prepare_input($HTTP_POST_VARS['password
_current']);
    $password_new =
tep_db_prepare_input($HTTP_POST_VARS['password
_new']);
    $password_confirmation =
tep_db_prepare_input($HTTP_POST_VARS['password
_confirmation']);
    $error = false;
    if (strlen($password_current) <
ENTRY_PASSWORD_MIN_LENGTH) {
      $error = true;

      $messageStack->add('account_password',
ENTRY_PASSWORD_CURRENT_ERROR);
    } elseif (strlen($password_new) <
ENTRY_PASSWORD_MIN_LENGTH) {
      $error = true;

      $messageStack->add('account_password',
ENTRY_PASSWORD_NEW_ERROR);
    } elseif ($password_new !=
$password_confirmation) {
      $error = true;

      $messageStack->add('account_password',
ENTRY_PASSWORD_NEW_ERROR_NOT_MATCHING);
```

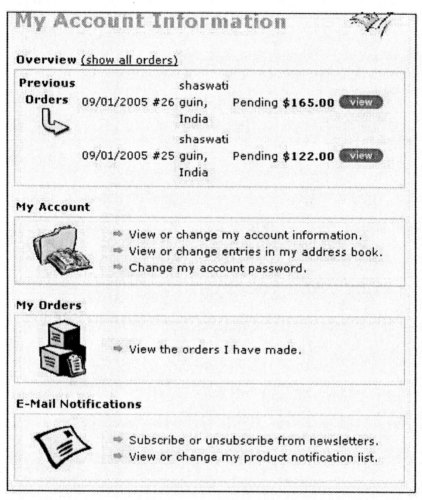

Figure 3.18. My Account Information page.

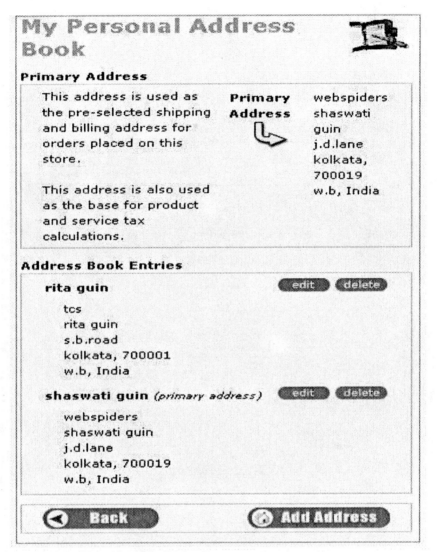

My Personal Address Book

Primary Address

This address is used as the pre-selected shipping and billing address for orders placed on this store.

This address is also used as the base for product and service tax calculations.

Primary Address →

webspiders
shaswati
guin
j.d.lane
kolkata,
700019
w.b, India

Address Book Entries

rita guin   edit   delete

tcs
rita guin
s.b.road
kolkata, 700001
w.b, India

shaswati guin *(primary address)*   edit   delete

webspiders
shaswati guin
j.d.lane
kolkata, 700019
w.b, India

Back   Add Address

Figure 3.19. My Personal Address Book page.

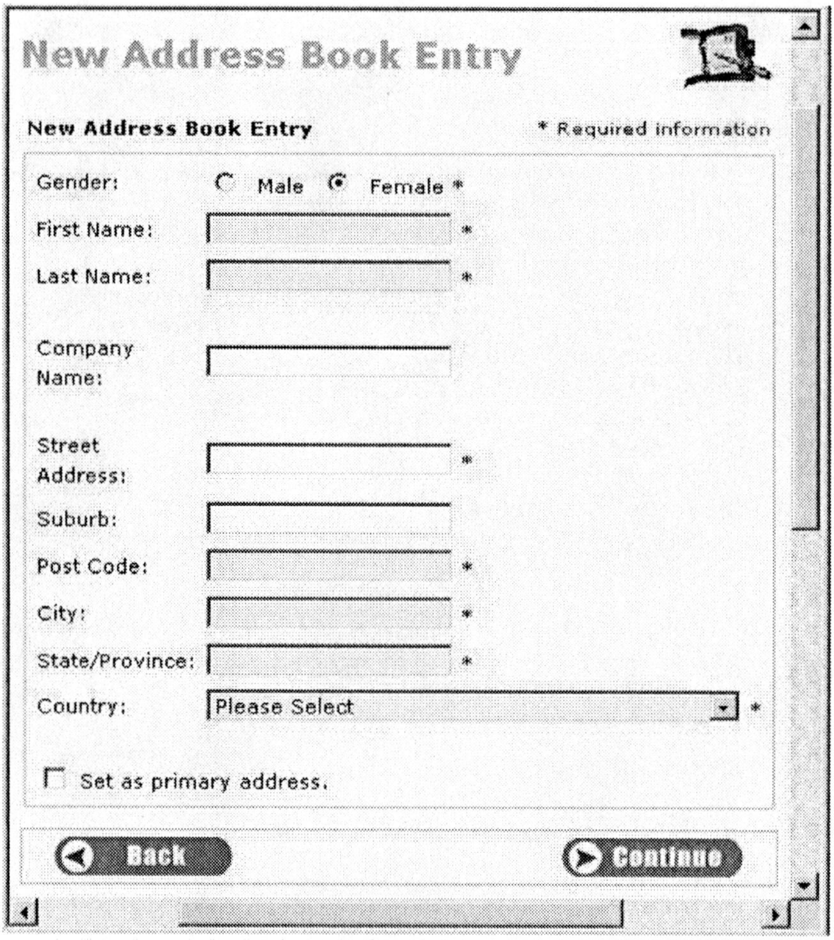

Figure 3.20. New Address Book Entry form.

```
    }
    if ($error == false) {
        $check_customer_query =
tep_db_query("select customers_password from "
. TABLE_CUSTOMERS . " where customers_id = '"
. (int)$customer_id . "'");
        $check_customer =
tep_db_fetch_array($check_customer_query);

        if
(tep_validate_password($password_current,
$check_customer['customers_password'])) {
            tep_db_query("update " .
TABLE_CUSTOMERS . " set customers_password =
'" . tep_encrypt_password($password_new) . "'
where customers_id = '" . (int)$customer_id .
"'");

            tep_db_query("update " .
TABLE_CUSTOMERS_INFO . " set
customers_info_date_account_last_modified =
now() where customers_info_id = '" .
(int)$customer_id . "'");

$messageStack->add_session('account',
SUCCESS_PASSWORD_UPDATED, 'success');


tep_redirect(tep_href_link(FILENAME_ACCOUNT,
'', 'SSL'));
        } else {
            $error = true;

            $messageStack->add('account_password',
ERROR_CURRENT_PASSWORD_NOT_MATCHING);
        }
    }
}
```

When the password is changed, the tables "customers" and "customers_info" are updated.

3.2.2. My Orders

This section stores the orders that are made by a customer. When the **View the orders I have made** link is clicked by the customer, the code written in the /catalog/account_history.php file is executed. Figure 3.21 shows a list of customer orders via the My Order History page.

Figure 3.21. My Order History page.

To show the orders in the My Order History section, the following MySQL queries are needed.

```
$history_query_raw =
"select o.orders_id, o.date_purchased,
o.delivery_name, o.billing_name, ot.text as
order_total, s.orders_status_name from " .
TABLE_ORDERS . " o, " . TABLE_ORDERS_TOTAL . "
ot, " . TABLE_ORDERS_STATUS . " s where
```

```
o.customers_id = '" . (int)$customer_id . "'
and
o.orders_id = ot.orders_id and ot.class =
'ot_total' and
o.orders_status = s.orders_status_id and
s.language_id = '" . (int)$languages_id . "'
order by orders_id DESC";

$history_split = new
splitPageResults($history_query_raw,
MAX_DISPLAY_ORDER_HISTORY);

$history_query = tep_db_query($history_split-
>sql_query);

while ($history =
tep_db_fetch_array($history_query))
    {
        $products_query = tep_db_query("select
count(*) as count from " .
TABLE_ORDERS_PRODUCTS . " where orders_id = '"
. (int)$history['orders_id'] . "'");

    $products =
tep_db_fetch_array($products_query);
.....................................................................................
.....................................................................................
    }
```

In addition, the following tables are necessary to perform the above queries: "orders," "orders_total," "orders_status," and "orders_products." The administrator can set the number of orders that are to be shown in the order history page in the following section: Admin > Configuration > Order History.

When a customer clicks on the **View** button to the right of a particular order, the code written in /catalog/account_history_info.php is executed, and the customer sees their order information details, such as shipping and billing. To show these details, we need the following tables: "orders," "orders_status," and "orders_status_history."

3.2.3. E-mail Notifications

Generally, this section consists of the following parts: **Subscribe or unsubscribe from newsletters** and **View or change my product notification list.**

3.2.3.1. Subscribe or unsubscribe from newsletters

If this link is clicked, the Newsletter Subscriptions page, shown in Figure 3.22, will appear. If, at the time of account creation, the customer selects the newsletter option, then it will be seen checked, as in Figure 3.22, and the customer will be able to get news about the store, new products, etc. through e-mail. If the check box is selected or deselected in this section, the code written in /catalog/account_newsletters.php is executed to update the "customers" table. The code follows.

```
$newsletter_query = tep_db_query("select
customers_newsletter from " . TABLE_CUSTOMERS
. " where customers_id = '" .
(int)$customer_id . "'");
  $newsletter =
tep_db_fetch_array($newsletter_query);

  if (isset($HTTP_POST_VARS['action']) &&
($HTTP_POST_VARS['action'] == 'process')) {
    if
(isset($HTTP_POST_VARS['newsletter_general'])
&&
is_numeric($HTTP_POST_VARS['newsletter_general
'])) {
      $newsletter_general =
tep_db_prepare_input($HTTP_POST_VARS['newslett
```

Figure 3.22. Newsletter Subscriptions page.

```
er_general']);
    } else {
      $newsletter_general = '0';
    }
    if ($newsletter_general !=
$newsletter['customers_newsletter']) {
      $newsletter_general =
((($newsletter['customers_newsletter'] == '1')
? '0' : '1');

      tep_db_query("update " . TABLE_CUSTOMERS
. " set customers_newsletter = '" .
(int)$newsletter_general . "' where
customers_id = '" . (int)$customer_id . "'");
    }

    $messageStack->add_session('account',
SUCCESS_NEWSLETTER_UPDATED, 'success');


tep_redirect(tep_href_link(FILENAME_ACCOUNT,
'', 'SSL'));
  }
```

3.2.3.2. View or change my product notifications list

Customers can get notifications about selected products, or all products depending on their choices, through e-mail (e.g., up-to-date information on products). When this link is clicked, the Product Notifications page, shown in Figure 3.23, will appear in the browser.

If the **Continue** button is clicked after selecting the global product notifications check box, the following code, written in the /catalog/ account_notifications.php file, is executed, and the "customers_info" table is updated. If customers select particular products for notification at the time of product browsing, then the data is saved in the "products_notifications" table (Figure 3.24). A list of notified products is shown on the Product Notifications page. The following code is used for global product notifications.

```
$global_query = tep_db_query("select
global_product_notifications from " .
TABLE_CUSTOMERS_INFO . " where
customers_info_id = '" . (int)$customer_id .
"'");
  $global = tep_db_fetch_array($global_query);

  if (isset($HTTP_POST_VARS['action']) &&
($HTTP_POST_VARS['action'] == 'process')) {
    if
(isset($HTTP_POST_VARS['product_global']) &&
```

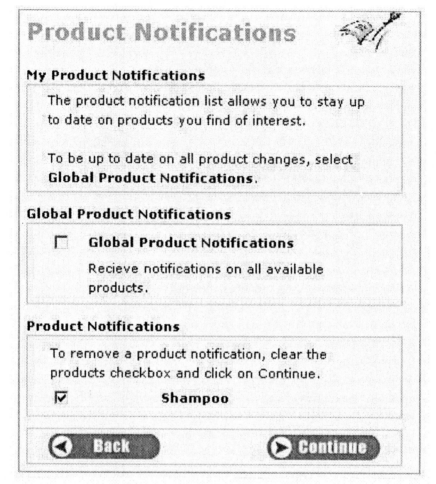

Figure 3.23. Product Notifications page.

products_id	customers_id	date_added
29	7	2005-09-07 12:43:19
28	7	2005-09-07 11:20:27

Figure 3.24. Table "products_notifications."

```
is_numeric($HTTP_POST_VARS['product_global']))
{
        $product_global =
tep_db_prepare_input($HTTP_POST_VARS['product_
global']);
    }
 else {
        $product_global = '0';
    }
   (array)$products =
$HTTP_POST_VARS['products'];

    if ($product_global !=
$global['global_product_notifications']) {
        $product_global =
(($global['global_product_notifications'] ==
'1') ? '0' : '1');

        tep_db_query("update " .
TABLE_CUSTOMERS_INFO . " set
global_product_notifications = '" .
(int)$product_global . "' where
customers_info_id = '" . (int)$customer_id .
"'");
    }
    }

    $messageStack->add_session('account',
SUCCESS_NOTIFICATIONS_UPDATED, 'success');


tep_redirect(tep_href_link(FILENAME_ACCOUNT,
'', 'SSL'));
    }
```

Also, from this page, customers can remove their product notification choices. If the customer wants to remove a particular product notification choice, the following code in the /account_notifications.php file is executed, and the related data is deleted from the "products_notifications" table.

```
if (sizeof($products_parsed) > 0)
{
        $check_query = tep_db_query("select
count(*) as total from " .
TABLE_PRODUCTS_NOTIFICATIONS . " where
customers_id = '" . (int)$customer_id . "' and
products_id not in (" . implode(',',
$products_parsed) . ")");
        $check =
tep_db_fetch_array($check_query);
```

```
if ($check['total'] > 0)
{
        tep_db_query("delete from " .
TABLE_PRODUCTS_NOTIFICATIONS . " where
customers_id = '" . (int)$customer_id . "' and
products_id not in (" . implode(',',
$products_parsed) . ")");
    }
  }
}
else
{
    $check_query = tep_db_query("select
count(*) as total from " .
TABLE_PRODUCTS_NOTIFICATIONS . " where
customers_id = '" . (int)$customer_id . "'");
    $check =
tep_db_fetch_array($check_query);

    if ($check['total'] > 0)
{
        tep_db_query("delete from " .
TABLE_PRODUCTS_NOTIFICATIONS . " where
customers_id = '" . (int)$customer_id . "'");
    }
}
```

3.3. SHOPPING AND THE SHOPPING CART

Customers can shop online using the Shopping Cart. After selecting a product to buy, when the customer clicks the **Add to Cart** button, that product is added to the customer's shopping cart, and the code written in the /catalog/shopping_cart.php file is executed. This file includes another file called /catalog/includes/application_top.php. To develop the Shopping Cart, the following PHP code is written therein.

```
// create the shopping cart & fix the cart if
necessary

if (tep_session_is_registered('cart') &&
is_object($cart))
{
    if (PHP_VERSION < 4)
    {
        $broken_cart = $cart;
        $cart = new shoppingCart;
```

```
          $cart->unserialize($broken_cart);
        }
      }
    else
    {
        tep_session_register('cart');
        $cart = new shoppingCart;
    }
```

The "shoppingCart" class is defined in the /catalog/includes/classes/shopping _cart.php file.

```
class shoppingCart {
    var $contents, $total, $weight, $cartID,
$content_type;
.......................................................................
............................................................. ..
function add_cart($products_id, $qty = '1',
$attributes = '', $notify = true) {
    global $new_products_id_in_cart,
$customer_id;

    $products_id =
tep_get_uprid($products_id, $attributes);
        if ($notify == true) {
        $new_products_id_in_cart =
$products_id;

tep_session_register('new_products_id_in_cart'
);
        }

        if ($this->in_cart($products_id)) {
        $this->update_quantity($products_id,
$qty, $attributes);
        } else {
        $this->contents[] =
array($products_id);
        $this->contents[$products_id] =
array('qty' => $qty);
// insert into database
        if
(tep_session_is_registered('customer_id'))
tep_db_query("insert into " .
TABLE_CUSTOMERS_BASKET . " (customers_id,
products_id, customers_basket_quantity,
customers_basket_date_added) values ('" .
(int)$customer_id . "', '" .
tep_db_input($products_id) . "', '" . $qty .
"', '" . date('Ymd') . "')");
```

```
        if (is_array($attributes)) {
            reset($attributes);
            while (list($option, $value) =
each($attributes)) {
                $this-
>contents[$products_id]['attributes'][$option]
= $value;
// insert into database
                if
(tep_session_is_registered('customer_id'))
tep_db_query("insert into " .
TABLE_CUSTOMERS_BASKET_ATTRIBUTES . "
(customers_id, products_id,
products_options_id,
products_options_value_id) values ('" .
(int)$customer_id . "', '" .
tep_db_input($products_id) . "', '" .
(int)$option . "', '" . (int)$value . "')");
            }
        }
    }
    $this->cleanup();

// assign a temporary unique ID to the order
contents to prevent hack attempts during the
checkout procedure
        $this->cartID = $this-
>generate_cart_id();
    }
...........................................................................................
...........................................................................
}
```

The data related to the Shopping Cart are saved in the "customers_basket" (Figure 3.25) and "customers_basket_attributes" (Figure 3.26) tables. In these tables the "products_id" is a combination of fields "products_id," "options_id," and "options_values_id," which are present in the "products_attributes" table shown in Figure 3.27.

In the above code, "$products_id" is created using the "tep_get_uprid ($products_id, $attributes);" function, which is written in the /catalog/includes/functions/general.php file. The code follows.

```
function tep_get_uprid($prid, $params)
{
    $uprid = $prid;
    if ( (is_array($params)) &&
(!strstr($prid, '{')) )
    {
```

customers_basket_id	customers_id	products_id	customers_basket_quantity	final_price	customers_basket_date_added
23	7	28{1}4	1	0.0000	20050908
9	7	34{3}7	1	0.0000	20050829

Figure 3.25. Table "customers_basket."

customers_basket_attributes_id	customers_id	products_id	products_options_id	products_options_value_id
25	7	28{1}4	1	4
26	7	34{3}7	3	7

Figure 3.26. Table "customers_basket_attributes."

products_attributes_id	products_id	options_id	options_values_id	options_values_price	price_prefix
35	29	2	5	0.0000	+
41	31	1	1	0.0000	+
32	29	1	2	0.0000	+
31	29	1	3	0.0000	+
30	29	1	1	0.0000	+
40	28	1	4	0.0000	+
36	34	3	7	1.0000	+
37	34	3	9	1.0000	-

Figure 3.27. Table "products_attributes."

```
        while (list($option, $value) =
each($params))
        {
            $uprid = $uprid . '{' . $option .
'}' . $value;
        }
    }
    return $uprid;
}
```

The actions related to the Shopping Cart are coded in the /catalog/includes/ application_top.php file.

```
// Shopping cart actions
  if (isset($HTTP_GET_VARS['action'])) {
// redirect the customer to a friendly cookie-
must-be-enabled page if cookies are disabled
```

```
        if ($session_started == false) {

tep_redirect(tep_href_link(FILENAME_COOKIE_USA
GE));
        }

    if (DISPLAY_CART == 'true') {
        $goto =  FILENAME_SHOPPING_CART;
        $parameters = array('action', 'cPath',
'products_id', 'pid');
    } else {
        $goto = basename($PHP_SELF);
        if ($HTTP_GET_VARS['action'] ==
'buy_now') {
        $parameters = array('action', 'pid',
'products_id');
    } else {
        $parameters = array('action', 'pid');
    }
    }
    switch ($HTTP_GET_VARS['action']) {
    // customer wants to update the product
quantity in their shopping cart

    case 'update_product' :

.......................................................................................  . .


....................................................................................... .
                                    break;
    // customer adds a product from the
products page

case 'add_product' :    if (is-
set($HTTP_POST_VARS['products_id']) &&
is_numeric($HTTP_POST_VARS['products_id']))
 {
    cart-
>add_cart($HTTP_POST_VARS['products_id'],
$cart-
>get_quantity(tep_get_uprid($HTTP_POST_VARS['p
roducts_id'], $HTTP_POST_VARS['id']))+1,
$HTTP_POST_VARS['id']);
}
    tep_redirect(tep_href_link($goto,
tep_get_all_get_params($parameters)));
                                    break;

    // performed by the 'buy now' button in
product listings and review page
```

```
    case 'buy_now' :
        if (is-
set($HTTP_GET_VARS['products_id']))
        {
            if
(tep_has_product_attributes($HTTP_GET_VARS['pr
oducts_id']))
            {

tep_redirect(tep_href_link(FILENAME_PRODUCT_IN
FO, 'products_id=' .
$HTTP_GET_VARS['products_id']));
            }
        else
        {
            $cart-
>add_cart($HTTP_GET_VARS['products_id'],
$cart-
>get_quantity($HTTP_GET_VARS['products_id'])+1
);
        }
    }
    tep_redirect(tep_href_link($goto,
tep_get_all_get_params($parameters)));
                        break;
........................................................................ .
........................................................................ . .
    }
```

To count the total number of products in the cart, the following function is used, which is located in the /catalog/shopping_cart.php file.

```
$cart->count_contents()
```

The function "count_contents()" is defined in the /catalog/includes/classes/shopping_cart.php file.

```
function count_contents() {  // get total
number of items in cart
    $total_items = 0;
    if (is_array($this->contents)) {
        reset($this->contents);
        while (list($products_id, ) =
each($this->contents)) {
            $total_items += $this-
>get_quantity($products_id);
        }
    }
```

```
        return $total_items;
    }
```

3.4. CHECKOUT AND PAYMENT INTEGRATION

3.4.1. Delivery Information

When a customer clicks on the **Checkout** button in the My Cart section, a Delivery Information page will open (Figure 3.28), the code for which is written in the /catalog/checkout_shipping.php file. By default, the customer's address is selected as the shipping address, but the customer can change the shipping address by clicking the **Change Address** button (Figure 3.29) and either selecting an address from his address book or adding a new shipping address. To process the selected shipping address, the following code, written in the /catalog/checkout_shipping_address.php file, is executed.

```
$reset_shipping = false;
    if (tep_session_is_registered('sendto'))
{
        if ($sendto !=
$HTTP_POST_VARS['address']) {
            if
(tep_session_is_registered('shipping')) {
            $reset_shipping = true;
            }
        }
    } else {
        tep_session_register('sendto');
    }

    $sendto = $HTTP_POST_VARS['address'];

    $check_address_query =
tep_db_query("select count(*) as total from "
. TABLE_ADDRESS_BOOK . " where customers_id =
'" . (int)$customer_id . "' and
address_book_id = '" . (int)$sendto . "'");
        $check_address =
tep_db_fetch_array($check_address_query);

        if ($check_address['total'] == '1') {
            if ($reset_shipping == true)
tep_session_unregister('shipping');

tep_redirect(tep_href_link(FILENAME_CHECKOUT_S
HIPPING, '', 'SSL'));
        } else {
```

Figure 3.28. Delivery Information page.

```
        tep_session_unregister('sendto');
        }
    } else {
        if
(!tep_session_is_registered('sendto'))
tep_session_register('sendto');
        $sendto = $customer_default_address_id;


    tep_redirect(tep_href_link(FILENAME_CHECKOUT_S
HIPPING, '', 'SSL'));
    }
    }
```

```
// if no shipping destination address was
selected, use their own address as default
    if (!tep_session_is_registered('sendto')) {
        $sendto = $customer_default_address_id;
    }
```

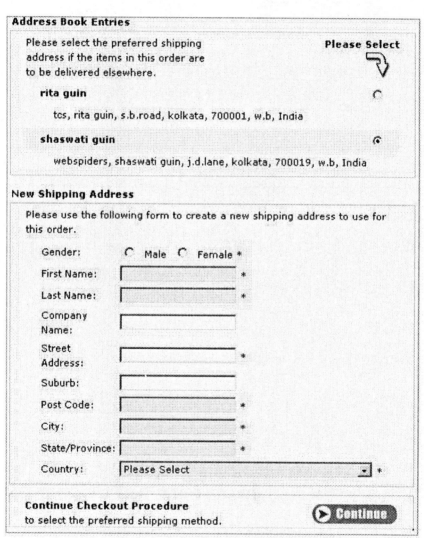

Figure 3.29. New Shipping Address form.

Similar code is written to process a new shipping address. In Figure 3.28 we see the Shipping Address section, but to show this, the address needs to be verified. For this the following code from the /catalog/checkout_ shipping.php file is used.

```php
// if no shipping destination address was
selected, use the customers own address as
default
  if (!tep_session_is_registered('sendto')) {
    tep_session_register('sendto');
    $sendto = $customer_default_address_id;
  } else {
// verify the selected shipping address
    $check_address_query =
tep_db_query("select count(*) as total from "
. TABLE_ADDRESS_BOOK . " where customers_id =
'" . (int)$customer_id . "' and
address_book_id = '" . (int)$sendto . "'");
    $check_address =
tep_db_fetch_array($check_address_query);

    if ($check_address['total'] != '1') {
      $sendto = $customer_default_address_id;
      if
(tep_session_is_registered('shipping'))
tep_session_unregister('shipping');
    }
  }
```

To show the shipping address, the following code is used.

```php
<tr>
    <td class="main" align="center"
valign="top">
        <?php echo '<b>' .
TITLE_SHIPPING_ADDRESS . '</b><br>' .
tep_image(DIR_WS_IMAGES .
'arrow_south_east.gif'); ?>
    </td>
    <td>
        <?php echo
tep_draw_separator('pixel_trans.gif', '10',
'1'); ?>
    </td>
    <td class="main" valign="top">
        <?php echo
tep_address_label($customer_id, $sendto, true,
' ', '<br>'); ?>
    </td>
```

```
    <td>
    <?php echo
tep_draw_separator('pixel_trans.gif', '10',
'1'); ?>
        </td>
    </tr>
```

Shipping methods are installed by the administrator, and to enable these, the following code is needed, which is written in the /catalog/checkout_ shipping.php file.

```
// load all enabled shipping modules
    require(DIR_WS_CLASSES . 'shipping.php');
    $shipping_modules = new shipping;

    if (
defined('MODULE_ORDER_TOTAL_SHIPPING_FREE_SHIP
PING') &&
(MODULE_ORDER_TOTAL_SHIPPING_FREE_SHIPPING ==
'true') ) {
        $pass = false;

        switch
(MODULE_ORDER_TOTAL_SHIPPING_DESTINATION) {
            case 'national':
            if ($order->delivery['country_id'] ==
STORE_COUNTRY) {
                $pass = true;
                }
            break;
            case 'international':
            if ($order->delivery['country_id'] !=
STORE_COUNTRY) {
                $pass = true;
                }
            break;
            case 'both':
            $pass = true;
            break;
        }

        $free_shipping = false;
        if ( ($pass == true) && ($order-
>info['total'] >=
MODULE_ORDER_TOTAL_SHIPPING_FREE_SHIPPING_OVER
) ) {
            $free_shipping = true;

            include(DIR_WS_LANGUAGES . $language .
'/modules/order_total/ot_shipping.php');
```

```
    }
  } else {
    $free_shipping = false;
  }
```

The code for processing the selected shipping option is also written in this page. In the above code the class named "shipping" is defined in the /catalog/includes/classes/shipping.php file.

3.4.2. Payment Information

When the **Continue** button is clicked on the Delivery Information page, the Payment Information page, shown in Figure 3.30, will open. The customer sees those payment options which have been installed by the administrator and selects one payment method.

In Figure 3.30 we see two payment methods: credit card and cash on delivery. This means that these two methods are enabled. To load all enabled payment modules, an object "$payment_modules" is created of class "payment." The class "payment" is defined in /catalog/includes/classes/payment.php.

```
class payment {
    var $modules, $selected_module;

// class constructor
    function payment($module = '') {
        global $payment, $language, $PHP_SELF;

        if (defined('MODULE_PAYMENT_INSTALLED')
&& tep_not_null(MODULE_PAYMENT_INSTALLED)) {
            $this->modules = explode(';',
MODULE_PAYMENT_INSTALLED);

            $include_modules = array();

            if ( (tep_not_null($module)) &&
(in_array($module . '.' . substr($PHP_SELF,
(strrpos($PHP_SELF, '.')+1)), $this->modules))
) {
                $this->selected_module = $module;

                $include_modules[] = array('class'
=> $module, 'file' => $module . '.php');
            } else {
            reset($this->modules);
            while (list(, $value) = each($this-
>modules)) {
```

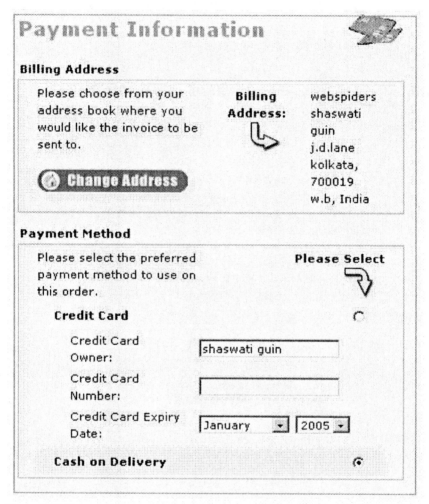

Figure 3.30. Payment Information page.

```
        $class = substr($value, 0,
strrpos($value, '.'));
        $include_modules[] = array('class'
=> $class, 'file' => $value);
      }
    }

    for ($i=0,
$n=sizeof($include_modules); $i<$n; $i++) {
```

```
        include(DIR_WS_LANGUAGES . $language
. '/modules/payment/' .
$include_modules[$i]['file']);
        include(DIR_WS_MODULES . 'payment/'
. $include_modules[$i]['file']);


$GLOBALS[$include_modules[$i]['class']] = new
$include_modules[$i]['class'];
      }
```

....

....

```
    }
  }
```

....

....

....

```
}
```

Now, we are going to discuss the credit card payment module. To integrate the credit card payment method, a class "cc" is implemented in the file /catalog/includes/modules/payment/cc.php. To modify the credit card module, customize the code written in the /catalog/includes/modules/payment/ cc.php and /catalog/includes/modules/classes/cc_validation.php files. There is a function "pre_confirmation_check()" in the class "cc" written in /catalog/includes/modules/payment/cc.php. An object "$cc_validation" of class "cc_validation" is created within this function, and this function is used to check the credit card details such as the credit card number and expiry date. The class "cc_validation" is defined in /catalog/includes/modules/payment/ cc_validation.php.

```
class cc {
    var $code, $title, $description, $enabled;
................................................................................... . .
...............................................................................
function pre_confirmation_check() {
    global $HTTP_POST_VARS;

    include(DIR_WS_CLASSES .
'cc_validation.php');

    $cc_validation = new cc_validation();
```

```
        $result = $cc_validation-
>validate($HTTP_POST_VARS['cc_number'],
$HTTP_POST_VARS['cc_expires_month'],
$HTTP_POST_VARS['cc_expires_year']);

        $error = '';
        switch ($result) {
          case -1:
            $error =
sprintf(TEXT_CCVAL_ERROR_UNKNOWN_CARD,
substr($cc_validation->cc_number, 0, 4));
            break;
          case -2:
          case -3:
          case -4:
            $error =
TEXT_CCVAL_ERROR_INVALID_DATE;
            break;
          case false:
            $error =
TEXT_CCVAL_ERROR_INVALID_NUMBER;
            break;
        }

        if ( ($result == false) || ($result < 1)
) {
          $payment_error_return = 'pay-
ment_error=' . $this->code . '&error=' . ur-
lencode($error) . '&cc_owner=' . urlen-
code($HTTP_POST_VARS['cc_owner']) .
'&cc_expires_month=' .
$HTTP_POST_VARS['cc_expires_month'] .
'&cc_expires_year=' .
$HTTP_POST_VARS['cc_expires_year'];


tep_redirect(tep_href_link(FILENAME_CHECKOUT_P
AYMENT, $payment_error_return, 'SSL', true,
false));
        }

    $this->cc_card_type = $cc_validation-
>cc_type;
    $this->cc_card_number = $cc_validation-
>cc_number;
    }
.................................................................. .
.......................................................... .
}
```

```php
class cc_validation {
    var $cc_type, $cc_number,
$cc_expiry_month, $cc_expiry_year;

    function validate($number, $expiry_m, $expiry_y) {
        $this->cc_number = ereg_replace('[^0-9]', '', $number);

        if (ereg('^4[0-9]{12}([0-9]{3})?$',
$this->cc_number)) {
            $this->cc_type = 'Visa';
        } elseif (ereg('^5[1-5][0-9]{14}$',
$this->cc_number)) {
            $this->cc_type = 'Master Card';
        } elseif (ereg('^3[47][0-9]{13}$',
$this->cc_number)) {
            $this->cc_type = 'American Express';
        }
        ..................................................................... .
        ..................................................................... . .
else {
            return -1;
        }
        if (is_numeric($expiry_m) && ($expiry_m
> 0) && ($expiry_m < 13)) {
            $this->cc_expiry_month = $expiry_m;
        } else {
            return -2;
        }

        $current_year = date('Y');
        $expiry_y = substr($current_year, 0, 2)
. $expiry_y;
        if (is_numeric($expiry_y) && ($expiry_y
>= $current_year) && ($expiry_y <= ($current_year + 10))) {
            $this->cc_expiry_year = $expiry_y;
        } else {
            return -3;
        }

        if ($expiry_y == $current_year) {
          if ($expiry_m < date('n')) {
            return -4;
          }
        }

        return $this->is_valid();
    }
```

```php
function is_valid() {
    $cardNumber = strrev($this->cc_number);
    $numSum = 0;
    .................................................... . .
    .................................................... . .

}

}
```

In the above the credit card payment module is used as an example, but there are more payment modules whose PHP files are in the folder /catalog/includes/modules/payment/, including PayPal, Authorize.net, etc. These files can be customized according to your requirements.

3.4.3. Order Confirmation

After completion of the payment process, customers will be sent to the Order Confirmation page. From here a customer can edit her shipping and billing information. Ultimately, when orders are confirmed by customers, the data is saved in the following tables: "orders," "orders_total," and "orders_status_history." Also, the customer will receive a confirmation e-mail containing the order information. The code to perform these actions is written in /catalog/checkout_process.php. This file can be modified as per your requirements.

To hold order and customer information, we need an array, which is shown below.

```php
$sql_data_array = array('customers_id' =>
$customer_id,
                        'customers_name' =>
$order->customer['firstname'] . ' ' . $order->customer['lastname'],
                        'customers_company'
=> $order->customer['company'],

'customers_street_address' => $order->customer['street_address'],
                        'customers_suburb'
=> $order->customer['suburb'],
                        'customers_city' =>
$order->customer['city'],

.................................................... . .

.................................................... . .
```

```
                                        'delivery_name' =>
$order->delivery['firstname'] . ' ' . $order-
>delivery['lastname'],
                                        'delivery_company'
=> $order->delivery['company'],

'delivery_street_address' => $order-
>delivery['street_address'],
                                        'delivery_suburb' =>
$order->delivery['suburb'],
                                        'delivery_city' =>
$order->delivery['city'],
                                        'delivery_postcode'
=> $order->delivery['postcode'],

..............................................................................

..............................................................................
                                        'billing_company' =>
$order->billing['company'],

'billing_street_address' => $order-
>billing['street_address'],
                                        'billing_suburb' =>
$order->billing['suburb'],
                                        'billing_city' =>
$order->billing['city'],
                                        'billing_postcode'
=> $order->billing['postcode'],

..............................................................................

..............................................................................
                                        'cc_type' => $order-
>info['cc_type'],
                                        'cc_owner' =>
$order->info['cc_owner'],
                                        'cc_number' =>
$order->info['cc_number'],
                                        'cc_expires' =>
$order->info['cc_expires'],
                                        'date_purchased' =>
'now()',
                                        'orders_status' =>
$order->info['order_status'],
                                        'currency' =>
$order->info['currency'],
                'currency_value' => $order-
>info['currency_value']);
```

Object "$order" is of class "order," and this class is defined in /catalog/includes/modules/classes/order.php. In the /checkout_process.php file the following four class files are included.

```
// load selected payment module
require(DIR_WS_CLASSES . 'payment.php');
$payment_modules = new payment($payment);

// load the selected shipping module
require(DIR_WS_CLASSES . 'shipping.php');
$shipping_modules = new shipping($shipping);

require(DIR_WS_CLASSES . 'order.php');
$order = new order;

// load the before_process function from the
payment modules
$payment_modules->before_process();

require(DIR_WS_CLASSES . 'order_total.php');
$order_total_modules = new order_total;

$order_totals = $order_total_modules-
>process();
```

These class files can also be modified.

3.5. CUSTOMIZING THE CSS

A single CSS file controls the style and colors of your store: /catalog/stylesheet.css. The features of a CSS are encapsulated within a class name, so to use the features of the class within an HTML file, first insert the following tag into your HTML pages.

- CSS stands for cascading style sheets
- Styles define how to display HTML elements
- Styles are normally stored in style sheets
- External style sheets can save you a lot of work
- External style sheets are stored in CSS files
- Multiple style definitions will cascade into one

```
<link rel="stylesheet" type="text/css"
href="stylesheet.css">
ClassName{

    Features1;
    Features2;
    Features3;
}
```

Examples are given below. The following is the original code (see Figure 3.31).

```
.boxText { font-family: Verdana, Arial, sans-
serif; font-size: 10px; }

.infoBox {
  background: #b6b7cb;
}

.infoBoxContents {
  background: #f8f8f9;
  font-family: Verdana, Arial, sans-serif;
  font-size: 10px;
}

TD.infoBoxHeading {
  font-family: Verdana, Arial, sans-serif;
  font-size: 10px;
  font-weight: bold;
  background: #bbc3d3;
  color: #ffffff;
}
```

To change the font, colors, etc., follow the below code and view the changes in your browser (Figure 3.32).

Figure 3.31. Information box.

Figure 3.32. Modified Information box.

```
.boxText { font-family: Verdana, Arial, sans-
serif; font-size: 11px; }

.infoBox {
background: #bbbbbb;
}

.infoBoxContents {
background: #888889;
font-family: Verdana, Arial, sans-serif;
font-size: 9px;
}

TD.infoBoxHeading {
font-family: Verdana, Arial, sans-serif;
font-size: 10px;
font-weight: bold;
background: #bbbbbb;
color: #ffffff;
}
```

3.5.1. Changing the Font and Color of the Page Header

To change the font and color of the header, change

```
TD.pageHeading, DIV.pageHeading {
    font-family: Verdana, Arial, sans-serif;
    font-size: 20px;
    font-weight: bold;
    color: #9a9a9a;
}
```

to the following:

```
TD.pageHeading, DIV.pageHeading {
    font-family: Verdana, Arial, sans-serif;
    font-size: 15px;
    font-weight: bold;
    color: #abcdef;
}
```

Using this class, you can change a table's heading as well as the div heading.

3.5.2. Changing the Font of the Sign In Page

To change the font used on the Sign In page, modify

```
TD.main, P.main {
    font-family: Verdana, Arial, sans-serif;
```

```
    font-size: 11px;
    line-height: 1.5;
}
CHECKBOX, INPUT, RADIO, SELECT {
    font-family: Verdana, Arial, sans-serif;
    font-size: 11px;
}
```

to read as follows:

```
TD.main, P.main {
    font-family: Verdana, Arial, sans-serif;
    font-size: 15px;
    line-height: 3;
}

CHECKBOX, INPUT, RADIO, SELECT {
    font-family: Verdana, Arial, sans-serif;
    font-size: 13px;
}
```

Using this class you can change a table's main font as well as a paragraph's main font.

3.5.3. Changing Other Style Elements

The "body" class is used to maintain the color of the body.

```
BODY {
    background: #ffffff;
    color: #000000;
    margin: 0px;
}
```

The "A" class is use to maintain the hyperlink text.

```
A {
    color: #000000;
    text-decoration: none;
}
```

The "A:hover" class is use to install a mouse-over effect on the hyperlink text.

```
A:hover {
    color: #AABBDD;
    text-decoration: underline;
}
```

The "Tr.header" class contains the header color of the table row header.

```
TR.header {
    background: #ffffff;
}
```

The "TD.headerError" class contains the background color, font height, width, alignment, and size of an error message.

```
TD.headerError {
    font-family: Tahoma, Verdana, Arial, sans-
serif;
    font-size: 12px;
    background: #ff0000;
    color: #ffffff;
    font-weight : bold;
    text-align : center;
}
```

The "TR.footer" class encodes the background color of a table row footer.

```
TR.footer {
    background: #bbc3d3;
}
```

The "TABLE.productListing" class contains the size of the border of a table product listing and its style, color, and spacing.

```
TABLE.productListing {
    border: 1px;
    border-style: solid;
    border-color: #b6b7cb;
    border-spacing: 1px;
}
```

The ".messageBox," ".messageStackError," ".messageStackWarning," and ".messageStackSuccess" classes contain the representative information of the message display.

```
.messageBox {
    font-family: Verdana, Arial, sans-serif;
    font-size: 10px;
}

.messageStackError, .messageStackWarning {
```

```
font-family: Verdana, Arial, sans-serif;
font-size: 10px;
background-color: #ffb3b5;
}
.messageStackSuccess {
font-family: Verdana, Arial, sans-serif;
font-size: 10px;
background-color: #99ff00;
}
```

In these ways the administrator can manipulate the fonts, colors, sizes, and styles used on the store pages. All the styles will "cascade" into a new, "virtual" style sheet through which the administrator will be able to access easily the CSS file from any PHP or HTML file within the project.

3.6. CUSTOMIZING THE PRODUCT LISTING PAGE

It is possible to modify the way the product list appears. Our discussion of the following code will give you a clear understanding of how to change the display format. The layout is changed by editing the following files: /catalog/index.php, /catalog/includes/application_top.php, /catalog/includes/classes/boxes.php, /catalog/includes/languages/English/index.php, and /catalog/includes/modules/product_listing.php. For example, before modification (Figure 3.33) the code of /catalog/index.php will appear as shown below.

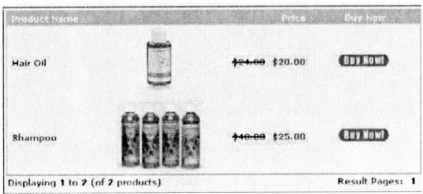

Figure 3.33. Product listing.

```
// create column list
    $define_list = array('PRODUCT_LIST_MODEL'
=> PRODUCT_LIST_MODEL,
                         'PRODUCT_LIST_NAME'
=> PRODUCT_LIST_NAME,

'PRODUCT_LIST_MANUFACTURER' =>
PRODUCT_LIST_MANUFACTURER,
                         'PRODUCT_LIST_PRICE'
=> PRODUCT_LIST_PRICE,

'PRODUCT_LIST_QUANTITY' =>
PRODUCT_LIST_QUANTITY,
                         'PRODUCT_LIST_WEIGHT'
=> PRODUCT_LIST_WEIGHT,
                         'PRODUCT_LIST_IMAGE'
=> PRODUCT_LIST_IMAGE,

'PRODUCT_LIST_BUY_NOW' =>
PRODUCT_LIST_BUY_NOW);

$select_column_list = '';

    for ($i=0, $n=sizeof($column_list); $i<$n;
$i++) {
        switch ($column_list[$i]) {
          case 'PRODUCT_LIST_MODEL':
            $select_column_list .=
'p.products_model, ';
            break;
          case 'PRODUCT_LIST_NAME':
            $select_column_list .=
'pd.products_name, ';
            break;
          case 'PRODUCT_LIST_MANUFACTURER':
            $select_column_list .=
'm.manufacturers_name, ';
            break;
          case 'PRODUCT_LIST_QUANTITY':
            $select_column_list .=
'p.products_quantity, ';
            break;
          case 'PRODUCT_LIST_IMAGE':
            $select_column_list .=
'p.products_image, ';
            break;
          case 'PRODUCT_LIST_WEIGHT':
            $select_column_list .=
'p.products_weight, ';
            break;
        }
```

```
        }
       switch ($column_list[$sort_col-1]) {
          case 'PRODUCT_LIST_MODEL':
             $listing_sql .= "p.products_model "
. ($sort_order == 'd' ? 'desc' : '') . ",
pd.products_name";
             break;
          case 'PRODUCT_LIST_NAME':
             $listing_sql .= "pd.products_name "
. ($sort_order == 'd' ? 'desc' : '');
             break;
          case 'PRODUCT_LIST_MANUFACTURER':
             $listing_sql .=
"m.manufacturers_name " . ($sort_order == 'd'
? 'desc' : '') . ", pd.products_name";
             break;
          case 'PRODUCT_LIST_QUANTITY':
             $listing_sql .= "p.products_quantity
" . ($sort_order == 'd' ? 'desc' : '') . ",
pd.products_name";
             break;
          case 'PRODUCT_LIST_IMAGE':
             $listing_sql .= "pd.products_name";
             break;
          case 'PRODUCT_LIST_WEIGHT':
             $listing_sql .= "p.products_weight "
. ($sort_order == 'd' ? 'desc' : '') . ",
pd.products_name";
             break;
          case 'PRODUCT_LIST_PRICE':
             $listing_sql .= "final_price " .
($sort_order == 'd' ? 'desc' : '') . ",
pd.products_name";
             break;
       }
```

However, you can modify the code to display the product image first, followed by the product name, price, and buy now option (Figure 3.34).

```
// create column list
   $define_list = array(
      'PRODUCT_LIST_MODEL' =>
PRODUCT_LIST_MODEL,
   'PRODUCT_LIST_IMAGE' => PRODUCT_LIST_IMAGE,
         'PRODUCT_LIST_NAME' =>
PRODUCT_LIST_NAME,
         'PRODUCT_LIST_MANUFACTURER' =>
PRODUCT_LIST_MANUFACTURER,
         'PRODUCT_LIST_PRICE' =>
PRODUCT_LIST_PRICE,
```

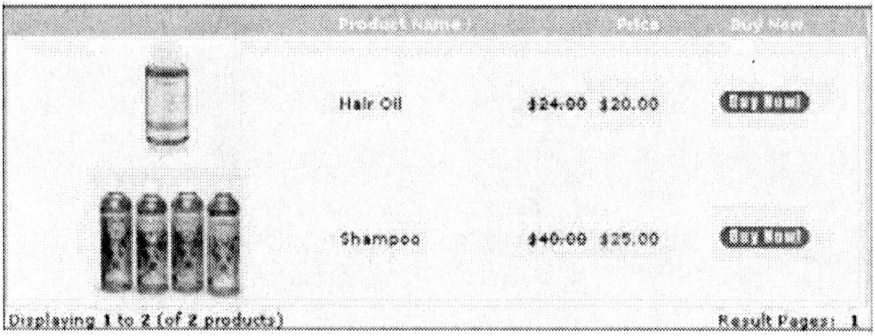

Figure 3.34. Modified product listing.

```
                'PRODUCT_LIST_QUANTITY' =>
PRODUCT_LIST_QUANTITY,
                'PRODUCT_LIST_WEIGHT' =>
PRODUCT_LIST_WEIGHT,
                'PRODUCT_LIST_BUY_NOW' =>
PRODUCT_LIST_BUY_NOW);

$select_column_list = '';

    for ($i=0, $n=sizeof($column_list); $i<$n;
$i++) {
        switch ($column_list[$i]) {
          case 'PRODUCT_LIST_MODEL':
            $select_column_list .=
'p.products_model, ';
              break;
          case 'PRODUCT_LIST_IMAGE':
            $select_column_list .=
'p.products_image, ';
              break;
          case 'PRODUCT_LIST_NAME':
            $select_column_list .=
'pd.products_name, ';
              break;
          case 'PRODUCT_LIST_MANUFACTURER':
            $select_column_list .=
'm.manufacturers_name, ';
              break;
          case 'PRODUCT_LIST_QUANTITY':
            $select_column_list .=
'p.products_quantity, ';
              break;
          case 'PRODUCT_LIST_WEIGHT':
            $select_column_list .=
'p.products_weight, ';
```

```
        break;
    }
}
switch ($column_list[$sort_col-1]) {
        case 'PRODUCT_LIST_MODEL':
            $listing_sql .= "p.products_model "
. ($sort_order == 'd' ? 'desc' : '') . ",
pd.products_name";
            break;
        case 'PRODUCT_LIST_IMAGE':
            $listing_sql .= "pd.products_name";
            break;
        case 'PRODUCT_LIST_NAME':
            $listing_sql .= "pd.products_name "
. ($sort_order == 'd' ? 'desc' : '');
            break;
        case 'PRODUCT_LIST_MANUFACTURER':
            $listing_sql .=
"m.manufacturers_name " . ($sort_order == 'd'
? 'desc' : '') . ", pd.products_name";
            break;
        case 'PRODUCT_LIST_QUANTITY':
            $listing_sql .= "p.products_quantity
" . ($sort_order == 'd' ? 'desc' : '') . ",
pd.products_name";
            break;
        case 'PRODUCT_LIST_WEIGHT':
            $listing_sql .= "p.products_weight "
. ($sort_order == 'd' ? 'desc' : '') . ",
pd.products_name";
            break;
        case 'PRODUCT_LIST_PRICE':
            $listing_sql .= "final_price " .
($sort_order == 'd' ? 'desc' : '') . ",
pd.products_name";
            break;
    }
```

3.7. Customizing the Product Information Page

You can also change the structure of the product information page (Figure 3.35), which contains detailed descriptions of products. For example, the code of the page, /catalog/product_info.php, appears as follows before modification.

```
<td class="pageHeading" valign="top"><?php
echo $products_name; ?></td>
```

Figure 3.35. Product information display.

Figure 3.36. Modified product information display.

```
    <td class="pageHeading" align="right"
valign="top"><?php echo $products_price;
?></td>
..........................
.......................... . .
.......................... . .
if
(tep_not_null($product_info['products_image'])
) {
?>
        <table border="0" cellspacing="0"
cellpadding="2" align="right">
            <tr>
            <td align="center"
class="smallText">
<script language="javascript"><!--
document.write('<?php echo '<a
href="javascript:popupWindow(\\\'' .
tep_href_link(FILENAME_POPUP_IMAGE, 'pID=' .
$product_info['products_id']) . '\\\')">' .
tep_image(DIR_WS_IMAGES .
$product_info['products_image'],
addslashes($product_info['products_name']),
SMALL_IMAGE_WIDTH, SMALL_IMAGE_HEIGHT,
'hspace="5" vspace="5"') . '<br>' .
TEXT_CLICK_TO_ENLARGE . '</a>'; ?>');
//--></script>
<noscript>
<?php echo '<a href="' .
tep_href_link(DIR_WS_IMAGES .
$product_info['products_image']) . '"
target="_blank">' . tep_image(DIR_WS_IMAGES .
$product_info['products_image'],
$product_info['products_name'],
SMALL_IMAGE_WIDTH, SMALL_IMAGE_HEIGHT,
'hspace="5" vspace="5"') . '<br>' .
TEXT_CLICK_TO_ENLARGE . '</a>'; ?>
</noscript>
```

```
                </td>
              </tr>
            </table>
<?php
    }
<p><?php echo
stripslashes($product_info['products_descripti
on']); ?></p>

<?php
    $products_attributes_query =
tep_db_query("select count(*) as total from "
. TABLE_PRODUCTS_OPTIONS . " popt, " .
TABLE_PRODUCTS_ATTRIBUTES . " patrib where
patrib.products_id='" .
(int)$HTTP_GET_VARS['products_id'] . "' and
patrib.options_id = popt.products_options_id
and popt.language_id = '" . (int)$languages_id
. "'");
    $products_attributes =
tep_db_fetch_array($products_attributes_query)
;
    if ($products_attributes['total'] > 0) {
?>
            <table border="0" cellspacing="0"
cellpadding="2">
              <tr>
                <td class="main"
colspan="2"><?php echo TEXT_PRODUCT_OPTIONS;
?></td>
              </tr>
<?php
    $products_options_name_query =
tep_db_query("select distinct
popt.products_options_id,
popt.products_options_name from " .
TABLE_PRODUCTS_OPTIONS . " popt, " .
TABLE_PRODUCTS_ATTRIBUTES . " patrib where
patrib.products_id='" .
(int)$HTTP_GET_VARS['products_id'] . "' and
patrib.options_id = popt.products_options_id
and popt.language_id = '" . (int)$languages_id
. "' order by popt.products_options_name");
```

The following code changes will modify the page view and arrangement of the page (Figure 3.36).

```
    <td class="pageHeading" valign="top"
bgcolor="#FFCCCC"><?php echo $products_name;
?></td>
```

```
    <td class="pageHeading" align="left"
valign="top"><?php echo $products_price;
?></td>
.............................
............................. . .
............................. . .
if
(tep_not_null($product_info['products_image'])
) {
?>
        <table border="1" cellspacing="0"
cellpadding="2" align="left">
            <tr>
              <td align="center"
class="smallText">
<script language="javascript"><!--
document.write('<?php echo '<a
href="javascript:popupWindow(\\\'' .
tep_href_link(FILENAME_POPUP_IMAGE, 'pID=' .
$product_info['products_id']) . '\\\')">' .
tep_image(DIR_WS_IMAGES .
$product_info['products_image'],
addslashes($product_info['products_name']),
SMALL_IMAGE_WIDTH, SMALL_IMAGE_HEIGHT,
'hspace="5" vspace="5"') . '<br>' .
TEXT_CLICK_TO_ENLARGE . '</a>'; ?>');
//--></script>
<noscript>
<?php echo '<a href="' .
tep_href_link(DIR_WS_IMAGES .
$product_info['products_image']) . '"
target="_blank">' . tep_image(DIR_WS_IMAGES .
$product_info['products_image'],
$product_info['products_name'],
SMALL_IMAGE_WIDTH, SMALL_IMAGE_HEIGHT,
'hspace="5" vspace="5"') . '<br>' .
TEXT_CLICK_TO_ENLARGE . '</a>'; ?>
</noscript>
              </td>
            </tr>
          </table>
<?php
    }
<p><?php echo "<b>Description</b> : ".
stripslashes($product_info['products_descripti
on']); ?></p>

<?php
    $products_attributes_query =
tep_db_query("select count(*) as total from "
. TABLE_PRODUCTS_OPTIONS . " popt, " .
```

```
TABLE_PRODUCTS_ATTRIBUTES . " patrib where
patrib.products_id='" .
(int)$HTTP_GET_VARS['products_id'] . "' and
patrib.options_id = popt.products_options_id
and popt.language_id = '" . (int)$languages_id
. "'");
    $products_attributes =
tep_db_fetch_array($products_attributes_query)
;
    if ($products_attributes['total'] > 0) {
?>
        <table border="0" cellspacing="0"
cellpadding="2" bgcolor="#66CCCC">
          <tr>
            <td class="main"
colspan="2"><?php echo TEXT_PRODUCT_OPTIONS;
?></td>
          </tr>
<?php
    $products_options_name_query =
tep_db_query("select distinct
popt.products_options_id,
popt.products_options_name from " .
TABLE_PRODUCTS_OPTIONS . " popt, " .
TABLE_PRODUCTS_ATTRIBUTES . " patrib where
patrib.products_id='" .
(int)$HTTP_GET_VARS['products_id'] . "' and
patrib.options_id = popt.products_options_id
and popt.language_id = '" . (int)$languages_id
. "' order by popt.products_options_name");
```

By this process you can change the layout of the /product_info.php page.

3.8. Customizing the New Products Section

3.8.1. New Products Box on Index Page

The path of the New Products box is /catalog/includes/modules/
new_products.php. You can change the heading and display format of this
page without changing the CSS file. To change the heading, modify the code of
the file /catalog/includes/languages/english/index.php.

```
define('TABLE_HEADING_NEW_PRODUCTS', 'New
Products For %s');
```

Alternatively, to increase the number of columns and change the background color, change the code of the /catalog/includes/modules/new_products.php file.

```
$row = 0; $col = 0;
$info_box_contents = array();
while ($new_products =
tep_db_fetch_array($new_products_query)) {
    $new_products['products_name'] =
tep_get_products_name($new_products['products_
id']);
    $info_box_contents[$row][$col] =
array('align' => 'center',
                        'params' =>
'class="smallText" width="33%"
valign="top",'text' => '<a href="' .
tep_href_link(FILENAME_PRODUCT_INFO,
'products_id=' . $new_products['products_id'])
. '">' . tep_image(DIR_WS_IMAGES .
$new_products['products_image'],
$new_products['products_name'],
SMALL_IMAGE_WIDTH, SMALL_IMAGE_HEIGHT) .
'</a><br><a href="' .
tep_href_link(FILENAME_PRODUCT_INFO,
'products_id=' .
$ducts['products_id']) . '">' .
$new_products['products_name'] . '</a><br>'
. $currencies-
>display_price($new_products['products_tax_cla
ss_id']))));
$col ++;
    if ($col > 2) {
            $col = 0;
            $row ++;
    }
}
```

```
define('TABLE_HEADING_NEW_PRODUCTS', '<font
color=red>New Products For %s</font>');
```

Then, go to the Admin page, click on the **Configuration** link, and from the left menu bar, click **Maximum Value** and edit the value of the New Products module (Figure 3.37), which specifies the total number of products to be displayed. For example, if you want to display eight products in the New Products section, four items per row, then you will need to change the values in two

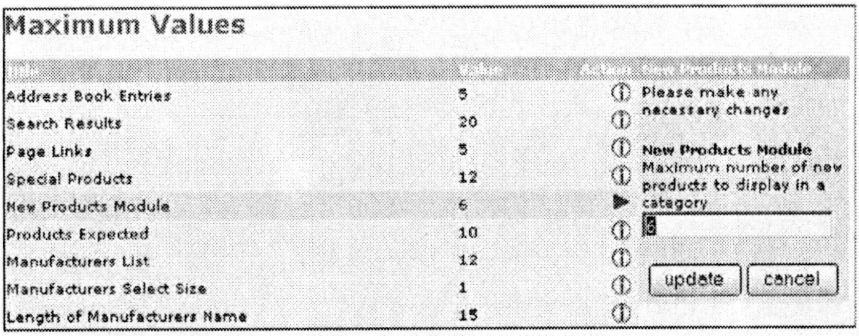

Maximum Values		
Title	Value	Action
Address Book Entries	5	ⓘ
Search Results	20	ⓘ
Page Links	5	ⓘ
Special Products	12	ⓘ
New Products Module	6	▶
Products Expected	10	ⓘ
Manufacturers List	12	ⓘ
Manufacturers Select Size	1	ⓘ
Length of Manufacturers Name	15	ⓘ

New Products Module
Please make any necessary changes

New Products Module
Maximum number of new products to display in a category

[6]

[update] [cancel]

Figure 3.37. Changing the number of new products to display via the Admin panel.

ways: by altering the values in the Admin page and by changing the code in the files /catalog/includes/languages/english/index.php and /catalog/includes/modules/new_products.php.

```
$row = 0; $col = 0;  $info_box_contents =
array();
   while ($new_products =
tep_db_fetch_array($new_products_query)) {
     $new_products['products_name'] =
tep_get_products_name($new_products['products_
id']);
     $info_box_contents[$row][$col] =
array('align' => 'center',
   'params' => 'class="smallText" width="33%"
valign="top" bgcolor="#CCCCFF"', 'text' => '<a
href="' . tep_href_link(FILENAME_PRODUCT_INFO,
'products_id=' . $new_products['products_id'])
. '">' . tep_image(DIR_WS_IMAGES .
$new_products['products_image'],
$new_products['products_name'],
SMALL_IMAGE_WIDTH, SMALL_IMAGE_HEIGHT) .
'</a><br><a href="' .
tep_href_link(FILENAME_PRODUCT_INFO,
'products_id=' . $new_products['products_id'])
. '"><b>' . $new_products['products_name'] .
'<b></a><br><font color=red>' . $currencies->
display_price($new_products['products_price'],
tep_get_tax_rate($new_products['products_tax_c
lass_id'])).'</font>');
     $col ++;
        if ($col > 3)
        {
           $col = 0;
```

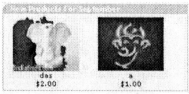

Figure 3.38. New Products display area.

Figure 3.39. Modified New Products display area.

```
            $row ++;
        }
    }
```

Figure 3.38 shows the original appearance of the New Products section, while Figure 3.39 shows the modified appearance.

3.8.2. What's New Box

The path of the What's New box is /catalog/includes/boxes/whats_new.php. This file is called by the /catalog/includes/column_left.php page. To change the original appearance of the What's New box (Figure 3.40), you will need to alter the following code.

```
if
(tep_not_null($random_product['specials_new_pr
oducts_price'])) {
        $whats_new_price = '<s>' . $currencies-
>display_price($random_product['products_price
'],
```

Figure 3.40. What's New box.

```
tep_get_tax_rate($random_product['products_tax
_class_id'])) . '</s><br>';
      $whats_new_price .= '<span
class="productSpecialPrice">' . $currencies-
>display_price($random_product['specials_new_p
roducts_price'],
tep_get_tax_rate($random_product['products_tax
_class_id'])) . '</span>';
    } else {
      $whats_new_price = $currencies-
>display_price($random_product['products_price
'],
tep_get_tax_rate($random_product['products_tax
_class_id']));
    }
.................
.................
    $info_box_contents = array();
    $info_box_contents[] = array('align' =>
'center',
                              'text' => '<a
href="' . tep_href_link(FILENAME_PRODUCT_INFO,
'products_id=' .
$random_product['products_id']) . '">' .
tep_image(DIR_WS_IMAGES .
$random_product['products_image'],
$random_product['products_name'],
SMALL_IMAGE_WIDTH, SMALL_IMAGE_HEIGHT) .
'</a><br><a href="' .
tep_href_link(FILENAME_PRODUCT_INFO,
'products_id=' .
$random_product['products_id']) . '">' .
$random_product['products_name'] . '</a><br>'
. $whats_new_price);
```

Suppose that you want to change the color of the product name (without changing the CSS) and that you want to hide the product price. The changed code would be as follows.

```
/*     if
(tep_not_null($random_product['specials_new_pr
oducts_price'])) {
        $whats_new_price = '<s>' . $currencies-
>display_price($random_product['products_price
'],
tep_get_tax_rate($random_product['products_tax
_class_id'])) . '</s><br>';
        $whats_new_price .= '<span
class="productSpecialPrice">' . $currencies-
>display_price($random_product['specials_new_p
roducts_price'],
tep_get_tax_rate($random_product['products_tax
_class_id'])) . '</span>';
    } else {
        $whats_new_price = $currencies-
>display_price($random_product['products_price
'],
tep_get_tax_rate($random_product['products_tax
_class_id']));
    }
*/
//Block the code
...............
...............
    $info_box_contents = array();
    $info_box_contents[] = array('align' =>
'center',
                                'text' => '<a
href="' . tep_href_link(FILENAME_PRODUCT_INFO,
'products_id=' .
$random_product['products_id']) . '">' .
tep_image(DIR_WS_IMAGES .
$random_product['products_image'],
$random_product['products_name'],
SMALL_IMAGE_WIDTH, SMALL_IMAGE_HEIGHT) .
'</a><br><a href="' .
tep_href_link(FILENAME_PRODUCT_INFO,
'products_id=' .
$random_product['products_id']) . '"><font
color="#CC00FF">' .
$random_product['products_name'] .
'</font></a><br>' . $whats_new_price);
```

You can thus change the appearance of the What's New box by changing this file.

3.8.3. New Products Page

This file path for the New Products page is /catalog/products_new.php. To change the display style of this page (Figure 3.41), alter the following code.

```
        <td><table border="0" width="100%"
cellspacing="0" cellpadding="2">
<?php
   if ($products_new_split->number_of_rows > 0)
{
     $products_new_query =
tep_db_query($products_new_split->sql_query);
     while ($products_new =
tep_db_fetch_array($products_new_query)) {
        if ($new_price =
tep_get_products_special_price($products_new['
products_id'])) {
           $products_price = '<s>' . $currencies-
>display_price($products_new['products_price']
,
tep_get_tax_rate($products_new['products_tax_c
lass_id'])) . '</s> <span
class="productSpecialPrice">' . $currencies-
>display_price($new_price,
tep_get_tax_rate($products_new['products_tax_c
lass_id'])) . '</span>';
        } else {
```

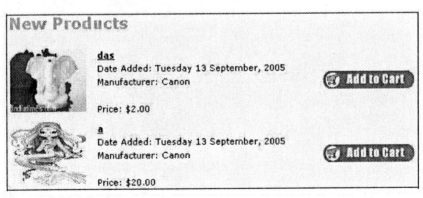

Figure 3.41. New Products page.

```
          $products_price = $currencies-
>display_price($products_new['products_price']
,
tep_get_tax_rate($products_new['products_tax_c
lass_id']));
      }
?>
          <tr>
          <td width="<?php echo
SMALL_IMAGE_WIDTH + 10; ?>" valign="top"
class="main"><?php echo '<a href="' .
tep_href_link(FILENAME_PRODUCT_INFO,
'products_id=' . $products_new['products_id'])
. '">' . tep_image(DIR_WS_IMAGES .
$products_new['products_image'],
$products_new['products_name'],
SMALL_IMAGE_WIDTH, SMALL_IMAGE_HEIGHT) .
'</a>'; ?></td>
          <td valign="top"
class="main"><?php echo '<a href="' .
tep_href_link(FILENAME_PRODUCT_INFO,
'products_id=' . $products_new['products_id'])
. '"><b><u>' . $products_new['products_name']
. '</u></b></a><br>' . TEXT_DATE_ADDED . ' ' .
tep_date_long($products_new['products_date_add
ed']) . '<br>' . TEXT_MANUFACTURER . ' ' .
$products_new['manufacturers_name'] .
'<br><br>' . TEXT_PRICE . ' ' .
$products_price; ?></td>
          <td align="right" valign="middle"
class="main"><?php echo '<a href="' .
tep_href_link(FILENAME_PRODUCTS_NEW,
tep_get_all_get_params(array('action')) .
'action=buy_now&products_id=' .
$products_new['products_id']) . '">' .
tep_image_button('button_in_cart.gif',
IMAGE_BUTTON_IN_CART) . '</a>'; ?></td>
        </tr>
        <tr>
          <td colspüan="3"><?php echo
tep_draw_separator('pixel_trans.gif', '100%',
'10'); ?></td>
        </tr>
<?php
    }
  } else { ?>
```

For example, suppose that you want to change the price color and the dimensions of the product display list (two products by two products, with the **Add**

to Cart button appearing below each) (Figure 3.42); the code would need to be changed as follows.

```
<td><table border="0" width="100%"
cellspacing="0" cellpadding="2"><tr>
<?php
  if ($products_new_split->number_of_rows > 0)
  {
    $products_new_query =
tep_db_query($products_new_split->sql_query);
    $i=1;
    while ($products_new =
tep_db_fetch_array($products_new_query)) {
      if ($new_price =
tep_get_products_special_price($products_new['
products_id'])) {
        $products_price = '<s>' . $currencies-
>display_price($products_new['products_price']
,
tep_get_tax_rate($products_new['products_tax_c
lass_id'])) . '</s> <span
class="productSpecialPrice">' . $currencies-
>display_price($new_price,
tep_get_tax_rate($products_new['products_tax_c
lass_id'])) . '</span>';
      } else {
        $products_price = $currencies-
>display_price($products_new['products_price']
,
tep_get_tax_rate($products_new['products_tax_c
lass_id']));
      }
?><td><table width="75%" border="0"
cellspacing="0" cellpadding="0">
  <tr>
```

Figure 3.42. Modified New Products page.

```
    <td rowspan="4" valign="top" width="<?php
echo SMALL_IMAGE_WIDTH + 10; ?>"
class="main"><?php echo '<a href="' .
tep_href_link(FILENAME_PRODUCT_INFO,
'products_id=' . $products_new['products_id'])
. '">' . tep_image(DIR_WS_IMAGES .
$products_new['products_image'],
$products_new['products_name'],
SMALL_IMAGE_WIDTH, SMALL_IMAGE_HEIGHT) .
'</a>'; ?></td>
 <td class="main"><?php echo '<a href="' .
tep_href_link(FILENAME_PRODUCT_INFO,
'products_id=' . $products_new['products_id'])
. '"><b><u>' . $products_new['products_name']
. '</u></b></a>';?></td>
  </tr>
<tr>
    <td class="main"><?=TEXT_DATE_ADDED . ' '
.
tep_date_long($products_new['products_date_add
ed'])?></td>
  </tr>
  <tr>
    <td class="main"><?=TEXT_MANUFACTURER . '
' . $products_new['manufacturers_name']?></td>
  </tr>
  <tr>
    <td class="main"><font
color="#FF0000"><?=TEXT_PRICE . ' ' .
$products_price?></font></td>
  </tr>
  <tr>
    <td class="main" align="center"
colspan="2"><?php echo '<a href="' .
tep_href_link(FILENAME_PRODUCTS_NEW,
tep_get_all_get_params(array('action')) .
'action=buy_now&products_id=' .
$products_new['products_id']) . '">' .
tep_image_button('button_in_cart.gif',
IMAGE_BUTTON_IN_CART) . '</a>'; ?></td>
  </tr>
</table>
        </td>
         <?php
         if($i%2==0) echo "<tr> ";
         $i++;  } ?>
        <tr><td colspüan="3"><?php echo
tep_draw_separator('pixel_trans.gif', '100%',
'10'); ?></td>
        </tr>
```

In this way the display and arrangement of this page can be changed.

3.9. REVIEWS SECTION

The file path for the Reviews section is /catalog/reviews.php. If you want to change the display of the Reviews section, for example, its color, without changing the CSS, you will need to change the code of this file. The original code appears as follows.

```
<tr><td><table border="0" width="100%"
cellspacing="0" cellpadding="2">
          <tr><td class="main"><?php echo
'<a href="' .
tep_href_link(FILENAME_PRODUCT_REVIEWS_INFO,
'products_id=' . $reviews['products_id'] .
'&reviews_id=' . $reviews['reviews_id']) .
'"><u><b>' . $reviews['products_name'] .
'</b></u></a> <span class="smallText">' .
sprintf(TEXT_REVIEW_BY,
tep_output_string_protected($reviews['customer
s_name'])) . '</span>'; ?></td>
          <td class="smallText"
align="right"><?php echo
sprintf(TEXT_REVIEW_DATE_ADDED,
tep_date_long($reviews['date_added']));
?></td></tr></table></td></tr> <tr>
          <td><table border="0" width="100%"
cellspacing="1" cellpadding="2"
class="infoBox">
          <tr class="infoBoxContents">
          <td><table border="0"
width="100%" cellspacing="0" cellpadding="2">
          <tr>
          <td width="10"><?php echo
tep_draw_separator('pixel_trans.gif', '10',
'1'); ?></td>
          <td width="<?php echo
SMALL_IMAGE_WIDTH + 10; ?>" align="center"
valign="top" class="main"><?php echo '<a
href="' .
tep_href_link(FILENAME_PRODUCT_REVIEWS_INFO,
'products_id=' . $reviews['products_id'] .
'&reviews_id=' . $reviews['reviews_id']) .
'">' . tep_image(DIR_WS_IMAGES .
$reviews['products_image'],
$reviews['products_name'], SMALL_IMAGE_WIDTH,
SMALL_IMAGE_HEIGHT) . '</a>'; ?></td>
```

```
                <td valign="top"
class="main"><?php echo
tep_break_string(tep_output_string_protected($
reviews['reviews_text']), 60, '-<br>') .
((strlen($reviews['reviews_text']) >= 100) ?
'..' : '') . '<br><br><i>' .
sprintf(TEXT_REVIEW_RATING,
tep_image(DIR_WS_IMAGES . 'stars_' .
$reviews['reviews_rating'] . '.gif',
sprintf(TEXT_OF_5_STARS,
$reviews['reviews_rating'])),
sprintf(TEXT_OF_5_STARS,
$reviews['reviews_rating'])) . '</i>'; ?></td>
                <td width="10"
align="right"><?php echo
tep_draw_separator('pixel_trans.gif', '10',
'1'); ?></td>
              </tr>
            </table></td>
          </tr>
```

The altered code appears below.

```
<tr>
        <td><table border="0" width="100%"
cellspacing="0" bgcolor="#CCCC00"
cellpadding="2">
          <tr>
            <td class="main"><?php echo
'<a href="' .
tep_href_link(FILENAME_PRODUCT_REVIEWS_INFO,
'products_id=' . $reviews['products_id'] .
'&reviews_id=' . $reviews['reviews_id']) .
'"><u><b>' . $reviews['products_name'] .
'</b></u></a><font color="red"> <span
class="smallText">' . sprintf(TEXT_REVIEW_BY,
tep_output_string_protected($reviews['customer
s_name'])) . '</span></font>'; ?></td>
            <td class="smallText"
align="right"><?php echo
sprintf(TEXT_REVIEW_DATE_ADDED,
tep_date_long($reviews['date_added']));
?></td>
          </tr>
        </table></td>
      </tr>
      <tr>
        <td><table border="0" width="100%"
cellspacing="1" cellpadding="2"
class="infoBox">
```

```
                    <tr class="infoBoxContents">
                        <td><table border="0"
width="100%" cellspacing="0" cellpadding="2"
bgcolor="#CC9999">
                            <tr>
                                <td width="10"><?php echo
tep_draw_separator('pixel_trans.gif', '10',
'1'); ?></td>
                                <td width="<?php echo
SMALL_IMAGE_WIDTH + 10; ?>" align="center"
valign="top" class="main"><?php echo '<a
href="' .
tep_href_link(FILENAME_PRODUCT_REVIEWS_INFO,
'products_id=' . $reviews['products_id'] .
'&reviews_id=' . $reviews['reviews_id']) .
'">' . tep_image(DIR_WS_IMAGES .
$reviews['products_image'],
$reviews['products_name'], SMALL_IMAGE_WIDTH,
SMALL_IMAGE_HEIGHT) . '</a>'; ?></td>
                                <td valign="top"
class="main"><?php echo
tep_break_string(tep_output_string_protected($
reviews['reviews_text']), 60, '-<br>') .
((strlen($reviews['reviews_text']) >= 100) ?
'..' : '') . '<br><br><i>' .
sprintf(TEXT_REVIEW_RATING,
tep_image(DIR_WS_IMAGES . 'stars_' .
$reviews['reviews_rating'] . '.gif',
sprintf(TEXT_OF_5_STARS,
$reviews['reviews_rating'])),
sprintf(TEXT_OF_5_STARS,
$reviews['reviews_rating'])) . '</i>'; ?></td>
                                <td width="10"
align="right"><?php echo
tep_draw_separator('pixel_trans.gif', '10',
'1'); ?></td>
                            </tr>
                        </table></td>
                    </tr>
```

It is also possible to change the display format, for example, to place two rated boxes in each row. To do so, just change the logic part of the above code.

The /catalog/product_reviews.php page will display the total review list of a particular product, and the /catalog/product_reviews_info.php will display one review from the above list. On both pages the **Write Review** and **Add to Cart** options are available, and you can change the color of or customize these elements as you wish. If you click on the **Write Review** button or click the **Write a review on this product** link on the index page, control will go to the /catalog/product_reviews_write.php page. To change the look and background color of the area box, change the coding style of the /catalog/ product_reviews_write.php page.

3.10. CUSTOMIZATION OF HEADER MENU

The file path of the header menu is /catalog/includes/header.php. To change the color of the text, the separator, and the arrangement of the menu (Figure 3.43) without changing the CSS, simply follow the code shown below in bold face. The original code is shown first.

```
<table border="0" width="100%" cellspacing="0"
cellpadding="1">
  <tr class="headerNavigation">
    <td
class="headerNavigation">  <?php
echo $breadcrumb->trail(' &raquo; '); ?></td>
    <td align="right"
class="headerNavigation"><?php if
(tep_session_is_registered('customer_id')) {
?><a href="<?php echo
tep_href_link(FILENAME_LOGOFF, '', 'SSL'); ?>"
class="headerNavigation"><?php echo
HEADER_TITLE_LOGOFF; ?></a>  | 
<?php } ?><a href="<?php echo
tep_href_link(FILENAME_ACCOUNT, '', 'SSL');
?>" class="headerNavigation"><?php echo
HEADER_TITLE_MY_ACCOUNT; ?></a>  | 
<a href="<?php echo
tep_href_link(FILENAME_SHOPPING_CART); ?>"
class="headerNavigation"><?php echo
HEADER_TITLE_CART_CONTENTS; ?></a>
 |  <a href="<?php echo
tep_href_link(FILENAME_CHECKOUT_SHIPPING, '',
'SSL'); ?>" class="headerNavigation"><?php
echo HEADER_TITLE_CHECKOUT; ?></a>
  </td>
  </tr>
</table>
```

```
<table border="1" width="100%" cellspacing="0"
cellpadding="1" bordercolor="#9966FF">
  <tr class="headerNavigation">
    <td
class="headerNavigation">  <font
```

Figure 3.43. Header bar.

```
color="#3333CC"><?php echo $breadcrumb-
>trail(' &raquo; '); ?></font></td>
    <td align="right"
class="headerNavigation"><font
color="#3333CC"><?php if
(tep_session_is_registered('customer_id')) {
?><a href="<?php echo
tep_href_link(FILENAME_LOGOFF, '', 'SSL'); ?>"
class="headerNavigation"><font
color="#3333CC"><?php echo
HEADER_TITLE_LOGOFF; ?></font></a>
 |  <?php } ?><a href="<?php echo
tep_href_link(FILENAME_ACCOUNT, '', 'SSL');
?>" class="headerNavigation"><font
color="#3333CC"><?php echo
HEADER_TITLE_MY_ACCOUNT; ?></font></a>
 |  <a href="<?php echo
tep_href_link(FILENAME_SHOPPING_CART); ?>"
class="headerNavigation"><font
color="#3333CC"><?php echo
HEADER_TITLE_CART_CONTENTS; ?></font></a>
 |  <a href="<?php echo
tep_href_link(FILENAME_CHECKOUT_SHIPPING, '',
'SSL'); ?>" class="headerNavigation"><font
color="#3333CC"><?php echo
HEADER_TITLE_CHECKOUT; ?></font></a>
  </font></td>
    </tr>
</table>
```

With this process you can change the header sections as per your requirements.

3.11. STS AND BTS

Basic Template Structure (BTS) and Simple Template System (STS) are the two major template systems used in osCommerce. To implement your own design, there are many files that will need to be changed in osCommerce, and a template system will help you to achieve the look and feel that you want for your site without changing all files. By using a template system, you can reduce your overhead while maintaining integrity in site design.

Both STS and BTS are contributions that can be downloaded from the osCommerce Web site.

3.11.1. Basic Template Structure BTS

BTS offers the ability to change the appearance of your store "on the fly"—and can allow the customer to choose how the store will present to them, if the store administrator so chooses.

BTS allows the development of PHP code for the store that can be independent of the HTML coding. It allows some parameters that would otherwise require users to edit files to be changed from the menu. It creates a friendlier store for the end user as well as for the accomplished Web designer.

3.11.1.1. Creating a new template

Creating a template is not as difficult as it sounds. Simply follow these steps.

1. Create a new directory inside the /catalog/templates/ directory. Choose the name carefully as it will become the name of your template. For example, if you choose MyWonderfulTemplate, the directory will be /catalog/templates/MyWonderfulTemplate/.
2. Select an existing template from which to start your modifications. Copy the contents of that template into your new template directory, and rename the template's SQL file to match the name of the directory. Case does matter. You should now have /catalog/templates/MyWonderfulTemplate/MyWonderfulTemplate.sql.
3. Now, edit the SQL file. The minimum change required is changing the name of the template screen shot to match the template name (e.g., change /Original.gif to /MyWonderfulTemplate.gif). You may want to alter any color changes or infobox parameters here to begin with.
4. Install your new template via the Admin panel. Go to Admin > Design Control > Template Admin, and click **Insert**. Follow the prompts, and your new template should now be available.

3.11.1.2. Files and directories used in a BTS template

This is a list of the files that are in a template directory and what they are used for.

- **/template/content/.** This is where the pages go for all templates. All templates pull their pages from here. You should not need to edit any files in this directory for your customized template. Note that some pages use files in the /includes/module/ directory.

Files placed in the /template/content/ directory are subject to being overwritten without notice during a patch procedure.

- **/templates/mytemplate/boxes.tpl.php.** This file contains code for the PHP class that generates boxes. It is used to produce the look and feel of your boxes. It places the images around the borders of the boxes, side and center.
- **/templates/mytemplate/extra_html_output.tpl.php.** Unless you are doing an advanced template, you will not need to edit this file. This file contains extra PHP functions for displaying images and buttons.
- **/templates/mytemplate/footer.php.** This is the footer for your template. If you do not want to use it, just include the information in the /mainpage.tpl.php file.
- **/templates/mytemplate/header.php.** This is the header for your template. If you do not want to use it, just include the information in the /mainpage.tpl.php file.
- **/templates/mytemplate/mainpage.tpl.php.** This is the bread and butter of your template. It sets up how your template will work and be displayed.
- **/templates/mytemplate/mytemplate.sql.** This file contains the code so that if you want to reload your template, you can. It should contain all of the initial settings for your template, including the information about side boxes. The name of the screen capture graphic should match the name of the SQL file, and this should match the name of the template directory.
- **/templates/mytemplate/mytemplate.css.** Each template has its own style sheet. The style sheet contains information about what fonts to use, their sizes and colors, backgrounds for HTML tables, rows, and cells, and other CSS-controlled features.
- **/templates/mytemplate/mainpage_modules/.** This is an optional directory. If your template requires the main page modules adapted so that they work with your template, then they will go in here. Otherwise, CRE Loaded will use the main pages in the

/includes/modules/mainpage_modules/ directory. By default, most templates use the /mainpage_modules/ directory for the whole store. If you need special main pages, they are placed here. When you create this directory in a template, this directory will become the default for your template, but only for the template where this directory resides.

- **/templates/mytemplate/boxes/.** All of your side boxes will go here, whether they are left or right boxes.
- **/templates/mytemplate/images/.** Any image that is unique to your template goes here. This includes things such as logos and the screen capture of what the template looks like for the Admin.
- **/templates/mytemplate/images/buttons/.** This is the place where all of your buttons for the template go.
- **/templates/mytemplate/images/infobox/.** Here is where the images that go around your side and center boxes should be found.

3.11.2. Simple Template System STS

The STS lets you create simple HTML templates to customize the look and feel of osCommerce. It does this by changing only a few /catalog/includes/ files, leaving all other files untouched and making it easy to add other contributions later. You simply create an HTML page that looks the way you want it to and put in placeholders for the various elements wherever you want to position them. For example, you would put "$cartbox" on the page in the position in which you want the Shopping Cart box to appear. Likewise, you would put "$categorybox" where you want the Categories box to appear and "$content" where you want the main page content to appear, etc.

The Header Tag Controller contribution lets you change headers without having to modify every file on the system. Just copy the Header Tag Controller's include files into place, and STS will automatically add them to all pages. Use the following process and files to modify your site using the STS method: /application_top.php, /header.php, /column_left.php, /column_right.php, /footer.php, /application_bottom.php, /sts_start_capture.php, /sts_stop_capture.php, /sts_display_output.php, and /sts_template.html.

1. Add the following lines to the bottom of your existing /catalog/includes/configure.php file.

STS: ADD: Define Simple Template System files
```
define('STS_START_CAPTURE', DIR_WS_INCLUDES .
'sts_start_capture.php');
```

```
define('STS_STOP_CAPTURE', DIR_WS_INCLUDES .
'sts_stop_capture.php');
define('STS_RESTART_CAPTURE', DIR_WS_INCLUDES
. 'sts_restart_capture.php');
define('STS_TEMPLATE', DIR_WS_INCLUDES .
'sts_template.html');
define('STS_DISPLAY_OUTPUT', DIR_WS_INCLUDES .
'sts_display_output.php');
define('STS_USER_CODE', DIR_WS_INCLUDES .
'sts_user_code.php');
STS: EOADD
```

2. Modify the /catalog/includes/sts_template.html file to look however you want. Use style sheet settings or HTML settings to provide a custom look and feel to your site, and arrange elements however you like them. The code is given below.

If you want to add any new boxes or template variables, add them to the /sts_user_code.php file. If you upgrade to a later version of STS, be sure not to replace this file when you install the new version.

One trick you can use to make debugging the template easier is to make your image and style sheet links absolute URLs (with a leading slash or http://) instead of relative (no leading slash). This will allow you to simply view the template page in your browser exactly as it will appear on your site, as opposed to the version without images that you get with relative URLs.

```
<html><head><!--$headcontent--></head><body>
<table width="100%" border="1" cellpadding="3"
cellspacing="0">
  <tr class="header"><td><font size="1"
face="Arial, Helvetica, sans-serif"> $cata-
loglogo</font></td>
    <td><div align="right"><font size="1"
face="Arial, Helvetica, sans-
serif">$myaccountlogo $cartlogo $checkout-
logo</font></div></td>
  </tr></table>
<font size="1" face="Arial, Helvetica, sans-
serif"><br>
```

```
</font><table width="100%" border="1" cellpad-
ding="3" cellspacing="0"><tr
class="headerNavigation"><td><font size="1"
face="Arial, Helvetica, sans-
serif">$breadcrumbs</font></td>
    <td><div align="right"><font size="1"
face="Arial, Helvetica, sans-serif">$myaccount
| $cartcontents | $checkout</font></div></td>
  </tr></table><font size="1" face="Arial,
Helvetica, sans-serif"><br>
</font><table width="100%" border="1" cellpad-
ding="3" cellspacing="0"><tr> <td width="125"
valign="top">
    <p><font size="1" face="Arial, Helve-
tica, sans-serif"> $category-
box</font></p><p><font size="1" face="Arial,
Helvetica, sans-
serif">$manufacturerbox</font></p> <p><font
size="1" face="Arial, Helvetica, sans-
serif">$whatsnewbox</font></p><p><font
size="1" face="Arial, Helvetica, sans-
serif">$searchbox</font></p> <p><font size="1"
face="Arial, Helvetica, sans-
serif">$informationbox</font> </p></td><td
valign="top">
<p>$content</p>
    </td>
  <td width="125" valign="top">
    <p><font size="1" face="Arial, Helve-
tica, sans-serif">$cartbox</font></p>
    <p><font size="1" face="Arial, Helve-
tica, sans-serif">$maninfobox</font></p>
    <p><font size="1" face="Arial, Helve-
tica, sans-serif">$orderhistorybox</font></p>
    <p><font size="1" face="Arial, Helve-
tica, sans-serif">$bestsellersbox</font></p>
    <p><font size="1" face="Arial, Helve-
tica, sans-serif">$specialfriendbox</font></p>
    <p><font size="1" face="Arial, Helve-
tica, sans-serif">$reviewsbox</font></p>
    <p><font size="1" face="Arial, Helve-
tica, sans-serif">$languagebox</font></p>
    <p><font size="1" face="Arial, Helve-
tica, sans-
serif">$currenciesbox</font></p></td>
  </tr>
</table>
<br>
<table width="100%" border="1" cellpadding="3"
cellspacing="0">
  <tr>
```

```
    <td><div align="center"><font size="1"
face="Arial, Helvetica, sans-
serif">$footer</font></div></td>
  </tr>
</table>
<br>
<table width="100%" border="1" cellpadding="3"
cellspacing="0">
  <tr>
    <td><div align="center"><font size="1"
face="Arial, Helvetica, sans-
serif">$banner</font></div></td>
  </tr>
</table>
<font size="1" face="Arial, Helvetica, sans-
serif"><br>
</font>
<table width="100%" border="1" cellpadding="3"
cellspacing="0">
  <tr>
    <td><font size="1" face="Arial, Helvetica,
sans-serif">$date</font></td>
    <td> <div align="right"><font size="1"
face="Arial, Helvetica, sans-
serif">$numrequests</font></div></td>
  </tr>
</table>
<font size="1" face="Arial, Helvetica, sans-
serif"><br>
</font>
<table width="100%" border="1" cellpadding="3"
cellspacing="0">
  <tr>
    <td><font size="1" face="Arial, Helvetica,
sans-serif"> </font></td>
    <td> <div align="right"><font size="1"
face="Arial, Helvetica, sans-serif">Simple
Template System by <a
href="http://www.yourpage.com/">Your
Page</a></font>
</div> <div align="right"></div></td>
  </tr>
</table>
<p> </p>
</body>
</html>
```

You'll be able to view your template page with the URL http://www.YourDomain.com/YourCatalogPath/includes/sts_template.html. To view it with the style sheets visible, go to your /catalog/ directory and type the following (this needs to be done from a UNIX prompt): ln -s includes/sts_template.html sts_template.html. This will create a symbolic link to your template file in the directory that contains the style sheet (CSS) file. Then, you can use the URL http://www.YourDomain.com/YourCatalogPath/sts_template.html/, and your style sheet settings will be visible.

The tags supported during template creation are discussed below.

- **$headcontent.** Put this string in your "<head>" section so that it can insert the dynamic head content and javascript on pages that require it. This will probably require putting the "$headcontent" in the "<head>" section of the source code. You can use the commented format of "$headcontent" ("<!--$headcontent-->") to keep the word "$headcontent" from displaying in your Web authoring software. Do not put "<title>...</title>" tags in your header; they will be added as part of the "$headcontent" variable, along with the description and keywords meta tags.
- **$cataloglogo.** The osCommerce logo and link.
- **$urlcataloglogo.** The URL used by the "$catalog" logo.
- **$myaccountlogo.** The My Account graphic and link.
- **$urlmyaccountlogo.** The URL used by the My Account function.
- **$cartlogo.** The Shopping Cart graphic and link.
- **$urlcartlogo.** The URL used by the Shopping Cart function.
- **$checkoutlogo.** The Checkout graphic and link.
- **$urlcheckoutlogo.** The URL used by the Checkout function.
- **$breadcrumbs.** The breadcrumbs text and links, showing the user the path taken through the site, e.g., Top > Catalog > . . . .
- **$myaccount.** The text version of My Account and its link; the link changes to **Logoff** if logged on.
- **$urlmyaccount.** The URL used by the My Account function.
- **$cartcontents.** The text version of the Cart Contents function.
- **$urlcartcontents.** The URL used by the My Account function.
- **$checkout.** The text version of the Checkout function.
- **$urlcheckout.** The URL used by the Checkout function.
- **$categorybox.** The Category box.
- **$manufacturerbox.** The Manufacturer box.
- **$whatsnewbox.** The What's New box.
- **$searchbox.** The Search box.
- **$informationbox.** The Information box.
- **$cartbox.** The Shopping Cart box.

- **$maninfobox.** The Manufacturer Info box (blank if not used on a page).
- **$orderhistorybox.** The Order History box (blank if not used on a page, i.e., user not logged in).
- **$bestsellersbox.** The Best Sellers box.
- **$specialfriendbox.** Either the Specials box or the Tell-A-Friend box (depending on page viewed).
- **$reviewsbox.** The Reviews box.
- **$languagebox.** The Languages box.
- **$currenciesbox.** The Currencies box.
- **$content.** The main content of the page (the middle of the page).
- **$date.** The current date.
- **$numrequests.** The "NUMBER requests since DATE" text.
- **$counter.** The page view counter.
- **$footer.** The footer output from /footer.php.
- **$banner.** The banner output from /footer.php.
- **$sid.** The string for the session ID in the format "SessionIdVar-Name = WhateverTheSessionIdIs."
- **$urlcat_Category_Name.** The URL to link to the category name; spaces in the category name must be replaced with underscores, for example, for a link to the category Video Cards you would use the template variable "$urlcat_Video_cards." Variable names are case-insensitive.
- **$urlcat_x_y_z.** The URL to link to the category by cPath string: you can use this to link to a category by the numeric values of the categories as shown by the cPath variable in the URL. The benefit of this is that it will still work if you change the names of the categories, which would break the "$urlcat_Category_Name" format.
- **$cat_Category_Name.** Same as "$urlcat_Category_Name."
- **$cat_x_y_z.** Same as "$urlcat_x_y_z."

In the /catalog/includes/application_bottom.php file you can see the following settings (near the top of the file).

```
$display_template_output = 1;
$display_normal_output = 0;
$display_debugging_output = 0;
```

"Display_Template_Output" (the default setting) will cause the template versions of the pages to be displayed. "Display_Normal_Output" will cause the nontemplate versions of the pages to be displayed. "Display_ Debugging_Output" will cause debugging information to be displayed, showing all of the blocks of data that are being used and how they are translated into template variables.

You can use any or all of the settings in any combination. If you have both normal and template output specified, the template output will be displayed first.

The use of BTS or STS depends on your needs and on which template system you prefer. It is suggested that you try both before deciding on one. Although both can be used for the same objectives, two points should be kept in mind: STS is easier and faster to use, but BTS allows for greater flexibility and customization.

You can toggle the debugging options via URL options. You can use the following parameters in your URL to turn the options on or off:

- **sts_template=1.** Turns on the template display.
- **sts_template=0.** Turns off the template display.
- **sts_normal=1.** Turns on the normal display.
- **sts_normal=0.** Turns off the normal display.
- **sts_debug=1.** Turns on the debugging display.
- **sts_debug=0.** Turns off the debugging display.
- **sts_version=1.** Turns on the version number display.
- **sts_version=0.** Turns off the version number display.

Index

Functions

D

E

F

G

H

Printed in the United States
50890LVS00003B/33